MW01063279

Lone Wolf

One of auto racing's most compelling characters tells his story

Doug Wolfgang

with Dave Argabright

Lone Wolf

By Doug Wolfgang
with Dave Argabright

© 2007 Dave Argabright

ISBN-13: 978-0-9719639-4-8
ISBN-10: 0-9719639-4-0

Published by:
American Scene Press
P.O. Box 84
Fishers, IN 46038

www.americanscenepress.com

Front cover image of Doug Wolfgang by Gene Marderness
Back cover image by Jack Kromer

Printed with pride in the USA by Print Communications, Inc.
Indianapolis, Indiana

Acknowledgements

The project of writing and publishing *Lone Wolf* began in May 2006, and from that point a number of people were extremely helpful in making this book possible.

Jeri Wolfgang was a gracious host during many visits to Sioux Falls, and Allie and Robby Wolfgang were patient and uncomplaining as our project often interrupted their busy schedules. However, in the process Robby gained an occasional stooge to help scrape mud from his motocross bike, so I guess that makes us even.

Many people provided background information for this book, including Bob Wilson, Bill Wright, Bryan Householder, Jim LeConte, Bob Trostle, Bill Smith, Jeff Olson, and Jack Trigg, among others. A special thank-you goes to Kevin Eckert for providing year-by-year statistics, which was a great help in confirming dates and places of various anecdotes.

A number of colleagues helped with proofreading and guidance in the early stages. Bruce Ellis in particular was very helpful in this regard, as well as providing insight into Doug's racing years in Pennsylvania. Bones Bourcier and Rob Sneddon also helped us through the early stages of the writing process.

Several photographers made an extra effort, some in the late stages, to provide a number of images you see in this book. Gene Marderness, Jack Kromer, Tony Martin, John Mahoney, Bill Taylor, Jim Fleming, and Max Dolder were particularly supportive. Jarl Sjovold was also quite helpful in providing the Wolfgang family photo found in the *Lone Wolf* photo gallery.

Even though he was in the thick of his racing season, Steve Kinser took time to write the foreword found here. Rob McCuen, who has been a Wolfgang fan since the beginning, was also helpful in providing a viewpoint that we've included in this book.

Corinne Economaki continued to provide her steady, guiding touch as she edited this book. Stacey Davis provided a great effort in helping to transcribe the mountain of interview tapes. Randy Steenbergen, Mike Herman, Kane Neese, and the gang at Print Communications continue to be invaluable partners in the production and printing process. Linda Burchette of Print once again came through with a top-notch cover design, as well.

A number of people have helped us get the word out on this book, in particular Doug Auld of *Sprint Car and Midget Magazine*, who also offered generous help on some technical issues related to photos. And kudos to Jeff Walker and Kathie Collins of Jeff's Storage for their ongoing support.

Finally, my wife, Sherry, and our children were very patient as the stress and strain of producing this book mounted. They provided love and support and without them *Lone Wolf* would not be possible.

Dave Argabright

Contents

Foreword

I've raced against a lot of guys in my career, that's for sure. Seems like just the other day that I was just getting started, but now I look up and realize I've been racing for more than 30 years. That means there have been a ton of guys with me on the race track, all of us fighting and scratching to win.

Of all those people—I'd guess it numbers in the thousands—I don't think there was one who was tougher and more skilled than Doug Wolfgang. If he isn't the toughest I've raced against, I don't know who would be. Doug was a guy who was intense and wanted to win just as badly as I did, every night.

I can't pinpoint exactly the first time I met Doug. I guess it's one of those things where I was aware of who he was, because he was winning races when I got started. I raced around home a lot, but I read the *Speed Sport* and had an idea of who was good at the time in various parts of the country. Doug's name was circulating a little bit and he'd come run in our area now and then. In fact, I remember someone telling me Doug showed up at Kokomo one Sunday night and got upside-down in hot laps. I wasn't there, but I distinctly remember someone telling me about it, so we definitely must have known who he was at the time. And I might have raced against Doug when we went to Florida and things like that, but I really only knew him from a distance.

Once I got into Karl Kinser's car and started racing with the World of Outlaws in 1978, that's when I got to know Doug. We got to talking and hanging out a little bit, and our friendship immediately clicked. We were friends, but we definitely raced each other hard! You know, people talk about me and Sammy Swindell racing against each other for all those years, but I'll bet I had just as many hard races with Doug as I did with Sammy. I mean, among the three of us, I KNOW we had some hard races! Doug and I, our race styles were a little bit different than Sammy, and maybe that's one more reason why we kind of clicked as friends. We were actually a lot alike in some ways.

Doug's style was really solid. He was a guy who ran hard, hit his lines, and knew what he was supposed to do. He was smooth, but if it came down to a dogfight to win, he was up to the task. He didn't get into that a whole lot, but he was willing if he had to. But he wasn't a guy who wanted to race like that—rough and tumble—every night. He was more apt to get his car working good, handling well, and beat you like that.

The big thing with Doug was confidence. When he had confidence in himself and his race car, he was probably the best there was at the time. Then again, he's like all of us: We all go through periods when you're struggling with your equipment and you start doubting yourself. He was probably harder on himself than most people during those times. But if he was up, and confident, it was a handful to beat him.

Doug talks in the book about that trip we made to Australia many years ago, and I remember it well. It was one of the first times we got to go down there, and I made the trip with Doug and his family. It was a really enjoyable trip, although the only bad thing was that the race cars weren't nearly as nice as the trip! But it was still memorable. We had to try and have fun, because we were all down there for like two months, traveling around. We had a lot of good times then, not just on that trip but through all the years after.

Matter of fact, we used to do more fun stuff, not just with Doug but with everybody. Back in the 1980s, it seemed like we might even have a card game going on before the races, everybody having a good time. I can remember Lee Osborne, Karl, Doug, and myself sitting there playing cards. We'd do all kinds of things to try and beat each other. Flipping coins, whatever, anything to have a little competition. But you don't see much of that any more. I know I don't do much. I don't know if that kind of thing has just left us or what, but guys aren't doing that stuff these days. It's more serious, more like business.

I guess that's what you miss about good times like that. When I say I miss seeing Doug every day, that's true. But what I also miss is the way things were back then. We were all younger and it seemed like we had lots more fun. For example, when I think about those times I can't help but smile, because, boy, we had a lot of good times. Not really hell-raising things, just joking around and laughing and getting after each other. Those were really good times.

You kind of get caught up in racing and going up and down the road, and you don't get a chance to stay in touch with people like you want to. I actually feel kind of bad that I don't get to stay in touch with Doug and his family as much as I'd like. Hey, we've been through a lot together. The day at Kansas City when he got burned, I was there in the hospital with him that night. He's a very special person and his family is special to me also, and I know my wife Dana feels the same.

I guess some of that is because he was a good influence on me, and taught me some things. Doug is just a little bit older than I am, and he already had children when our kids came along, so he was a person who you'd kind of look up to because he had already done some of those things. For example, the very first time I ever played racquetball, it was Doug who taught me how to play. Of course, he played a lot, so it wasn't much of a game for him that day. But it was enough competition that I really liked it, I guess I was intrigued about how I could get better and beat this guy. At first I got skunked every time, but it got me interested enough that I started playing, and I've played ever since. That's just one thing I can trace back and say that Doug pointed me in the right direction. I know there have been many things and that's just one.

After Doug got burned in 1992, he had a very, very tough road to try and come back. Doug always kept himself in shape—I'll bet he still does to this day—and that probably helped him some. But he definitely went through a lot after that crash. All the rehabilitation, all those surgeries, it would have been easy to give up, but Doug isn't that kind of person. He is tough and determined and he wasn't going to give up that easily.

I admire the fact he could come back after the crash and win races. That's pretty impressive to me. I think the timing for him was different, and it wasn't quite the same, but still it was impressive. And then he had that accident at Granite City in 1997 and that was it.

I think Doug quit racing mainly because his family probably felt like they didn't want to go through all of that again. Doug probably saw that, and I'm sure it influenced his decision. It was probably more for his family than for himself, which again is something you admire about Doug.

The thing I'll always remember is just how well our families clicked. I mean, all of us really cared a lot for each other. Me and Dana, Doug and Jeri, our kids, their kids, we all really thought the world of each other. Even when we don't see each other for a while, when we cross paths we pick right up with our conversation and it's like we saw each other just last week. That's when you know your friendship is something special.

I hope you like reading Doug's story. He really is an interesting person. When you're finished, I'll bet you respect Doug just as much as I always have. He worked hard at what he was doing, and he always tried to be the best. He was a great racer and a great friend of mine. And he always will be.

Steve Kinser
20-time World of Outlaws champion
Bloomington, Indiana
June, 2007

Introduction

Doug Wolfgang's life has certainly been eventful, hasn't it? He rose from humble beginnings to experience a powerful passion for auto racing as a teen-aged kid, putting forth a determined struggle to establish his driving career. His soaring debut almost immediately took him to the pinnacle of sprint-car racing. He followed that up with nearly 16 straight years of success at the very peak of the sport, winning hundreds of races and becoming a household name in short-track racing. Then came the devastating 1992 crash that nearly took his life, prompting an inspiring recovery and comeback, followed by a controversial lawsuit. Finally came the dramatic crash in 1997 that ultimately ended his career.

Amid all the miles and wins and people he met along the way, Wolfie grew and matured and was shaped into a complex, fascinating character, the kind of multi-dimensional leading man you'd find in a Hollywood movie. He's a bit too rugged to be a saccharine good-guy, and far too pleasant to be cast as the heavy. In the end he became the type of man we tend to be drawn to, complicated and interesting and awfully difficult to define.

Wolfgang can be many personalities, reflective of the moment and the mood and the setting. He can be blunt and direct when he's angry, but the next conversation might find him warm and supportive and generous. He has little tolerance for those who seek to exploit him or anyone else, and he is powerfully loyal to his friends.

In the beginning of his career he was naïve, which is actually a healthy trait that brings its share of disappointments. Wolfie had a simple view of a complex world, and through the years that view was hardened and shaped by the bumps and bruises that come with living. Luckily, he discovered that being hard and rugged isn't really the answer, so he learned to sort through his many emotions and heartbreaks, letting go of the anger and bitterness, forgiving others and forgiving himself.

Doug's racing career was remarkable on many fronts, the first being his sudden rise to prominence. In just three seasons he went from unknown beginner, begging rides at Knoxville Raceway, to the most successful sprint-car driver in America. That amazing debut earned him a legion of loyal fans, and they have stuck with him through thick and thin.

Another element that immediately separated this Wolf from the pack was his articulate interviews. He often jokes about being "just a dumb race driver from South Dakota," but in reality he is an exceptionally bright man. His views on the world are honest, realistic, and straightforward, offered with a unique and fractured vernacular peppered with double-negatives. "Ain't got no chance," he might say. Others might take two paragraphs to describe someone's intelligence, while Wolfie would effectively sum it up much more concisely: "He ain't dumb."

His fractured vernaculars mask the fact that he is a highly intelligent and perceptive man. Wolfgang still sees himself as a blue-collar everyday guy, and his fractured grammar softens any perception that he's suddenly gone big-time on us. In nearly every way he is the same man as when he began his career, never allowing his dazzling success in racing to polish away the homespun grit that is an essential part of his soul.

From the very beginning, Wolfie established himself as his own man. When big-time independent sprint-car racing was organized under the World of Outlaws banner in 1978, Wolfie kept himself at arm's length from any formal organization. Throughout his career he would maintain that dogged independence, even if it meant more travel or less money. If he was going to make it in this business, he believed, he would do it on his own terms.

People saw that, and loved it. He was the outlaw's outlaw, choosing his own schedule, his own venues, and his own terms. They recognized him as perhaps the sport's last rugged individualist, quietly resisting a reformed, administrative world. It endeared him to tens of thousands of fans, who loved the fact that "their guy" was somehow above and beyond all the rest.

There was always something of a mystique surrounding Doug. Maybe it started with the name: "Wolfgang." It's a mysterious, unusual name, and it sounds strong. It's a name you might hear in an old Bela Lugosi/Boris Karloff movie, surrounded by dark night forests and fog that hangs at the ground. And the nickname, "Wolfie," or just "Wolf," which tightly associates the man with that proud and distant animal of the same name. And funny stuff, too; Wolfie had a way with words, and when he tells the story of wearing glasses: "I wore glasses until I got gonked on the head in a crash in the late 1970s, and it corrected my vision." Gonked? Corrected his vision? That's just funny, and a superstar wouldn't tell that story. But stories like that reminded us that Doug is just an average guy living a very un-average life.

None of this, of course, would have mattered very much if he hadn't been a winner. But when he consistently backed up the mystique and the everyman persona with hundreds of victories from coast-to-coast, the package was complete.

Throughout his 22-year career, Doug was consistently a winner. However, there were three truly extraordinary periods. The first was with car owner Bob Trostle in 1976 and '77, when they won 21 and 45 races in respective back-to-back seasons. The next was with Bob Weikert from 1984 to '87, when Wolfie won 130 races in that span. The third was his brilliant 1989, when he won 43 races and more than a half-million dollars with car owner Danny Peace. Those seasons were dotted with wins at the sport's most significant events: the Knoxville Nationals, the King's Royal, the Williams Grove National Open, the Syracuse Supernationals, on and on.

Any *one* of those stints would put a guy in the Hall of Fame. Wolfie did all three, along with plenty of success in between.

His devastating, fiery 1992 crash at Kansas City resonated throughout the sport, and effectively ended his ability to perform at the top level of competition. The lawsuit that followed made him arguably the most misunderstood man in all of motorsports. He was vilified endlessly in print and on the air, primarily because most of us didn't understand his reasoning and motives.

The harsh criticism stung Doug mightily, and threatened to change the very heart and soul of the man. Verbally beaten into submission, sinking into bitterness, he withdrew from most of the world in the late 1990s, struggling to understand why he had been vilified for doing what he steadfastly believed was right. He developed a tough, rugged exterior and spoke as though the criticism was no big deal. The fact is, the period hurt him deeply.

Had the story ended there, it would have been a sad outcome for a great champion. Luckily, time began the process of healing, both within Doug Wolfgang and throughout the sport. Today, we can look much more clearly at his life, his decisions, and his motives for what they really were, not spun in the emotional cauldron of 1995. For his part, Wolfie has come to terms with the pain and controversy of the period, and is today much more forgiving and understanding of the situation. Time has healed much of the suffering, and forgiveness has swept away any lingering anger or bitterness.

Perhaps that is Wolfgang's most impressive, important accomplishment. He could have remained an embittered outcast, but he rose above that, and in the process was delighted to discover that his friends are all still here, happy to see him, happy to shake his hand, happy that he's still an important part of our sport.

More than anything, his fans still adore him. They still talk glowingly of his powerful performances at Knoxville, at Williams Grove, at East Bay, at Manzanita. They remain in awe of his barnstorming travels across America. They speak reverently of his phenomenal victory totals. They relish the long-ago night when he shook their hand and signed their t-shirt, making them feel like a million bucks. Making them feel like he cared about them. The fact is, he *did* care about them. And he still does.

My take? Here is the simple assessment of a complex man: He is a bit suspicious of strangers, but once you earn his trust he is powerfully loyal. He was a gifted racer, yet is reluctant to blow his own horn. He loves sprint-car racing and it pains him when he talks of the sport's flaws. He is a keen, articulate observer of human nature. He is a profoundly loyal father and husband who cherishes each day with his close-knit family, a unit that is filled with loving relationships. He is a racer who saw exciting and wonderful peaks, but also lived through terribly painful valleys. He is a self-made man with a deeply imbued sense of determination, tenacity, and toughness. Finally—and the statistics back this up—he was a great, immensely talented champion.

From the moment we began this book, Doug was open and supportive. He never once hesitated to speak honestly and directly, or asked that we spin something to soften it up. He was candid of his own foibles as well as those he encountered along the way, and also readily offered praise when it was due.

At the outset, I didn't know him well. Like most others, I had been a distant admirer of Doug Wolfgang the racer, but knew little of the man inside. Through the months that followed our initial discussion, a thousand miles of travel, a hundred conversations, and meals that ranged from a McDonald's drive-thru to pleasant sit-downs at nice restaurants, the man who is Doug Wolfgang began to appear in clear focus. The words began to dot the page with my fervent hope that they would somehow be adequate to help you get to know him with the same deep understanding that I had.

As we progressed it was quickly evident that this project was a healing, cathartic effort for Doug. For that I am happy and deeply grateful, because it offers the perspective that even difficult stories can have a happy ending.

So read on, fellow travelers. Ride along with Wolfie as he takes you through his life and his career, when he left a powerful mark on a powerful sport, but always on his own terms. He's a survivor. He's his own man. He's a lone wolf.

Dave Argabright
May, 2007

Viewpoint

As a race car driver, Doug Wolfgang was both an icon and an enigma. Fiercely independent, intense, braver than Godzilla and off-the-charts smart, Wolfie was the real deal, the genuine article. He was an old-school throwback to another era, yet completely timeless. Wolfgang's meteoric rise to the upper echelons of sprint-car racing would no doubt have happened regardless of which period in history he arrived. If he wasn't absolutely the greatest dirt-track wizard I've ever had the pleasure of witnessing, it's only because I also got to watch super-studs like Steve Kinser, Tom Bigelow, Pancho Carter, Richie Vogler, and Jan Opperman during the heights of their powers.

God only knows how much higher the Wolf might've soared had that hell-on-earth inferno in Kansas City not come within a whisper of killing him on that cold and cruel April afternoon back in 1992. A lesser man would have never walked again, but Doug Wolfgang ain't no lesser man. He bit the bullet, dug deep down inside and *willed* himself into becoming a racer all over again. The prolific trips to victory lane were over, but Wolfie's return to sprint cars was nothing short of miraculous. His comeback was one for the ages and it was rife with dignity, grace and class—just like the man who engineered it. "Heal yourself, boy," his old man used to say to his only son. Doug might've been just another punk kid who thought he knew the score, but he must have heeded his dear old dad's advice. In more ways than we could ever know, Wolfgang is still healing himself.

But you surely already know what a bad motor-scooter the Wolf was in a sprint car or you wouldn't have bought this book.

That part of the story is for Doug himself to tell. What I wanna get to is something else entirely. Wolfgang is without a doubt one of the most complex individuals I have ever known; a deep sea of contradictions and curve balls. When it was time to play the star, nobody did it better. But don't kid yourself: Wolfie is an exceedingly proud and private man and he never drops his guard unless he's had the chance to size you up. If you're lucky enough to pass his "inspection," and his finely honed instincts tell him that you're worthy of his trust, he won't hesitate to let it all hang out and you'd have to be an idiot not to shut up and glue your ears to his every word. Wolfie's got wisdom to burn and moreover, his gift for expressing himself is right up there with Mark Twain, Will Rogers, or any other wise old sage. Hell, yeah, he was an amazing race car driver, a mega-legend and a Hall-of-Famer many times over, but where Doug Wolfgang really shines is simply as a human being. They say heroes are hard to find but I'm not buying it for a minute. You just have to know where to look.

Doug and I have been crossing paths since 1976, the year he somehow landed in Bob Trostle's highly sought-after sprint car. We didn't actually meet until 1983, and the circumstances were both classic and hilarious. I was at the now-shuttered Santa Fe Speedway in suburban Chicago for a World of Outlaws race, and Wolfgang was wheeling the Gambler house car. For whatever reason, and in spite of my old racing buddy Eric's pleas to reconsider, I was determined to sneak into the pits and enjoy the program on Ted Johnson's dime. I was already up in a tree looking for my chance to jump the barbed-wire fence when along comes Wolfgang. Now keep in mind, Wolfie didn't know me from Herman Munster so this was a real leap of faith on my part. "Hey man," I hissed under my breath. "Would you be my look-out? I don't have a pit pass and I'm tryin' to sneak in." Right away Wolfie started cackling like Eddie Haskell, scanned the pits for signs of trouble, and told me the coast was clear. Thanks largely to him, the caper didn't get me thrown out of the joint nor did I suffer the indignity of a night in the notorious Cook County Jail. More importantly, I had learned that Wolfgang wasn't hung up on some star trip and that he could still appreciate a bit of hi-jinx in the workplace. Whether he thought so or not, I felt like we were kindred spirits from that day forward.

Perhaps that chance encounter helped set the stage for what I considerer one of my watershed moments as a motorsports journalist. It was July 12, 1997, and Wolfgang's storied career had now come full circle. He was back running weekly shows at Knoxville for Minnesota car owner Dan Motter, struggling to rekindle the magic that had once come so naturally. I was writing for a now-defunct rag called *Mid-States Racing News*, and had a weekly column called "Open Wheel Fury." I was delighted early on to discover that as long as I made the Monday deadline, I could write anything I wanted. Week in and week out, I ranted and raved with a complete absence of fear, and to say that I took editorial liberties would be putting it mildly. Little—if anything—was sacred. The money they were paying me was a joke, but the gig had its upside for sure. One upside was that I could approach Wolfgang about an interview.

The downside of course, was that I was a virtual nobody in the sprint-car universe. Somehow I had to convince Wolfgang of two things: One, now was the time to tell his story. The fire, his brush with the grim reaper, the legal quagmire that followed, the whole kit and caboodle. Two, that I was the only logical man for the job, even though I represented a paper that was practically invisible.

But there were complications, of course. Wolfie's self-imposed five-year code of silence with the press seemed etched in stone. He'd already shut down every big-name, hot-shot scribe in the business so what chance did I have? But I was bolder than Batman in those days and had absolutely nothing to lose. This mission was a long-shot and I figured my odds were about the same as successfully launching myself to Uranus on a rock-o-plane.

To this day, I continue to marvel over having pulled it off. I still have my original tape of our two-hour conversation, and a signed copy of the four-page cover story that we released just in time for the 1997 Knoxville Nationals.

Since then, I've written volumes about the Wolf for *Flat Out Magazine* and even had the distinct honor of writing his induction biography in 2003 when he was enshrined into the National Sprint Car Hall of Fame on the first ballot. Whenever we talk these days, we rarely discuss racing. We talk about life; about sticking your neck out and having the courage of conviction to do what you want to do. We talk about the fine line that exists between being a responsible adult and taking chances and the importance of having passions in your life. Wolfie's passion nearly killed him twice (at least!). Some days I could swear that passions are trying to snuff me out too, but I've known all along that rock-and-roll ain't for the faint of heart. Every choice we make in this life has its consequences, for better or worse.

We each talk of losing our mother to cancer, and how awful it is it is to helplessly watch someone suffer. We have each also lost our father, and Doug's take on that bummer is something I'll always hold close to my heart. His words will forever remain between us, but trust me, it was beautiful stuff and he helped ease some of the hurting. We prattle on forever about our only sons, each of whom just turned 16. Wolf's kid Robby is an aspiring motocross racer, and my boy Sean is an honor student and a guitarist/songwriter in a band called "The Wandering Monsters." Neither of us could be any more proud. By no means do we get all heavy every time we speak and to be truthful, our conversations are somewhat rare these days. But frequency doesn't matter and nobody is keeping score. He always takes my calls and that's good enough for me.

Sometimes, when he gets on a roll or if we hit upon a hot-button topic, Wolfgang can be a riot, a wisecracker of the highest order. He teases me about being a middle-aged rock star and tells me I should never quit chasing my dreams. I tell him I'm too dumb and stubborn to quit anyway. Recently, he offered this tidbit of twisted wisdom: "If you ever need any help with all the bureaucratic bullshit when you hit the top, don't ask me. I ain't gonna be no help!" Priceless. And here's one more pearl of wisdom from the world according to Wolfgang: "You're all right, McCuen. You're a hippie but I ain't talkin' about what most people think about hippies. I'm talkin' about people who think for themselves and ain't afraid to live outside the norm. I like that. People like French Grimes—now there's a hippie!"

I once told Wolfgang that the reason I still wear my stupid-looking black-framed glasses is because he used to have a similar pair when he first started running Knoxville in the mid-1970s. So what if it's only partially true and that they're actually more of my personal tribute to Buddy Holly? That's one more thing I admire about the Wolf—he refuses to take himself too seriously. He doesn't mind having his ego stroked now and again, but he certainly doesn't require it. In the final analysis, Wolfie has a keen sense of who he is and remains committed to making the most out of every minute of every day, never losing sight of how dangerously close he came to being either an invalid or a dead man. He's still in his shop every day crankin' out WolfWeld chassis with his boyhood buddy Jack Trigg, still playin' racquetball and takin' no prisoners, ridin' bikes and lovin' his family with everything he's got. Sometimes you don't have to go to the movies to find a story with a happy ending.

Rob McCuen
May, 2007

Lone Wolf

To Allie and Robby, who didn't get to know the great Doug Wolfgang, only the guy who was their dad;

and to the fans, who stuck with me through thick and thin.

Prologue

The sprint car grinds to a stop on the race track, a twisted, wrecked mass of steaming metal. My limp body is still strapped tightly in the cockpit, my head sagging against my chest and my arms hanging lifelessly at my side.

People rush toward the car, coming to my aid. EMT staff, fellow racers, onlookers. In a moment their strained voices echo across the infield and pit area at Lakeside Speedway in Kansas City, Kansas.

"It's Wolfgang! Looks like he's hurt bad!"

It was late on a Friday afternoon, April 3, 1992. We were practicing on a newly paved track surface, in anticipation for a World of Outlaws race set the following day. Just after taking the checkered flag to end my session, I turned the wheel tightly to steer my car into the third turn. Several old tires were imbedded in the ground along the inside of the track, serving as infield markers. My car clipped one of those tires, breaking my front suspension, sending me careening into the outside wall at a very high rate of speed.

The impact was loud, and violent. The forces were so extreme; my body was bent at an impossible angle and stretched out the right side of the car, where my head literally bounced off the outside wall. I suffered a serious head injury, my neck was broken, and my sternum—that's the bone in the center of your chest—was split perfectly down the middle, like you'd snap a wishbone on Thanksgiving.

As quickly as the people got to my car, they instinctively recoiled. Their shrill voices cried out, "Fire! The car's on fire!"

The impact had knocked off a fuel line, which ran under my seat and between my knees. Methanol racing fuel poured from the broken line, spilling onto the rear brake rotor, which was nearly red hot. The heat of the rotor ignited the methanol, and the burning fuel began to pool in the belly pan of the car.

There were screams of horror, and anguish. Several people, primarily my fellow race drivers, ran back to the pit area, stripping fire extinguishers from their trailers and tow rigs. They hurried to my car, desperately emptying the small units on the fire. The fire would briefly stop, and they would try to remove the steering wheel of my car and unfasten my safety belts, but in a moment the fire would flare back to life, forcing them back.

In the middle of the chaos, someone was holding a screaming, hysterical woman. My wife Jeri, who was seven months pregnant, tugged and strained to try to come to my aid. Onlookers clutched her arms, trying to keep her back, knowing that the moment she reached the car her clothing would ignite and she would also be badly burned.

For me, it was silence. Nothing but empty blackness, with my eyes closed, oblivious to the terrible burns being inflicted on my legs and feet. While the scene played out all around me, I knew only the floating numbness of the unconscious mind. Pain, misery, anger, sadness, all of that would come later; at this moment, it was only silence, pure and still.

After two minutes the car was a hot, burning hell. Several racers, wearing their full safety gear, tried valiantly to help me. Several times the scenario was repeated: The fire would be knocked down, and they would lean into the cockpit, only to be repulsed as the fire regained life.

The air was filled with smoke, and the stench of burning rubber, paint, and flesh mixed with the horrified screams of people trying to help me.

If my mind had been functioning, I might have been thinking, "So this is how it ends…after 39 years on earth, and a racing career that spanned all of my adult life, this is the final day. On a Friday afternoon in Kansas, it's time for my exit."

I would have probably wanted to say goodbye to Jeri, and our children. And maybe just one more embrace for my mother, and to shake my father's hand, and say farewell to a few close friends. But now, sitting there with the fire consuming me, I was never going to have that opportunity.

Even though the scene was chaotic, time was moving very slowly. More than eight minutes passed, with the fire dancing and burning greedily at my legs and feet. Finally, the people trying to help me managed to extinguish the fire once and for all, and the EMT folks leaned in to begin prying me from the car.

After a few minutes they carefully lifted me onto a stretcher. They had called an air ambulance to transport me to the hospital, and they placed the stretcher into the helicopter. They slammed the door closed and the rotor blades immediately sped up, and we slowly lifted off the ground. There was only the dying sound of the helicopter as it faded away into the distance.

For a lot of the people there, their instincts told them it was my last ride. They were probably shaking their head, knowing they just watched Doug Wolfgang burn to death.

This was the end, they figured. I probably would have figured it, too.

But my story wasn't quite over. Not yet. Now I'm finally ready to tell it, the best way I know how.

1

Roots

The haze of the November morning hangs close to the ground as I drive my pickup truck onto I-90. It's early, and I'm headed east out of Sioux Falls, S.D. In a few miles I'll cross the Minnesota state line, but it won't look much different. Just a rolling prairie that looks like it goes on forever.

You know what else looks like it goes on forever? This ol' interstate highway. I look out across the hood of the truck and the road is wide, straight, and flat, and it looks endless. But it ain't really endless; if you keep going east, you'll dead end in Boston, at the Atlantic Ocean. If you turn around and go west, you'll ride this highway clear out to Seattle, and the Puget Sound. I know, because I've traveled the road clear out to the end in both directions, chasing the rainbow.

Well, really, not just the rainbow, but the pot of gold, too.

You know how far it is out to Alger, Wash.? The atlas says it's 1,605 miles, but I don't have any idea if that's right. All I know is that it's 34 hours. I never measured those drives by miles, but by hours. That one is 34. I know from experience.

When you look at a map of the United States, Sioux Falls looks like it's in the middle of the country in terms of the two oceans. But it ain't. It's close, but it's not as far to Boston as it is to Seattle.

For most of my life, I was consumed by racing, and that led me far, far away from home. From the very beginning, when I was a young man, I rode this highway, I-90. At first it was just a short jump over to Minnesota, to the towns of Fairmont or Jackson, but later I went a lot farther. Sometimes I'd go south on I-29, depending on where I was headed. But it seemed that every trip started on one of these interstates coming out of Sioux Falls.

It's funny how fate put me here. I guess a guy can be from anywhere, can't he? But me, I'm from Sioux Falls. Even when my family and I moved away for a little while, we still considered Sioux Falls our home. When we'd say, "We're goin' home," that's what we meant.

I'll tell you how I happened to be from Sioux Falls. It's kind of interesting, I think.

My dad, Ed Wolfgang, grew up in Kansas. He had 11 brothers and sisters, and this was when the Great Depression was in full swing. He lived in Frankfort, a little town about 15 miles southeast of Marysville.

My dad had a very difficult childhood, but I didn't know much about his life until after he passed away a few years ago. In fact, I'm still learning things about my dad. He always kind of kept to himself, and didn't talk much about things like this. But after he died in 1995, I grew closer with his brother Gerald—everybody calls him Jake—who shared with me a lot of the details of my dad's early years.

My dad was born in 1923, and by the time he was in seventh grade the Great Depression had put the hurt on his family. Unfortunately, my dad was the wrong age for the hand-me-down stuff, because everything was either too big or too small. He was too big for the little ones and there was nothing left from the older ones. So when he started seventh grade he had no shoes. Literally, he had nothing to put on his feet.

The kids walked to school then, and when the weather started getting colder the teacher took my dad aside and said, "Ed, if you don't have any shoes, you can't come to school. It's too cold to walk that far."

They lived about a mile and a half from the school, so my dad walked home that day and told his dad what had happened. My grandfather looked at him and said, "I'll tell you what, son, I understand but you can't live here. If you're not going to school any more, I can't afford to put you up. We don't have enough food, and you can't just hang around."

So my dad went to live with his uncle, about five miles away. He never once went home again. Just never did. All of this seems impossible by today's standards, but this was a different time, a different world. Being displaced like that had a major effect on my dad, and for the rest of his life he always had a very deep and powerful fear of being left out. When my uncle told me this story, it helped me understand my dad a lot more.

My dad went to work on his uncle's farm, and never went back to school. He didn't see any of his brothers or sisters until everybody was grown. Remember, he lived five miles away; that was a big trip in those days.

All his brothers and sisters finished high school, and right after graduation Jake tracked my dad down and they reconnected. My dad wasn't close to his brothers and sisters, except Jake. They weren't just brothers, but good friends.

My dad was still very young when he got a job working on a harvesting crew. If you've ever been to Kansas, or the other states in the Great Plains, you've seen the vast wheat fields of the region. Harvesting all that grain is a big operation, and in those days very few farmers could afford a combine—a giant tractor-like machine that cuts the wheat and separates the grain. So a wealthy company would own and operate a half-dozen big machines, and they would travel during the summer, harvesting wheat. They'd start way up in Winnipeg, Canada, and work their way back down. They'd spend several months on the road, eventually getting back to Kansas, and then farther south.

When Japan attacked Pearl Harbor in 1941 and the war was on, a lot of young guys flocked to the enlistment offices. Both my dad and Jake signed up, and I suspect for most guys their rush to sign up was about more than wanting to be a red-blooded American hero. The military was kind of an escape from the Depression; in the army they'd get enough to eat, and they'd get paid, and that was more than a lot of guys had going for them at the time.

My dad didn't want to be in an airplane, and he wasn't interested in being a foot soldier, so he joined the navy in 1942. He later told me that if you're in a plane that's shot down, you're done; but since he knew how to swim, he figured he could jump in the water and swim if the ship sank.

As it turned out, that's pretty much what happened.

He ended up serving on a small boat, like a PT boat, near the Philippines. The Japanese still held the islands, and my dad's boat would patrol the coastlines, engaging the enemy and looking for big ships to attack. But on one patrol they brushed a mine, and it blew their boat in half.

My dad and a couple of the other crewmen—along with their pet monkey—managed to launch a life raft before they went down. They were in a bad spot; they were within sight of the shore, but they didn't dare go inland or they'd be captured by the Japanese. But if they drifted out to sea with the tides, they'd probably never be rescued.

They spent three days adrift before they were finally picked up. It really was a lucky break that they made it. My dad was shipped back to be reassigned, but by that time the Japanese were nearly finished. Before he could be redeployed, the Japanese surrendered, and his war was over.

When my dad mustered out of the navy, the first place he headed was the little town of Andover, S.D. Before the war he had met a young girl there, and while he was overseas she was evidently on his mind quite a lot.

Andover was my mother's home town, a tiny burg about 40 miles east of Aberdeen in the northern part of the state. Her name was Anita Engelson, and her dad owned and operated the Andover pool hall. The major east-west mode of transportation during those years was the railroad, and the main line of the Minneapolis-Seattle route passed through Andover, where trains made their first fuel stop on the western run. The aircraft industry was booming in Seattle, and a lot of people were taking the train to Seattle in hopes of finding work.

This little town probably didn't have but 15 houses, and when the train stopped most of the passengers got off to stretch their legs, basically doubling or tripling the town's population. The first place they'd go was the pool hall. Why? Because the pool hall served beer. In a town like Andover, this was the place to hang out.

One afternoon my dad and his harvesting crew were passing through when they visited the pool hall. My dad would have been maybe 17 at the time, and my mom—she was probably 13 years old—was there working that day.

I doubt my dad had even had a girlfriend at that point in his life. I don't know, but he was never around very many people, and he was shy anyway. He kept to himself, like my uncle says, and he never had much to say. My mom must have made quite an impression on him, because he carried her memory with him for three years, halfway around the world. Now he was coming home, older, wiser, hoping to find this young girl.

I don't know, but I suspect he was very nervous when he made that trip. Maybe she wasn't there any more, or maybe she'd already gotten married. After all, in those times lots of kids got married when they were 15, 16 years old. But fate came through for them both, because they got together and soon enough got married.

Right away, my dad needed to find work. Not long after they were married, he learned that the John Morrell packing plant in Sioux Falls was hiring, because business was booming. All these boys came home from the war, and suddenly everybody was getting married and building stuff and having kids. Business was really taking off.

Dad got the job at the packing plant, and he and Mom moved to Sioux Falls. Soon a couple of her sisters and brothers moved here as well, so our family put down roots. Later on a couple of dad's sisters and brothers—including Jake—also moved to Sioux Falls.

Working at the packing plant didn't agree much with ol' Ed, and after a couple of years he quit. But since so many family members had also settled down here, my parents didn't even consider moving anywhere else. Sioux Falls was their home, and both of 'em spent the rest of their lives here.

So that's the story on how Doug Wolfgang happened to be from Sioux Falls, S.D.

I didn't come along until July 26, 1952. I'm an only child, and the only thing I remember from my very early years is that my dad went to work in the morning and came home at night.

We lived in a middle-class neighborhood near 4th Street and French, and my life was pretty much like all the other kids. We'd play at the playground, stuff like that. I liked sports, and played on different teams through my early school years. I wasn't a bad little basketball player as a kid, but I never got the size you need to be really good.

One of the boys who lived nearby was Doug Clark, who became my very close friend. Doug is black, but we were so little when we first met we didn't even notice that stuff. He and I were good buddies. We spent a lot of time together, and had a lot in common. Later on we were both ate up with racing, and while I decided to be a race driver Doug chose to be a flagman, and a damned good one. He was probably the most prominent flagman of his generation.

I remember once when we were very little, playing out on the playground. Doug's older brother James came walking over—he wasn't much older than us—and he explained that Doug and I couldn't be friends any more. We both came to a standstill and looked at James and said, "Why not?"

"'Cause you're white, and he's black, you big dummies," he said. "Everybody knows a black kid and a white kid can't be friends."

I remember Doug and I standing there, bawling our eyes out, because we couldn't be friends any more. I guess James's comments didn't stick with us very long, though, because right away we were back to being good friends, and we're good friends to this day.

When I was in third or fourth grade we moved out to Mitchell, about 70 miles west of Sioux Falls. My dad worked at several different places, doing custodial work at schools, heating and air conditioning work, stuff like that. We were only in Mitchell a year or so, and eventually moved back to Sioux Falls.

When I was in ninth grade, my dad had a job opportunity in Beloit, Wis. so we packed up and moved. Sometimes it's hard to pinpoint an event that literally changed your destiny, but I look back at that move to Beloit as a turning point in the course of my life.

To begin with, any ideas I had of being a serious athlete went out the window. I was a competitive kid, and I liked sports. I was pretty decent in basketball and track, and I was all right in football. When I say "pretty decent" or "all right," I mean I was probably good enough to be on the starting five at Lincoln High School in Sioux Falls. But at Beloit I attended a huge high school, and everything was different.

I was probably 5-foot-5 my sophomore year, and maybe weighed 140, 150 pounds. When I tried out for football I saw kids who were 6-9 and weighed 270. I had never even *seen* anybody that big, let alone been hit by 'em. And in basketball I couldn't even touch the net, and these guys were dunking the ball. I was nowhere near competitive, and I could see the writing on the wall. I was outclassed.

I didn't feel all that comfortable there, anyway. It was a weird time for a lot of things in America, probably an awkward time for me to make the transition to a school like that. Our school was 50/50 racially mixed between blacks and whites, and here I am from very white South Dakota. I didn't have any trouble with anybody—white, black, whatever—because I kept a low profile and never had a problem. But that year Martin Luther King, Jr. was assassinated, and it made everybody act really weird toward one another. I think the blacks hated the whites because they thought the whites hated them; and the same was true for the white kids. They assumed the blacks hated them, so they acted accordingly.

The whole thing was weird and I didn't understand it. I don't think anybody did.

Whatever the reason, I never felt like I fit in there in Beloit. But looking back, moving there was still the greatest thing that ever happened to me.

A couple of blocks from my house there was a little Rexall drug store with a magazine rack. I discovered a newspaper there called *Midwest Racing News*, a weekly racing paper. Each week I'd walk down and buy my copy.

Boy, that opened my eyes. I discovered that racing was going on all over the country! When we lived in Sioux Falls, sometimes my dad would take me to the modified races in our area, but I never dreamed anybody was actually racing beyond Jackson, Minn. Never dreamed it could be!

Living in Wisconsin changed everything. *Everything!* We weren't far from Milwaukee, and my dad took us to some of the races at the Milwaukee Mile. Suddenly I got to watch A.J. Foyt, Johnny Rutherford, Parnelli Jones, Mario Andretti, Lloyd Ruby, Jim Hurtubise…those were the guys who ran the Indianapolis 500! And stock car drivers like Norm Nelson, Bay Darnell, Don White, Roger McCluskey. They all came to Milwaukee, and I'd sit in those grandstands and eat it up.

But the biggest factor was in the town of Sun Prairie: Angell Park Speedway. That's the place that really lit my fire. Angell Park is a third-mile dirt track west of Milwaukee, where they have kick-ass midget racing every Sunday night. That was true then and it's still true today.

My dad worked the second shift at the Fairbanks-Morris plant, which meant he didn't have to get up early on Monday morning. For an entire summer—maybe two, I don't exactly remember—we'd go to Sun Prairie every Sunday night to watch the midgets.

It was spectacular. There was a guy there, Billy Wood—he won a bunch of championships during this period—who was unbelievable. The cars didn't have cages, but he'd whistle that sumbitch into the corner like a daredevil. Man, it was exciting. He was a real racer, man, wicked-ass bad.

I sat up there in the stands, and I watched Billy Wood, and suddenly I wanted to be like him. I wanted to put my hands on that steering wheel, and feel the air washing over me down the straightaway, and hear that engine screaming, and turn the wheel and slide through the corner. Billy Wood was *the man*. My eyes would hardly leave his car when it was on the track. I was dazzled by the whole deal.

I'd see Billy Wood's name in the paper every week, and I thought he was God. Other guys I remember well were Tom Bigelow and Billy Engelhart. They were also very good. And Todd Barton, whose real name was Owen Snyder. He raced under an assumed name, which was kind of mysterious and very cool. It's funny, but later on Owen's daughter Dana married my friend Steve Kinser. Small world. Owen was a fine racer, and won a couple of Badger midget titles in the 1960s and '70s.

When I saw Billy Wood and Todd Barton and those guys pitch it into turn one at Sun Prairie, my sports days were over. I knew right then and there what I wanted to do with the rest of my life. Period.

I haven't said much about my mom, but I want to tell you about her. She was a very cool lady. Actually, my dad was cool, too. I'm sure we all had our moments but I liked my parents. Of course I loved them, but I liked them, too.

With my dad working the night shift, that meant Mom and I would have the evenings to ourselves. This gave us a chance to get closer, and we had a lot of fun. When the weather was mild, and in the fall and spring when the sunset was late enough, we would cruise out to the edge of town in our '55 Chevy and Mom would let me drive.

It was cool, being 14, 15 years old and driving that old Chevy. We'd get a hamburger at some little Dairy Queen or whatever, and Mom and I would sit and have our dinner and talk, then we'd head out in the country with me behind the wheel.

They had a lot more blacktop roads in Wisconsin than we had in South Dakota—certainly at that time—but sometimes we'd find a gravel road and my mom would let me slide the corners. I'm haulin' that '55 Chevy into the corner, leaning up on that big ol' steering wheel, feeling how the wheel moved the car around, feeling it with the seat of my pants. Mom taught me how to brake, and shift, and how the car felt when you slid. She showed me how you don't panic when the car was sliding; you stay calm and keep it under control.

A lot of times on Friday night we would drive down to Rockford Speedway in Illinois. My dad worked on Friday, so those trips were just my mom and I. We'd get there around 7:30, and she would park that old Chevy right by the pit fence. I'd hop the fence and help a couple of the guys—namely the late model guy, Joe Shear, and Jimmy Caruthers when the USAC midgets came to town—by bustin' tires, carrying fuel, whatever. Nobody even knew my name, I was just that kid who came and helped them. My mom sat in the car and read a book, or worked on her knitting, whatever it is that moms do while their sons are helping work on a race car.

Many years later I ran into Joe Shear—who had a tremendous career as a pavement late model guy, and he lived in Beloit—at a race track somewhere, and introduced myself. By then I had a pretty good career going myself, and Joe recognized me from seeing my name and picture in the racing papers. I asked Joe if he remembered me when I was a little kid. He looked at me with a blank expression and said, "No, I sure don't."

"I lived in Beloit for a while, and I rode my bike to your shop," I said. "I'd bust tires and hang around your shop."

Joe stared at me real intently, and then he began to smile and nod his head.

"I *do* remember you!" he said. He got the biggest kick out of that. It was pretty neat.

Another important thing that happened at Beloit came at the school library. Beloit is only 95 miles from Chicago, which is only 180 miles from Indianapolis. One of the newspapers they carried in our library was the *Indianapolis Star*, which did a great job in May covering the Indianapolis 500. I'd see the names, and some of 'em I had seen the previous summer at the Milwaukee Mile. And I recognized some of the names from when we lived back in Sioux Falls and I listened to the race while we had a Memorial Day picnic. Back then, while everybody else was playing games and stuff, I'd sit in the car so I could hear the race broadcast.

By this time those names, and that race, was starting to ring a bell with me. I'd read every line of that sports page, and every word made me want more than ever to be one of the drivers in the Indianapolis 500.

I didn't have any idea how much money a professional race driver made, and I didn't care. It wasn't about the money. It was about being a great racer. That's what I wanted to be. And that's all there was to it.

If you're going to be something, you ought to try and be the best. At that time, around 1968, 1969, the best drivers raced at Indianapolis. That's how it was, and there was no debate or argument. I wasn't just gonna be a race driver; I was gonna be one of the best, and that meant getting to Indianapolis. My mind was made up. Now all I had to do was figure out how.

2

The Plan

At 16 years old, I had a plan. An ironclad, foolproof plan: I was gonna race in the Indianapolis 500. All I had to do, I figured, was make enough money to buy an old race car for the modified races they had in my area, win a few races, and I'd be on my way.

Yeah, I know; it sounds dumb today, but that's exactly how I had it figured at the time.

I was still a teenager, and I didn't know anything. But I had figured out this much: If I wanted to get to Indianapolis, I'd have to work my way up through the minor leagues, kind of like you do in baseball. Working my way up meant total focus, and setting aside any other interests I might have had. So forget about sports, or hobbies, or anything like that, and concentrate on the things that would get me into a race car.

After one year my dad's job opportunity in Beloit didn't pan out like he had hoped, so we moved back to Sioux Falls. I didn't care one way or another, because where we lived didn't really matter. I was going to somehow connect with racing, and I could do that almost anywhere.

All I had to do was get some laps in a race car—any kind of race car—and I'd be on my way.

Of course, it isn't that simple. But I didn't know that. I didn't know *anything*. I was young and naïve and dumb as a bag of rocks.

Back in Sioux Falls, I re-connected with my childhood friends. Just down the street from our old house, a guy named Darryl Dawley opened up a transmission shop. Now, I didn't care anything about transmissions, but there was something else parked in one of those service bays: a race car!

Darryl raced the car at Jackson and Fairmont, both in Minnesota. The car wasn't legal at our local track, and it was kind of what you'd call a supermodified, with a roll cage but no wing. Every weekend Darryl would haul that thing down I-90 to Minnesota, and pretty soon he was one of the bad-ass racers in the area.

Which impressed the hell out of us kids. We'd hang on his every word, because he was real. He was actually racing, and winning, so that elevated him beyond belief in our eyes.

Darryl allowed me to hang out at the shop, and even gave me a part-time job cleaning transmission parts. I had been taking shop classes in high school, figuring that would help prepare me for working on race cars. Plus, I like working with my hands, so I really didn't mind fooling with those greasy transmissions.

Each evening after school I'd go work in Darryl's shop, and listen to the racing talk. My good friend Doug Clark hung out there too. We traipsed around like big shots, like we were plugged into the racing deal. Darryl was well-respected, and a lot of local racers would stop by his shop. It was soon something of a hub for racing activity here in Sioux Falls.

Doug and I stayed in the background, but we soaked up all that conversation, trying to learn as much as we could. I hung around the shop through my high school years, and Darryl taught me a lot about basic mechanics. Pretty soon I was doing more work for him, always with one eye on that race car.

When I was maybe 17, 18 years old I rode out to California with a friend of mine. I didn't have any real purpose for going, other than I just wanted to experience California. I had just graduated from high school, and we visited Ascot Park and saw 'em racing midgets and sprint cars. My God, I couldn't stand it! That kind of fired me up even more; I had such a powerful desire to race it was about to eat me up.

There was a little bar in Sioux Falls called the Beer Spot, and even though I wasn't yet of legal drinking age I would sometimes hang out there. One day I found myself in a game of "pitch," a simple little card game that was usually played for low stakes, nickels and quarters and beers. I was still a teenager, a broke teenager, so you sure as hell weren't gonna find me in a *high-stakes* card game.

But this fellow was pretty sure he had the better hand, so he asked if I'd be willing to take his race car as a wager. *What??!!* A race car? Are you kiddin' me? Hell yes, I'll take your race car as a wager!

Sure enough I suddenly found myself the proud owner of a '37 Plymouth coupe race car.

Damn, this was big time. My very own race car!

Actually, the thing was complete junk, and there were times when I wondered if the guy lost the card game on purpose. It couldn't finish a race, and I didn't know enough to figure out how to keep it running.

They wouldn't let me run the old car at Huset's Speedway—our local track in Sioux Falls—because they said I was a hazard. I probably *was* a hazard. So me and my buddies—I had a bunch of high school pals who were all excited about being on a real-life pit crew—took the car down to Scotland, S.D., for our first race.

Scotland is about 100 miles from Sioux Falls, and it felt like you had to go to the end of the earth to get there. This was just a dusty little race track out in the middle of a cornfield. You probably could have divided all the cars there into three divisions: Junk, Truly Junk, and Hopelessly Junk. Our old Plymouth would have fit into the third division, for sure.

You know how a young kid says he's so desperate to race, he'd drive anything? Well, this old car was even less than anything.

But I climbed in for the first time, and got out onto the race track for my heat race. I'm whistling along, maybe going 40 miles an hour, kind of nodding my head and thinking, "I'm getting better…I'm doing *all right*!"

All of a sudden I felt this hot liquid all over my crotch. Immediately I'm thinking, "Oh, my God, I've got so scared I've wet my pants!" All I could think about was how I was going to explain this to my high school buddies back in the pit area.

What had actually happened was that the radiator overflow hose wasn't tied down, and it was swinging around under the hood, spewing hot water. The water was coming through a hole in the dash and squirting me right in a very important and sensitive area.

When I got back to the pits and realized what had happened, it suddenly seemed funny. It wasn't so funny a few minutes earlier when I thought I had pissed my pants.

To say I was less than stellar is a pretty big understatement. It was the debut of the great Doug Wolfgang, but the world was immediately underwhelmed.

But I wasn't discouraged. Not at all. Hey, I was racing. That's all that mattered, getting there. You start somewhere, and then you've got to get yourself going better. Then you think about the right color of helmet, and the uniform has got to be nice, stuff like that. After a while, you're interested in getting a better car. It's probably like that in anybody's business or sport. You begin as a peon, then you work to get on a better pickup team, then an organized team, then score the most points.

It's that way in racing, too. In the beginning you just want to be a part of it. It doesn't matter if you're any good, but you're out there, you're doing it.

I raced that old coupe four or five times, and finally gave up on the damned thing. It was so bad; I took it back to the guy from the card game and gave it back. I've sometimes wondered if some other poor sap came along behind me and found themselves the lucky owner of a '37 Plymouth coupe race car.

By this time I had a full-time job at a local auto parts house, working in the machine shop. They did machine work on engines, valve jobs and stuff like that, and they were going to teach me the ropes. It wasn't a bad job. I did learn some stuff and they were okay to me.

I still hung around Dawley's shop, and also at Ron Larson's service station a couple of blocks from my parent's house. Ron wanted to build a modified, and we got to talking about his idea. He asked if I'd be willing to come over and help him build this thing.

Soon Ron got covered up in his business, and he didn't have time for the race car. We were working in a small two-car garage behind his house, a little place with a tiny kerosene heater. Got kind of chilly in the wintertime, but we managed. When Ron got busy, it kind of fell into my lap to build the new car. I don't know how I did it, but I somehow got it finished. I had learned just enough to know how to cut a piece of tubing, and how to grind it so that it fit with another piece. I have no idea how I got it square or level, but I must have been fairly close.

We were nearly finished with the car, and spring was right around the corner. Ron said he'd maybe let me drive the car a time or two, but by this time all the racers were coming out of the woodwork, checking out each other's race cars. This car had turned out semi-nice, and Ron decided to let Bill Hill, a pretty good local racer, drive it that summer. I wasn't sore, because

Bill was an established racer and I understood that Ron would put the more experienced guy in the seat.

Bill was maybe ten or 15 years older than I was. He was originally from California, and came through town while racing the fair circuit with the IMCA. Bill liked Huset's, and decided to settle down here. He opened up a service station about two blocks from Dawley's, and always had race cars in there. That was also a cool place to hang out.

One Friday morning Darryl called me at the machine shop. Looking back, I've got to say it was one of those phone calls that truly changed my life. Darryl was telling me I ought to come to work for him full-time in his transmission shop. I hem-hawed a little bit, because the machine work was a little more appealing to me than working on those greasy transmissions. But then Darryl said, "I'll tell you what: You come to work for me, and I'll let you drive my modified."

I hung up and quit my job on the spot! Hell, I didn't know anything about giving a notice or anything like that. Besides, Darryl had recently bought a sprint car, and now his modified was just sitting. He needed somebody to go with him that night to Mid-America Fairgrounds in Topeka, Kan., and that would be me.

My job at Darryl's meant I'd work on transmissions during the day, and at night help with the race car. I made $50 a week, but the money didn't matter. The big draw for me was that modified sitting over there in the corner. I was pretty sure this was my first break in getting to Indy.

Darryl had won the track championship for something like three years running, so I knew this was a good car. It had been torn down, and it was my responsibility to get it put back in race-ready condition. Darryl also provided a trailer, but it was up to me to get something to tow it with.

On one of my first outings in the car, we took it over to Jackson. I started 10th in a 10-car heat race, and I was probably running second going down the back straightaway on the first lap. I mean, totally out of control. I got down to the third turn, and never hesitated, just drove 'er straight in. The front end pushed right out and I hit the fence, bending the right front corner of the car.

I didn't bend the frame, but really did a number on the front axle. I was pretty concerned about how I was going to tell Darryl about this, and on the ride home decided, hell, maybe I didn't have to tell him anything. I'd fix the car real quick, and he'd never know the difference. Right?

We hurried to the shop and got a good look at the car, and the right front wheel was pushed so far back it's sitting on the magneto. I fired up the porta-power and the torches, got everything heated up, and started straightening. Pretty soon the thing looked semi-okay, and after it cooled I sprayed a coat of paint on and rolled 'er back up on the trailer. Darryl was running his sprint car at Knoxville, and I knew he wouldn't be getting home until around six a.m.

So I'm figuring everything is cool, like nothing is going to be said. But one of Darryl's daughters had seen me out there working on the car, and the next morning said something like, "Say, Dad, did you know Doug wrecked your car last night? He was out here all night working on it."

Darryl gave me all kinds of hell, but not really. I think he kind of understood, and I suppose he realized how hard I had worked to try and make it right. But was I dumb, thinking I'm going to cover this baby up.

I worked 90 hours a week, just to be able to drive that race car. I'd work my full week for Darryl, and the rest of the time I'd spend on the car. But I considered myself very lucky to get a break like this. See, I had no idea how to get started on my own. The '37 Plymouth had shown me that it was harder to get going than I had imagined. When Darryl opened the door for me, it allowed me to take my first itty-bitty steps in the direction of being a race driver. I wasn't much good right off, but that was beside the point. I was driving a race car, and starting to learn a little bit here and there.

I got going pretty good later in the year, and actually won a race at the South Dakota State Fair. All of a sudden, Indy didn't seem so far away after all.

3

It's a Grown-Up World

When I began working for Darryl Dawley in his transmission shop, the fact that I could drive his modified was truly the greatest fringe benefit he could have given me.

But I learned an important lesson in the process: Nothing lasts forever. Even though we were friends, and I felt like I was doing him a good job in the shop, we split up after that first season and went our separate ways.

That left me without a race car to drive. I'd like to say all I had to do was take the phone calls from eager car owners wanting to hire me, but the silence from that phone was deafening. Kind of like that country song: "My phone ain't ringin' so I assume it ain't you," or something like that.

Not only was I out of a ride, I was also unemployed. So I took a job at a wrecking yard about 10 miles west of town. Yes, sir, I was moving up in the world.

Since I wasn't exactly overwhelmed with offers to drive somebody else's car, I figured my best option was to get my own race car. So I scrounged up what little money I could and bought a wrecked race car from a local guy. It was pretty torn up, but since I had learned to use a welder and a cutting torch at the junk yard, I had my basic education pretty much handled. After all, with those old cars you could fix almost anything on the car with a torch or welder.

One other challenge—I had a lot of challenges, it seems like—was a place to work on the car. My dad had a tiny garage he eventually let me use, and because of the tight space I'd usually have to drag the pieces out into the alley to work on 'em. Late at night I'd be out there, freezing, sweating, cussing, hammering away.

Luckily I had a bunch of friends who helped me. It was fun, really, with those guys hanging around. We had a good time. I was all of 19 years old, and life was pretty carefree. Of course, it's because we were all young and dumb and had no idea of anything.

We eventually got the old car running. Yeah, it was pretty basic, and I didn't set the world on fire, but I was racing. I raced several times in Sioux Falls, and a couple of times over in Minnesota. It was fun.

In a slow, subtle way, my life was changing. I was growing up. I was still young and dumb, but this was a period where I sort of stumbled into making grown-up decisions. I know I made lots of mistakes, but I was very, very lucky: The most important thing I got right on the first try.

The guys who helped me on my race car all had girl friends, and all these girls hung around as a group at school. The guys were friends and the girls were friends, a typical deal for kids this age. The guys had all graduated in the past year or two, and the girls were seniors in high school.

The girls would kind of hang around that old garage, waiting on the guys to finish working on the race car. Then they'd go to the lake or the movies or whatever, just mess around. Pretty soon I noticed another girl who was hanging around with them, a girl named Jeri Wegner. Pretty soon Jeri was coming to the races with us.

She didn't have a boyfriend, and I didn't have a girlfriend, so she'd sit up in the front seat with me. My dad let me use his 1960 Chevy station wagon as both my daily drive and our tow rig, and we'd pile four people in the front and four in the back, and fill the rear area with race car parts. That old wagon had a distinctive aroma, kind of a combination grease pit and brewery, because everybody was drinking beer. Things weren't quite very professional yet.

So Jeri got stuck sitting with me. There was an outdoor movie place in Sioux Falls, and on Wednesday night they had what they called "Buck Night," which meant everybody you could get into your car got in for a buck. They showed a double feature. I don't think anybody was actually watching the movies, but they were raising hell and it was a fun place to hang out.

So there was Jeri and me, kind of stuck sitting next to one another by default, while everybody else was boyfriend-girlfriend. After a while we started dating, I guess I asked her out a few times and we started going around together.

The summer faded away that year, and the South Dakota winter moved in. It got to be November, and Jeri and I were still dating, and all of a sudden she broke up with me. I didn't know why, but she seemed pretty upset and said she didn't want to see me any more. I couldn't understand this, because I liked her and I thought she liked me. We didn't date for about a month, although I'd bump into her around town when she was hanging out with her girl friends.

Sometime in December she called me. "Doug, we need to talk," she said, and she asked if we could sit down and meet. I told her that would be great, because I still liked her, a lot.

We went out that next Friday night, and sat and talked for a while, and finally she told me she was pregnant. Really, "we" were pregnant, but that's not how she said it. She was scared, afraid to tell her parents, and she didn't know what to do.

"Well, I know what to do," I told her.

She kind of looked up at me, and said, "What?"

"The first thing, you better go tell your mom and dad, and the second thing is we'll get married."

So that's what we did. In January 1973, we got married. Naturally, it was a hard thing for her parents to accept, because you have to understand that things were different at that time. People didn't live together, they got married. If a young girl was pregnant, it was considered a disaster, and a lot of times girls were sent away to some faraway relative's house to have the baby, because it was considered a scandalous thing. For a lot of parents, having a daughter get pregnant before she was married was considered almost the worst thing that could happen. It was like the end of the world.

Her mom warmed up to me okay, but her dad was never really cool with me, especially in the beginning. But I don't blame him. In his eyes, I was ruining his daughter's life because she wasn't able to go to college and have an education. Remember, she was right out of high school when this happened. Plus, he didn't know anything about me, and God, I didn't have a damned thing in terms of a future. I was broke, dumb, and had no idea of anything. I was working at a junk yard, and didn't even own a car. I had $150 to my name, and Jeri was making payments on a Chevy Malibu. To say we didn't have much is, well, a pretty big understatement.

Off we go, into the wild blue yonder.

You know, I look back today and realize that most of our friends—from that group of guys and gals riding in that old Chevy wagon to the drive in—have been married and divorced a couple of times over the past 34 years, but Jeri and I are still together. It's kind of amazing, when you think of the circumstances. But we stuck with each other, no matter what, and it's been the greatest thing for both of us, I think. I'm kind of proud of that.

When a young guy gets married, his life changes. We were going to have a baby right away, and it took every dime we made to stay alive. It was obvious that my days as a race-car owner were over; spending money on a race car didn't exactly fit with the priorities any more. Hell, keeping that old modified going had taken every dime I had the previous summer, so it wasn't hard to figure out there was no way I could do that again.

I don't remember being disappointed about it, I just accepted that's how it was and that was that. I hadn't given up on the idea of racing, but I knew I couldn't race out of my own pocket.

There was a little bar in Sioux Falls called the Pit Stop, where a lot of the racing people hung out (what an original name for a racing bar, huh?). I wasn't much of a beer drinker, but we stopped by there a couple of times a week during that winter to visit with racing people. Gary Bott, a local guy who drove his own modified, approached me and asked what I had going for the '73 season race-wise. I told him I had nothin', because I couldn't afford to run my own car. He told me he still had his car, but didn't think he'd have time to drive it the next season. He called me a couple of weeks later and offered the seat to me for the 1973 season.

"If you want it," he said.

Want it? Hell, yeah, I want it! It was an opportunity to race, without getting into my pocket. Actually, it was the only real opportunity I had.

By this time I had taken a job as a motorcycle mechanic, which turned out to be a big step up for us. My job at the salvage yard paid maybe $100 a week; it's amazing to think that a family could live on such a small amount, even at that time. But $100 paid the rent and bought food, so somehow we got by.

A friend of mine, Eddie Deubler, was a motorcycle racer, and he was working at Stitches Honda-Kawasaki in Sioux Falls.

One day Eddie called and asked if I liked working at the junk yard.

"Aw, it's okay, I guess," I said.

"You ought to come down here and work at our shop," he said. "We're looking for a good mechanic. I think you could make $200 to $300 a week here, fixing these bikes."

"Hell, Eddie, I don't know *anything* about motorcycles."

"Hey, you'll learn. I've watched you, and you'll be okay. Come on over and give it a try."

I wasn't much of a mechanic at that point; really, it would be a stretch to say I was a mechanic at all. I had a very basic understanding of things, and didn't understand how to properly use a lot of the various tools of the trade. But I wasn't completely dumb, and I did have some aptitude for mechanical work. The last two years of high school I had taken as many mechanical shop classes as possible, because I figured it would help me as a race driver, and get me to Indianapolis all the faster. Indy was still like a beacon to me; I hadn't lost sight of my goal to run the 500.

See, all this was part of my plan to work my way through the minor leagues. The minor leagues for Indianapolis in the years previously were midgets and sprint cars, but you didn't start there. In our region, you started in something like modifieds or some other class. So my plan was still pretty basic: win the championship around here in a modified, then I'd get me a sprint car and go down to Knoxville and win a championship down there, and like some guys before me—Joe Saldana and Jan Opperman, for example—that would get me to Indianapolis. Then I'd be set for the rest of my life, no sweat.

'Course, it doesn't exactly work like that, but I didn't know that. I laugh today at how dumb and naïve I was, thinking you waltz right to Indianapolis smooth as can be.

My job at Stitches turned out to be a great opportunity for me and Jeri. We were expecting our first child, so making enough money to support ourselves was very important. I was working on a shop rate, which basically means I worked on commission. I'm the kind of guy who will hustle, you know, I'll get with the program when things are rolling. I learned how to work very quickly, using air tools and stuff.

It was actually a fun environment, and a fun period. At that time, in-line four-cylinder Japanese motorcycles were the rage.

Honda had the 750 and several other bikes, and Kawasaki had the Z-1 900 which was a killer crotch-rocket. Truly a super bike, very fast and fun to ride. Most of the customers for these bikes were guys my age, anywhere from 19 to 25 years old. Lots of guys who raced also rode a bike for fun, and it seemed like everybody coming by the shop was involved in motorcycle racing or drag racing or oval racing. I thought all of this was great, and very interesting. I was *into* it! I liked the job, I liked the people, and I was eager to learn and get more efficient and make some money.

Boy, did those local boys and their crotch-rockets keep me busy. See, the Z-1 had a two-shaft transmission, if I'm remembering correctly, and when you went from third gear to fourth the process of shifting gears was a tiny bit balky, and guys would miss a gear. They were turnin' these things 12,000 RPM at the shift points, and when they missed a shift and the engine suddenly revved with no load on it, it would spin it to 15,000, 17,000 RPM. Today that probably wouldn't be as big a deal with modern synthetic oils and such, but at the time it was a very big deal because almost every time it would bend or break the valves.

It seemed like all these maniacs would do this at least once or twice, miss a shift and tear the shit out of the top end of the motor, or the transmission. So they'd haul their bike to our shop, and away I'd go.

First I'd yank the motor off the frame, tip it upside down and fix the transmission, then go through the motor. This job was rated at a specific number of hours, but I could do it in half that time. And do it right, too. My pay was based on the published rate, which meant I was making good money, sometimes as much as $400 or $500 a week. Damned good money in those days.

Those wild-ass boys on their Z-1's bought us a lot of diapers and baby food. God love 'em!

4

Breakthrough

Motivation came easy in early 1973, because I desperately wanted to prove to everybody that I could support my family on my own. Especially Jeri's dad, because I knew he was very skeptical.

I focused all that motivation into my job. I was a workin' fool on those motorcycles, boy. As fast as they'd bring 'em in for repairs, I'd fix 'em and try to beat the shop rate. As it turns out, I was probably making more money than Jeri's dad at the time.

I wasn't a real smart guy, but I could perceive that some people had me figured as a no-account lowlife. That bothered me, and I wanted to prove 'em wrong.

Six months after we got married, our daughter Niki was born, and a couple of months later we bought a house. They called them "1099 loan" houses or something like that, some kind of program to help first-time home buyers. We weren't exactly flush with cash, but we were doing all right.

I'll tell you a funny story from when Niki was born. I was driving Gary Bott's modified, and was doing a little better as the season went on. We usually ran a couple of times each weekend, and as the summer progressed I was improving but hadn't yet won any races.

Niki was born on July 18, 1973, and it just so happened that on that very night there was a special promotion at the local track. It benefited the local Sertoma Club, which went around selling all kinds of tickets and the turnout was very large. It was $600 to win the feature, damned good money for modified racing at the time. Actually, that's probably good money for modified racing yet today!

Gary Bott and his wife were a little older than Jeri and me, and were kind of gruff. We didn't pay much attention to that, just kind of learned to ignore it. Gary would give me hell about "stupid driving" and stuff like that, but I never took it personally.

On the night of the Sertoma race Gary approached me and said, "I'll tell you what, Sonny, I'll make you a deal: If you win tonight, I'll give you all the money. All $600. But if you don't win, you race for the next month for free. How about it?"

Remember, I hadn't won a race all year.

I just grinned at him. "I'll take that bet." 'Course, it didn't really matter, because it wasn't the end of the world if I didn't win. But I was damn sure motivated by the idea of winning $600.

Sure enough, I went out and won the race! I drove around to the frontstretch to get my trophy, and climbed out. You could hear Bott yelling from the top row of the grandstand: "You rotten son-of-a-bitch! You never won a race all year and you win this one!" I'll never forget it...I laughed and laughed. It was great. And you know, I didn't win another race for him until the very last race of the season, when they had a 35-lap championship race. Those ol' boats steered so hard, it was usually all you could do to make 20 laps, but I shined in those 35-lappers. I think I won that race three years running, in fact.

How about this: Niki cost us $667, and that $600 pretty much covered it. Had a baby born and almost paid for, on the same day. And that $667 was the TOTAL bill; Jeri and I didn't qualify for insurance because she was pregnant when we got married, and we had to pay the bill ourselves. Can you imagine paying $667 for a baby to be born? Two years later Cori was $2,000, some years later Allie was $7,000, and later still Robby was $12,000. None of them had any complications, so that was just basic cost. Luckily, we had insurance on the later ones.

The following winter Bott was hired as a mechanic on one of the better modifieds in town, and they hired me to drive for the 1974 season. We did pretty well, and won several races. I was starting to get my name out there in modified racing, but in our region there wasn't any question about what was considered the premier division: sprint cars. And I was keen on getting into a sprint car.

However, it's a big financial jump from modified racing to sprint car racing. Actually, it's not a jump, but more like a *leap*.

Buying a sprint car was out of the question for me personally, and again the silence from the telephone was deafening.

Then I finally got a break. In late 1974 I met Dick Morris, a Chevy dealer from Sioux City, Iowa. At the end-of-season banquet Dick said he had purchased a new sprint car from a builder in Lincoln, Neb., named Don Maxwell. I had heard of Maxwell but certainly had never met him.

I was pretty tuned in to what has happening in sprint cars, at least on a local basis. Each year they had a big two-day sprint car event called "Cheater's Day" which drew a lot of guys from out of town. Joe Saldana, Scratch Daniels, Itch Daniels, guys like that. Lots of those guys would hang out at Pete's Welding Shop, and of course my buddies and I would hardly leave Pete's while they were there, because we wanted to listen to them talk about sprint-car racing. We'd hover around, soaking up every word.

Dick explained he was going to Phoenix for the Western World Championship in November, which was one of the biggest sprint car races of the year. Man, I *knew* what the Western World was about. Dick was aware I wanted to go sprint-car racing eventually, and I think he was just being helpful and kind when he asked me to come along on the trip. Not to drive his car, but just to hang out with them. He used an old school bus to haul the race car, with the front part of the bus converted into kind of a motorhome. Not fancy by any means, but functional.

"You can throw a sleeping bag in the bus and ride along," he said. "I'll pay your way in to the races, and I'll even buy a hamburger now and again. It'll be a cheap trip and you'll get to meet some sprint car people."

Of course, I thought this idea was totally cool. Dick went on to tell me something else: Maxwell was looking for a welder in his shop.

"I've seen you weld, and I know you can work on stuff," he said. "If you got a job working on sprint cars, you might be able to get a car to drive. It's worth a shot, right?"

I told Jeri I was taking a week off to go out to Phoenix, and she was cool with that. So I rolled up my sleeping bag and climbed into that bus, and I guess that weekend trip to Phoenix changed my life forever.

It was a very different time for racing, different than the sport we know today. Things were a lot less organized, and more informal. People were down-to-earth, and not as professional. The Western World attracted guys from every part of the country, and I mean *every* part of the country. It was a big deal and I was fascinated with all the people.

A lot of racers stayed on this angled street near Manzanita Speedway; I think it was called Grand Avenue. Old motels lined the streets, and racing guys would sit out by the swimming pool until the wee hours of the morning, drinking beer and bullshitting. I loved it, obviously, because I could sit there and listen to important guys telling sprint car stories. Man, it was like heaven!

Each night after the races, Dick and his guys would drive back to the motel and retire to their room. But I'd hurry down to the pool, hoping some racers were hanging out, telling stories. Sure enough, the guy who ran second to Rick Ferkel was sitting there, his name was Rick Goudy. This particular hotel hosted most of the CRA guys from California, and several were sitting out there talking, drivers and crews and some fans. We sat there until four or five in the morning, drinking beer, but nobody got drunk. Just having fun, really. It was nice outside (meanwhile it was probably snowing back in Sioux Falls) and it all seemed incredibly exciting to me. I was getting sprint-car fever, big time.

That trip pushed the button. I mean, I was ready, and I wanted to race. But at the same time, it all seemed impossible. My life had changed, and the possibility of actually driving a sprint car seemed so far off you couldn't see it with the naked eye. I tried not to think about it, because it was so hopeless. But that trip to Phoenix fueled my passions, and motivated me. Seeing the great Western World, and seeing all these great racing guys, it inspired me.

(Three or four years later, when I was starting to do pretty good, several of those CRA guys remembered me from that night sitting around the pool. I thought that was very cool.)

As soon as we got back to Sioux Falls, I called Maxwell and asked about working for him. He kind of hem-hawed a little bit, and said yeah, they're building some cars and stuff, but he wasn't sure he needed that much help. I called him a few more times and finally drove down there, maybe pestering him a little.

I kept calling, and drove down there again, and finally in November he agreed to hire me.

Now I had a *full-time* job in racing. I was going to be building sprint cars for one of the most successful guys in the country, Don Maxwell. Suddenly, things had changed, and it was all starting to happen very quickly.

5

Life in Lincoln

Don Maxwell's shop was always busy, and I settled in and tried to listen and learn and contribute. Wealthy Pennsylvania car owner Al Hamilton had ordered a car, and we were immediately busy because the car had to be finished in time for the Florida races in February. Hamilton had hired Jan Opperman to drive the new car in Florida.

We worked through December and January, and every day I was still kind of in awe. There I was, immersed in sprint-car racing, with one of the top builders in the country. Maxwell's shop was located near I-80, a major east-west thoroughfare. Lots of racers would stop by while they were passing through, and maybe spend half a day hanging out. I got to meet Rick Ferkel, Opperman, and several others.

I was still pretty much in the background. I was this shit-dumb kid from South Dakota with long hair, who asked all these questions and told everybody he wanted to drive a sprint car. But people were nice to me and after a while people started recognizing me as "the kid who worked for Maxwell."

Life was good. However...

This was all a financial disaster for Jeri and me. The first couple of weeks I'd leave Sioux Falls each day around 4 a.m. and get to Lincoln around eight. I was driving back and forth a lot, and after a few weeks Jeri and I finally rented an apartment in Lincoln, a little duplex. We sold our house back in Sioux Falls and actually made a little money, but when we sat down at the end of the month to pay our bills we realized pretty quickly that we were probably going to go broke at this deal. Jeri had quit her job to move to Lincoln, so we were back to one income. The wage I earned at Maxwell's was actually very little, and I justified this by telling myself how much I was going to learn there.

Still, it was sobering, trying to figure out how we were going to survive. We had a baby girl, and we knew almost nobody in Lincoln, so it was pretty hard on Jeri. But I set all those things aside, because I really wanted to do this. You rationalize, you know, when you want something very badly. I was so excited about getting involved in big-time sprint-car racing; I was willing to sacrifice a lot. I knew back in Sioux Falls I didn't have any prospects of driving a sprint car, and at least this gave me a chance to be close to the sport, and at least get some exposure.

Jeri and I were still young and innocent, and when you're young and innocent and you're in love—with each other, and I was also in love with sprint car racing—you don't think about things like rent or insurance payments. I didn't know how we could make it, but I had to try. I just had to.

In January, just a couple of weeks before the races in Florida were set to begin, Jeri and I went back home for a weekend visit. To be honest, neither one of us were all that pumped up about living in Lincoln, and we missed our family back home. We were homesick. Plus, our folks liked seeing their grandbaby.

I stopped by Darryl Dawley's shop to say hello, and immediately he perked up.

"I'm leavin' for Florida!" he says. "C'mon and go with me!"

All of a sudden I'm thinking, "You know, I really need to go to Florida. I need to see what's going on, and socialize, meet some more sprint-car people, and also I could watch the new car we built, the one Opperman would be driving."

So I told Jeri what I was thinking, and she was okay with it.

Darryl told me he'd put me up if I'd help him, but he couldn't pay me anything. That was okay; hell, I was broke anyways, so a couple of more days living like a hobo didn't make a damned bit of difference. We loaded his stuff up and headed South.

We were staying at Robert Smith's place down in Gibsonton, not far from East Bay Raceway, although at that time the February races were still held at the old fairgrounds downtown called Plant Field.

If you've never met Robert, the best way I can describe him is that he was without a doubt the biggest hillbilly in the world. The biggest! I mean, he was great. He was a southern boy, through and through, and made no bones about it. He was a fun guy, and very generous. You'd lose count of all the racing people who stayed at his place down through the years. He was very hospitable and a lot of fun to be around.

The Florida races were like a convention of sprint-car people. You saw just about *everybody* down there, and you'd get to the track early in the day and visit, and after the races you'd hang around with everyone for a couple of hours. It was a great opportunity to meet lots of people. The Florida races had been a big deal for many years and everybody who was anybody had won a race down there.

I hung out in Opperman's pit, and got to know Joe Hamilton, Al's brother. Joe was a great guy, very kind, and treated me well. This confused me later on, because a couple of years later I met Al Hamilton, and he acted like a jerk from day one. Of course, that's just my opinion and it don't matter what I think.

Hanging out in Opperman's pit allowed me to meet a lot of great racers whom I was definitely in awe of. These were some of the best in the country at that time, and I thought it was cool to meet these guys. Opperman, Bubby Jones, Chuck Amati, Kenny Weld, Jerry Blundy, lots of heavy hitters. I knew who *all* those guys were, but they had never heard of me, of course.

I probably wore people out, telling them how bad I wanted to drive a sprint car. I don't know if it helped me any, but some people knew I worked for Maxwell, so at least I had a tiny bit of recognition.

On Tuesday night Robert got a big poker game going at his house, and everybody was drinking beer and having a good time. I'm not much of a beer drinker, and I can't stand to sit still and play cards (plus I had no money to gamble with), so I went out in the shop and rebuilt Darryl's engine. Not really a big deal, just put new rings and bearings in the motor.

Actually, the beer drinking and card games went on *every* night at Robert's. I slept out in Darryl's camper, but he stayed in the house. The next morning everybody was all hung over, and I'll be damned if Darryl didn't win the feature later that night. First time he had won in Florida and I had rebuilt his motor.

When the events wrapped up I helped Darryl load his gear and we headed for home. This had been a great trip, because I rubbed shoulders with some big-time people in sprint car racing. I don't imagine anybody thought twice about me, because I was still a nobody. But the important thing was that I was inching closer to being a sprint car racer. I was starting to get more involved, and working at Maxwell's helped me gain a lot of knowledge, not just of race cars but of the people who were important in the sport.

One of the key people who influenced me during this period was Jan Opperman. At that time, Opperman was like the gold standard that every aspiring racer compared himself to. I mean, the guy was the greatest of the day, no question about it. Whether you liked him or not, it didn't matter; you had to acknowledge his talent.

I guess in looking back, he was probably the closest thing I had to an idol. Everybody dreamed they might be as good as Opperman, and I was no different.

I actually had a little bit of history with Jan. It's funny now, but it wasn't very funny at the time.

When I was still a teenager, my buddies and I would often go to the races with Darryl. He was our guy; we figured he did everything but hang the moon. I was probably 16 years old, maybe 17.

One weekend we rode with Darryl to the Clay County Fair in Spencer, Iowa, which each fall hosted a big modified race. This was just before Jan went to Pennsylvania and really became famous, so most of us had not yet heard of Jan Opperman.

Opperman was there that day, and he's leading this modified race. Darryl was pretty much the king of modified racing then, at least in our region. He moved up to pass Jan, and clipped the back of Jan's car. They had graded a furrow at the bottom of the track, and Jan hooked this furrow and turned over.

Jan got out of the car, and boy was he was pissed at Darryl! I remember Jan was wearing a fireproof uniform, which was not yet common in our area. He had peace signs and stuff patched on his uniform, wore his hair long, and was different than anybody we had ever seen.

The field was circling around slowly while they cleared away Jan's wrecked car, and Jan—he's standing in the infield now, not far from where my friends and I were hanging out—started throwing mud clods at Dawley, kind of expressing his displeasure. This went on for five or six laps, and it started to tick me off.

I walked up to Opperman and tapped him on the shoulder.

"'Scuse me, sonny, but that's my driver out there, and I don't think you ought to be doin' that."

In defense of Jan, he didn't say anything. He didn't tell me to get out of his face, he didn't call me a punk kid, nothing. He just looked at me and I walked away.

Next lap, he picks up another mud clod and throws it at Dawley, aiming for the window opening. I tapped him on the shoulder again.

"Son, you ain't hearin' me now, that's my driver and you're makin' me mad. You don't need to be doin' that!" Still, nothing was said from Jan.

Third time by he throws another mud clod. This time I hurry over and crack him on the shoulder.

You know, by the time I blinked, he hit me twice in the face so hard it knocked me on my ass. And that was all there was to that.

While I'm sitting there on my ass, I immediately thought, "You know, to hell with Darryl, he can handle this himself!" Besides, I was riding in the back of the pickup anyways, because they wouldn't let me sit in the front. When you go to the Clay County Fair it's September, and it's about 40 degrees when you leave to go home. I froze my butt off. So I wasn't feelin' particularly eager to get my ass thoroughly whipped by this long-haired guy with peace signs on his uniform, when my stature on Darryl's team wasn't even enough to get me a seat in the cab of the truck.

About five years later, Jan came to Fairmont, Minn., to run a No. 4j sprint car for Fred Aden out of Lincoln, Neb. It was a July midweek race, and I was driving Gary Bott's modified at the time. We got off work that afternoon and my dad joined Bott and me to ride over to Fairmont to watch the races.

By this time Opperman was big-time famous. I mean famous like through all of sprint-car racing, across the entire country. He was a monster talent by then. He had spent a couple of years in Pennsylvania, won a bunch of races, won the Knoxville Nationals, and really had it goin'. He was a star.

We hung around his trailer that night, and there was always a big crowd around him. We could hang close enough to eavesdrop as he talked to others, and later on my dad talked about how much he enjoyed listening to Jan carry on a conversation. He really was skilled with people.

Little things like, "Oh, this motor ain't big but it's quick, and we'll be all right." Things that made him sound confident, but not bragging. People liked that.

I stared at that race car, and damn, I wanted to drive it so bad I was about to fall over. God, I dreamed of someday driving a car that good. I looked at everything about the deal: the car, Opperman, the trailer, his mechanic (Tommy Sanders, who later worked with me on a sprint car), the whole deal. It was everything in the world I wanted.

That night Jan started 18th and he dusted 'em. Drove around everybody and won going away, all the way from the back. It was impressive as hell.

I didn't know this, but Opperman knew what was going on. He looked like the kind of guy who would never read a race paper, but he did. He knew all about who was winning races, in all kinds of cars.

We're standing right at the trailer, looking things over, and he suddenly noticed me from across the way and walked over to me.

"Ain't you that boy from South Dakota?"

He knew who I was, and I don't know how he could have remembered that. Not only that, but by this time I had won a few modified races, and he evidently knew my name. I was so stunned, and surprised, I just shifted on my feet and stared straight ahead, absolutely at a loss for words. Jan Opperman is standing here, talking to *me*! What am I supposed to say?

"Yeah, ain't you that boy from South Dakota that would throw mud clods at me and now you're winning a few races?"

I shook my head just a little and smiled.

"I didn't throw mud clods at you."

He smiled, with a gentle laugh. "No, I guess you didn't."

"Yeah, I'm him," I said.

"They tell me you win a few races nowadays," he said, smiling. "In fact, they tell me you're pretty good."

Man, that felt good. Really, really good.

When I went to work at Maxwell's, I got to see a lot more of Opperman. He lived in Beaver Crossing, not far from Lincoln, and since Don built his race cars Jan often came by the shop to hang out.

I wasn't sure I liked his lifestyle. Actually, I'm not sure I *understood* his lifestyle. The long hair, talking about Jesus, talking about smoking marijuana, I didn't understand any of that stuff. I didn't see how it all mixed together.

The guys I knew in Lincoln did smoke some pot. They'd go up in Maxwell's office and smoke a little marijuana and I'd look the other way. I tried not to pay any attention. I wanted to do what I wanted to do, and I didn't want to get into any trouble or anything. And to tell you the truth, I was so green, I didn't know what any of it was. That's how stupid I was. I hadn't heard of cocaine yet, and I'd barely heard of marijuana, so I wasn't sure it was all a taboo deal. Something instinctive told me it wasn't right, but I didn't know *why* it wasn't right.

For me, and I guess for a lot of young kids at the time, it was all very confusing. You're taught to be this way or that way, and it seemed like everything around us was telling us the opposite. And you'd see guys talking about religion and crosses and Jesus, and on the other hand you'd hear rumors about them chasing women. I didn't know how it all mixed together.

So I kind of ignored all that stuff and let it go.

Opperman was the first guy I ever met who seemed larger than life. I had been around a lot of racers, and I knew all of them were way bigger than me, but nobody came anywhere close to having the presence of Opperman. It was like the seas parted when he walked in. It was like everybody stood in awe. It was like God, almost.

I don't know why everybody felt that way, but they did. And I did, too; even though I had only seen him race four or five times, I still felt that presence, that aura.

Maybe it was the times. Today, kids see everything instantly on television on the Internet. Well, we obviously didn't have the Internet, we didn't have cable TV, and there damn sure wasn't any racing on the few channels we had. We couldn't walk down to the 7-Eleven and buy a racing publication on the magazine rack, because there were no racing magazines. Hell, we didn't even have a 7- Eleven!

So most of what we heard was by word of mouth, and *Speed Sport News*. Yet Opperman's legend continued to grow. It was like you thought this guy was the greatest son-of-a-bitch ever and you just knew it. I don't know *how* you knew it, but you knew it. It was like he walked on water.

Funny thing was, I worked with a guy named Randy Hunt who grew up and went to school with Jan and his brother Jay.

And Randy was in awe of Jan, just like everybody else, even though he had known him since they were little kids.

Jan commanded a presence like nobody I had ever met. Charisma, I don't know exactly what you'd call it, but he definitely had it.

Even though I was in awe of the guy, and had the privilege of getting to know him a little bit, I didn't understand him. You know, wearing the cross on his uniform, the long hair, and calling a prayer session after the races were over. Baptizing people, the whole deal, then going up to smoke a joint with his buddies. I struggled to figure out how to respect and admire certain things, even though I wasn't in tune with other things.

After our Florida trip I went back to work, and Maxwell didn't seem to mind that I had taken a few days off. You know, looking back, Don really helped me. He hardly paid me a decent wage, that's true, but I can't complain. He didn't say much about me being gone, and he listened when I told him over and over about how much I wanted to race.

Don was clearly ahead of his time. He was a mechanical genius, and I mean that literally. The man had a brilliant mind. He was not a gifted businessman in terms of dollars and cents, but he had such a powerful understanding of how things worked, and how to build and create things, he was an amazing guy.

For example, later on Don did some very interesting things. He worked with several guys to put a small V8 engine—like a Chevy 283 or a Ford 289—into a P-51 Mustang airplane. This was a very complex project, and Don was one of the few guys who could design the intricate mounting and linkage issues involved.

Maybe his most impressive feat was the portable sound stage he created and sold to several top musicians and musical acts. For years these guys had like six semi-truck loads of gear to set up at each show; Don developed this deal where everything was integrated into a couple of semi-trailers, and they'd back it into place, fire up the hydraulics, and these huge arms would extend out and in a matter of minutes they had a sound stage. Maxwell looked at their old setup and figured there must be a better way, so he invented it. The guy really was amazing.

It can't hurt to hang out with a guy like that. It's hard to measure the impact this period had on my life, and my career.

There were things, knowledge and techniques and tools, I picked up there that serve me to this day. Plus, Don was a friend, and he helped me make the most important step of my racing career: I was about to become a sprint-car driver.

6

Sprint Car Break

At any one time, there are a bunch of sprint-car drivers around the country. I don't know the exact number, maybe a thousand, maybe two thousand. I have no idea. In the overall scheme of things, I guess, it's kind of a small number.

For every one driver, I'll bet there are five guys who work on the car in some capacity. A lot of those mechanics are frustrated race drivers, who either hope to get a ride or never did get a ride but still love the sport. It's always been like that; there are always a bunch of guys on the outside looking in.

That's where I was in early 1975. I was working for Don Maxwell, and had the opportunity to be around sprint cars, and sprint car people all day long, but I was still on the outside in terms of getting to drive. I'm sure at the time I felt like it was never going to happen.

Nobody publishes a handbook that tells you how to be a sprint-car driver. Nobody lists the things you need to do to find a ride. Of course, it's very different today because so many kids start out racing for their family. When I started, the way "in" was to get hired by a car owner. But how do you do that? I didn't know then, and I'm not even sure I could tell a guy today how to go about it. It's just a matter of trying to be in the right place at the right time, and meeting the right people.

I was frustrated, that's for sure. What was taking so long? Why wasn't I driving a sprint car yet? Even though I had lots going on in my life—I had only been married a couple of years, and was still pretty young—I couldn't stop thinking about sprint cars. Damn it, I knew I could be good, if somebody would give me a chance. I had a fierce, burning desire, but didn't have much to show for all that desire in terms of actually getting behind the wheel.

Right around the first of April, I got my first real break. Charlie Martin, a mechanic for a guy from Norfolk, Neb., (that's the town where Johnny Carson, the famous TV show host, grew up) decided to let me drive their car for the 1975 season opener at Knoxville. Charlie was from Lincoln, and had worked with Joe Saldana in past years. Charlie hung around Maxwell's shop now and then, mainly because that's where you could bump into interesting or famous sprint-car people.

The car was an old spring-front Roger Beck car, but Jan Opperman and Saldana both had won the Knoxville Nationals in a car with a similar narrow-spaced frame. It really was a beautiful car, and Roger Beck had a reputation as an impeccable welder and a great craftsman. And I was gonna make my debut in one of his chassis! Man-oh-man, we're on the road now!

Just as I was getting excited, however, the deal came crashing down. Charlie called and said the car owner had some financial difficulty and wasn't going to be able to race the car. In fact, the man was selling everything. Just like that, my big break evaporated. Poof!

My buddy from Sioux City, Dick Morris, decided to buy their stuff. He recognized that this was a very good car, and knew he could easily sell it. But he also wanted all the spares, so he bought the entire operation. As it turns out they had 25, maybe 30 Halibrand magnesium wheels with mounted tires, and a lot of good stuff that Dick could put on his other car, the Maxwell chassis.

At six a.m. on the morning of Knoxville's opening night, my phone rang. It's Dick. He tells me he's feeling kind of bad that he bought "my" car out from under me, but I explained he didn't need to feel bad at all. They weren't gonna race anyways, so I was done before I got started.

"I'll tell you what," Dick said, "if you'll tell me what gear you want and what four tires you want, I'll fill it up with fuel and bring it to Knoxville tonight and let you run it. Tonight only. We can't be changing gears and tires there at the track, but I'll get it ready here if you'd like to drive it. I'm going to sell this car right away, so if you wreck it you've got to fix it."

I hadn't driven at Knoxville yet; hell, I hadn't yet been in a sprint car! Not once!

I told Dick that I appreciated his offer, but I didn't have anything in terms of resources, and if I tore the car up there's no way I'd have the money to fix it. So I didn't feel like I ought to drive his car for that one night.

I hung up the phone, and Jeri and I were lying in bed, talking. After about one minute I just couldn't stand it, and I knew I had to drive that race car. I just had to. I called Dick back and said, "Okay, put in a 5:18 gear, and this tire on the right rear, that tire on the left rear…" and so on. I was basing all this on what guys told me they ran at Knoxville; I had no idea if any of this would work for me, but it was all I knew.

That night turned out pretty well. I timed second-quick, and ran second in my heat. They had a trophy dash, and I ran second in that, too.

One of the cars in the pits that night was the No. 4x sprint car owned by Bill Smith. Bill owned a very successful mail-order performance company, Speedway Motors, in Lincoln. Everybody called him "Speedy Bill," or just "Speedy." Now, believe me, at the time the 4x was one of the premier teams in the entire country. In fact, in our part of the country it absolutely *was* the premier team. Every sprint-car driver wanted to drive that car. That night Bill had hired Ray Lee Goodwin, a Missouri driver who had won the 1968 Knoxville Nationals.

While working for Maxwell, sometimes I'd go over and see Speedy Bill. Hell, he didn't know me from Adam, but I'd go see him anyways. I'd saunter into his office, flop down in one of his chairs, and pretend like I knew what I was doing.

"Sonny, you need to hire me," I'd say, trying not to act nervous.

"What for?"

"To drive that race car."

He'd just laugh.

"Maybe you ought to get some experience first."

"I don't need no experience. I could drive your race car."

Well, I kept trying. But Speedy was very nice to me and I figured we were buddies.

That night at Knoxville, I'm driving Dick's sprint car and I worked my way up to second place. Hell, I took to that car like I had been doing it for 30 years. It just felt…*comfortable*. I felt like I was doing what I was supposed to be doing.

Right in front of me was the 4x, with Ray Lee driving. I mean, I'm right on him. I'm thinking I can pass him, and win the race. But I eased up, because something inside of me said, "Sonny, you shouldn't be doin' that."

YET.

I finished second, which shocked the hell out of everybody. Nobody there even knew who I was. It was, "Who is this long-haired bum-lookin' guy who ran second? Where's he from? What's his name?"

I kept my mouth shut, but I wanted to tell everybody, "It's Wolfgang. W-O-L-F-G-A-N-G. Sioux Falls, South Dakota."

That night, I became somewhat credible. Or, maybe I took the first step toward being credible. I went back to Maxwell's on Monday morning and went to work, like nothing had happened. I didn't have another ride lined up, so as far as I knew this was the one shot of my lifetime and that might be it. I didn't really think that would be the case, but it was possible.

Boy, that was a looooonnnngggg week. I was dying to get back to Knoxville that next Saturday night, even though I had nothing going on. But I was itching to at least *try*.

On Saturday we drove back to Knoxville, and Jeri and Niki sat by themselves up in the grandstand while I went to the infield pits. I started at one end and worked my way down the line, talking to every single car owner and asking if I could drive their car. Of course, that ain't the best way to do it, but what did I know? Besides, what were my options? My phone still wasn't ringing off the hook just because I ran second the week before.

But at least some of them remembered me.

"You the boy who ran second last week?"

"Yeah."

"Oh. Well, I already got my driver."

And so on.

Pretty soon qualifying was over, and then the heat races. I was standing in the infield, kicking rocks and feeling disgusted, when Lenard McCarl came walking toward me. Lenard was a good racer from Des Moines who had been racing at Knoxville for a long time. Lenard drove his own No. 7x sprint car, but he evidently had the flu and was feelin' bad.

"Hey, you Doug Wolfgang?"

"Yeah."

"You think you could drive my car? It's the best car in the field, and it'll go faster than anything out there. I don't expect you to win, but buddy you'd better finish the race if you drive it. And it's got the biggest motor you've ever driven so it's gonna wear you out."

Ol' Lenard, he can be a little gruff.

They were already through the consolation race, so I barely had enough time to get into my uniform. I pulled my helmet on and I'm a little nervous, you know, because I'd only been in one sprint-car race in my life, and I didn't even get a warm-up lap in this thing.

I wound up running third or fourth, I'm not exactly sure. And Lenard was right, it was a bitch to drive. I mean, it steered so hard it flat wore me out. I was amazed, because Lenard isn't a big guy, and I had no idea how he could drive this thing.

Incidentally, that's the night I realized that if I was gonna drive sprint, I had to be in better physical shape. That's the night I knew it for sure. Not long after, I started working out, running, and concentrating on being in the best physical condition possible.

Like I said earlier: I was willing to do whatever it took to be successful. If that meant working out in a gym, fine. Whatever it takes.

Through the rest of that season I ran several different cars, but never did win any races. I crashed a couple times, and did okay a couple of nights, but after a few weeks I kind of had that sinking feeling that I was going nowhere fast. It felt like nothing solid was happening in terms of becoming a real-life, honest-to-God sprint-car driver.

A couple of good breaks had come my way, but everything was kind of scattered. It was like some small doors had opened, but no really big doors, you know? And I wanted it so bad, it was hard to be patient.

It's kind of like that cartoon with the two buzzards sitting on the limb, and one says, "Patience, my ass! If dinner doesn't come along soon, I'm gonna kill somethin'!"

Jeri and I hauled ourselves to something like 80 sprint-car races that summer, with me either driving a one-off deal or maybe not even finding anything that night. We were livin' like bums, really. We didn't have money for motels, so we'd sleep in a camper, in the cab of the truck, whatever, with Niki right there with us. Jeri never complained, never said anything about it. It was kind of amazing, I guess, how we got through that period. Of course, we didn't really have it all that bad. I don't remember even having one argument about it. We did argue later, but not then. We were still young kids in love and all that, so things didn't matter so much.

I do know this: If gas back then was as expensive as it is today, we would have gone broke. Period. There's no way we could have traveled like that, because we were razor-thin on money anyways.

Did Jeri like it? I don't know if she liked it or not. I never asked her. I don't know if she had an idea that this was going to be how it was *forever*. Maybe she had in her mind that this part—all the traveling, being tired and poor all the time—was only going to be for a little while, and then things would get better.

Besides, this was going to be my *job*. Racing was going to be how I made a living. And Jeri and I were both brought up that you respected what someone did for a living, and didn't really ask why.

Things did get better, eventually. But boy, those were some hard times we got through.

I had quit driving the modified back in Sioux Falls that summer, because it was too far to commute on Sunday nights. Even though I made good money in the modified, and won a number of races, I felt like if I was gonna be serious about sprint cars, I had to show a commitment. If a guy wanted me to run his sprint car some weekend and I said, "Well, okay, but I have to get back in time to run the modified in Sioux Falls on Sunday night..." I didn't figure that would send the right message to these car owners.

Toward the end of the season, I was second-guessing myself. I might have made a mistake, because I passed up a lot of opportunities to race the modified, yet still hadn't landed a steady sprint car ride. Plus, I was getting more frustrated with my financial situation. Our second daughter, Cori, came along on January 12, 1976, so now I had a wife and two little girls to provide for.

Winter set in and I was still working at Maxwell's, welding up race cars. Maybe I was down on myself, whatever, but all of a sudden I just couldn't see anything in the future, at least with how things were right then. It looked to me like I was goin' nowhere fast. I finally sat down and talked to Maxwell.

"Maxwell, I'm not goin' anywhere," I told him. "I'm tired of living like a bum. I can't get a race car to drive, I'm about to starve, and this just ain't workin' out like I figured it would.

"I think I'm gonna give you notice that this spring I'm going back home to Sioux Falls, because I can drive a modified there and go back to work at the motorcycle shop and make some good money."

I didn't want to leave Don in the winter, because that was by far his busiest time. So I figured I was doing right by him by letting him know three, four months ahead so he could plan for my leaving.

In my mind, my decision probably meant that my sprint-car career was not going to happen. I would be driving modifieds the rest of my career. But my destiny was still in sprint cars, and one key reason was that ultimately Don Maxwell was all right to me. As a matter of fact, Don Maxwell was damned good to me, and I am very grateful to him.

He understood where I was coming from, because I had told him—over and over again—for more than a year how much I wanted to race. And he wasn't dumb…he could see that with me having two kids, and knowing he couldn't afford to pay me more, it was only a matter of time before I'd have to leave and get another job, just to provide for my family.

But Maxwell really went to bat for me, and that was the big break that absolutely opened all the doors that mattered. Not long after he and I sat down and talked, Maxwell had a purely happenstance conversation with a guy who turned out to be just about the greatest thing that ever happened to me.

Maxwell had lots of different racing products, certainly not just chassis. He offered all kinds of components, including a plastic fuel tank that didn't require a bladder.

Bob Trostle was a successful car builder and owner from Des Moines, and he came up to Lincoln every now and then to buy pieces and components from Maxwell. Bob called one day and said he was coming up to pick up four or five of those plastic fuel tanks.

When Bob called that day, he was probably not in the finest of moods. His driver had just quit him, saying he wanted to go back to driving his own car. On top of that, just as Trostle received a big order for several cars, his welder left him to go back to the small-engine business.

Trostle was telling all this to Maxwell, and Maxwell kind of perked up.

"Hey, I've got just what you need," he said. "I've got a kid who is a sprint-car driver, who can weld! That's just what you're looking for!"

"Really? Who's that?"

"Doug Wolfgang. He works for me here, but he's already told me he's quitting because he wants to be a racer and he can't find a car to drive down here."

"Oh yeah? Can he weld?"

"Yeah, he welds real good!"

Yeah, Don Maxwell was all right. Totally, totally all right.

7

Trostle

You remember that phone I told you about, the one that was never ringing off the hook? Well, in early 1976 it rang. Not exactly off the hook, but when it finally rang with a car owner on the other end, it was a damned good car owner.

I picked up the receiver and heard Bob Trostle's voice on the other end. He had a proposal for me to think over.

"I just sold five cars to Kenny Woodruff to take to Australia and we've got to have them done in the next few weeks," he said. "You come over and do those cars for me, and you can drive my sprint car for the rest of the year."

Are you kidding me? At that time, Trostle was one of the most respected car owners in the business. He had some great racers in his cars through the years, guys like Jan Opperman, Dick Sutcliffe, and so on. And here I was, still pretty much a rookie. I had never even driven a car with upholstery before.

To say I had lucked out is a big understatement. I was so excited, I probably forgot to hang up the phone; I probably dropped the receiver, ran to the car, and hauled ass for Des Moines. Well, maybe it wasn't quite that frantic, but close.

I knew who Bob Trostle was, of course, but I had no idea what kind of a person he was. Was he a good guy, or a jerk? Quiet, or loud? I didn't really know what it would be like, working for him.

I soon discovered that I had nothing to worry about. Bob was very good to me, and we hit it off real nice. Over time he eventually got to where he was somewhat like a father to me in many ways. At the time I was 23 years old, and he was maybe 40, 45, so there was naturally a generation difference. He wasn't telling me how to live or anything like that, but he was just a good person, a good mentor and advisor to me. He provided me with a job, he paid me on time, gave me a race car to drive, and paid me 40 percent of what the car made. He did everything he said he'd do.

At that time, I believe his car was probably as good as any sprint car in the country. In fact, in 1976 his car was *as good as* anything in the country; but in 1977 it was the *best* car in the country. More on that in a little while.

The first few weeks I stayed at Bob's house, because Jeri had her hands full with two little girls back in Lincoln. She was taking care of all the details so we could move to Des Moines.

Each morning Bob and I got up around 7:30 or 8 a.m., and we'd work till 10 o'clock every night. Hey, we were under the gun, trying to get those five cars built for Kenny Woodruff. We really had it goin'.

I remember Bob walking by me, kind of kidding me, saying "I just hope you're as good a race driver as you are a welder, because you can definitely weld!"

"You ain't seen nothin' yet, Bob," I told him. "I'm twice as good a driver as I am a welder!"

You know how kids are. I could be a little bit cocky.

Our first weekend of racing was a whirlwind experience. We had spent several hard weeks in the shop, really humping. We got the cars finished for Woodruff on time, so that was a relief. Now my desire to go racing was about to boil over, and I was ready. I mean, *ready*. I had my mind in the right place, and I was focused. The time—my time—had come.

It was Easter weekend, 1976, and we loaded up and headed for Riverside Speedway in West Memphis, Ark., for a two-day show, Friday and Saturday night. After Saturday night's race we drove through the night and raced at Paragon, Ind., on Sunday afternoon, and as quickly as we finished racing at Paragon we hurried over to Tri-State Speedway near Haubstadt, Ind., for a Sunday night race. Then we drove through the night again to be back at Des Moines on Monday morning for work.

Right away, I saw how dedicated Bob was to racing. Really, I saw how dedicated almost *everybody* was. Looking back, I'm kind of amazed everyone had the stamina for it. To think about me being 40 or 45 and living and working like that, I don't think I could have done it. Even at 23, it just about wore me out. It didn't seem like a big deal at the time, but when I think about it today, wow!

Jeri left the kids with our folks and rode along with us, and we stopped in Kansas City on Friday morning to pick up some wheels from Weld Wheels. That was the first time I met Greg Weld, there in his factory.

I didn't win anything that first weekend, but we did all right. At West Memphis I was running second to Bobby Marshall when the yellow came out. I didn't know this, but at Riverside—everybody called the place "the Ditch"— local rules allowed you to race back to the yellow. Somebody passed me for the position, and then the yellow turned into a red. During the red I told Trostle I was gonna try to win this thing with a big slider from the bottom on the restart, but guess what: That didn't work. I dropped another spot and ended up fourth.

I was kind of disappointed because I thought we could have won. But I was also happy and relieved that we were competitive right out of the gate. That felt pretty good.

I should mention that Bob wasn't officially the car owner by himself. Dave Van Patten, who operated a mobile home dealership in Des Moines, was a partner with Trostle both on the car and in Trostle's chassis business. Dave bought the material for the cars and furnished all the gas for our traveling, and Trostle provided the tow rig. It was one of those give-and-take deals that are all over racing, and it worked pretty well.

The Paragon race was an afternoon deal, and the track slicked off big time, just slick as glass. We started back a ways—ninth, I think—and that's where we finished. Later that night at Haubstadt, Dick Gaines won and we ran fifth.

I don't figure we did too badly for our first weekend, considering that we were up against excellent competition. Gaines was in Karl Kinser's car for a couple of the races, and at West Memphis we were racing against Marshall, Bubby Jones, Sammy Swindell, Rick Ferkel, and many more. It wasn't like we were racing against a bunch of slugs. There were a lot of great racers there.

One thing that surprised me was Bob made it clear from the beginning that it was my car and I could do anything I wanted from the standpoint of setup. I don't think I did anything trick or spectacular, but I know for certain that Bob was very open to things, and definitely wasn't telling me I had to drive it any certain way. Of course he had lots of ideas, because he had far more experience than I did. He had worked with—and learned from—some of the greatest drivers of the day long before I came along. So we had a nice balance of his experience, my ambition and desire, and pretty good chemistry.

After our first weekend together we went home to Des Moines and worked for a week or two, preparing for the season opener at Knoxville Raceway.

Knoxville was without a doubt the biggest weekly program in our region. Guys would tow three, four, five, six hours every Saturday night to race there. It was a big, dangerous place that was fast, fast, fast. I liked it from the word go.

Bob and I went down to Knoxville that first Saturday afternoon—after towing to West Memphis on our first weekend together, we probably felt like we could have almost *walked* to Knoxville from Des Moines—and it was almost like the world threw the gate open for me, and got out of the way. We set fast time, won our heat, won the dash, and won the feature.

Boom. Just like that.

I remember Bob walking up to me in Victory Lane, and he looked at me real serious, and said something like, "You weren't kidding, were you?" I didn't understand, and I just said, "What?" He gave me a focused, intense look, and nodded his head, and just said, "You can drive."

The look on his face said it all: Now we're ready. Let's go racin'.

As 1976 progressed we got better and better. I was learning, and getting more confident. We won four of the first five races at Knoxville, and did the same at Fairmont, Minn. By the time the season wrapped up we won a total of 21 features, which was the most Bob had ever won in one season. He and Dick Sutcliffe had won 18 together, and we topped that, which was pretty cool.

We won seven races at Knoxville, and at the time it was a new single-season record. Several great drivers had won six in one season—Jerry Blundy, Bill Utz, Tiger Bob Williams, and Greg Weld—but we managed to get seven.

As I sit here today, 31 years later, I'm thinking about all this and marveling that it all happened so quickly. Am I surprised that things took off so strong, right away? I think I am now, but at the time I probably wasn't. I was very confident, and I expected to win. However, I don't think anybody *else* expected me to win. In a way that made it easier, because there weren't any outside expectations.

I can't say enough about how easy Bob was to work with. Oh, we had our moments, but he didn't dog on me or needle me or tell me I needed to drive harder. He was very good for my confidence, because he believed in me, and he put a great car under me. We worked well together and you could look forward to going racing with Bob. Throughout my career I worked with lots of different people, and just about every personality type you can imagine. Some of those guys were gruff and rough and pretty rugged, and they didn't mind getting on your ass for the smallest little thing, and really cut you down with their criticism.

Bob wasn't like that. If I made a mistake we could talk about things and he didn't make me feel like a piece of shit, you know? He treated me with respect, and in turn I respected him, very much.

Looking back, it's interesting that Bob was so willing to listen to my input on setting up the race car. I was still pretty green, but I was very eager to learn, and to try new things. And it was cool, because Bob was that way too. Hey, he had been racing at Knoxville since 1950 and had a sprint car in the first Knoxville Nationals in 1961. He could have beat his chest and told me how much he knew, but he didn't do that. He listened to my ideas, and I listened to what he knew, and together we came up with some good things. And the great thing was, we didn't keep score of whose idea it was. It wasn't like we were trying to outdo each other with knowledge; we just worked together to make the car better.

Sometimes my ideas were good. Not because I was smart, but because I didn't know very much of how it used to be done. See, a lot of times people will do the same thing over and over again, for years, because they believe that's the way it's done. For example, when I came along everybody ran soft tires when the track was tacky and grippy, and hard tires when it was slick. But I felt like that was backward; the gumball tires didn't necessarily help your car when it was tacky; but when the track got slow and slick and you needed traction, bolt on the gumball tires and hope they wear to the cords, because that means they're grabbing the track while the hard tires would just spin.

I'd make a suggestion like that to Bob, and he'd listen. Hell, let's try it. Sometimes when we did it the opposite of everybody else, we were way faster. Other times, we weren't. But you've got to try it to see what works. Some guys can't do that; they're too hardheaded. Not Bob; he was always willing to listen, and we weren't above drilling a hole in the frame to move the radius rods up or down, just to see if it helped the car.

He also taught me a lot of things people wouldn't understand. He taught me by example. If you raced late on Sunday night and didn't get home till 4 a.m. Monday morning, he was still at the shop at 7:30 a.m. He never said he expected me to be there; he never said I'd get fired if I came in late. But when you see him giving 100 percent, you feel like you should too. That's something I've never forgotten. Things aren't easy and sometimes things don't go right. But what are you going to do? Sit home and bawl about it? You ain't fixing anything if you do that.

Bob had a work ethic like you wouldn't believe. Just outstanding. And that taught me a lot. Just that one thing, right there, was a big influence in my life. There were many things he taught me, obviously, but just that one thing, the idea of working hard, was pretty important.

I grew very close to Bob, and considered him more than my car owner. He was a friend, almost like a relative. Like family. But something happened the following February that was an important lesson to me, something I never forgot throughout the rest of my career.

We were racing at East Bay for the annual February races, and I tangled with Paul Pitzer—he was driving Bob Weikert's car out of Pennsylvania—and broke my shoulder blade. We had been very good right out of the gate that year, winning at Phenix City, Ala., and winning a couple of the Florida races. What happened with my injury was very common at the time, because our seats were too low (we know that now, but we didn't know it then). When my car got upside down, and my body was stretched out because of the g-forces of the flipping car, my shoulder blade slipped up and over the top edge of the seat. When the car slammed into the ground—BAM!—it broke the tip off my shoulder blade.

It wasn't a bad injury, but it was enough that they hauled me to the hospital. This was the first ambulance ride of my career. I don't remember being scared, or feeling a lot of intense pain. Bob and the guys on our crew said they would pick me up later at the hospital, so I rode alone in the ambulance.

They did X-rays and all that stuff, and put my right arm in a sling and released me. I'm sitting there in the lobby, waiting for Bob and the guys. I'm waiting, and waiting, and waiting, and finally around two in the morning here they come. I was pretty upset by then, because I'm hurting and these guys left me sitting there by myself.

"What took you guys so long?" I said, probably sounding more than a little grouchy.

"Well, we put an axle in the car and hired Joe Saldana to run it the rest of the week," they said. "We couldn't leave until we had the car ready to race tomorrow night." They were actually surprised that I was irritated, and kind of gave me a funny look, like, "What did you expect us to do?"

What I expected was I would be their number one concern. I expected them to drop whatever they were doing and come take care of their driver. But that's not how it happened. And that was a genuine moment for me; like a bell going off, loud and crystal clear. The message that came ringing directly into my soul was, "Sonny, you are replaceable."

Welcome to the cold, hard world. Welcome to mortality. These are the facts of life: "You ain't God, and the world ain't stoppin' just because you got hurt." The car wasn't hurt bad, but the driver was out for a couple of weeks, at least. They wasted no time hiring a replacement.

Now, believe me, I'm not saying this to cut Bob Trostle, not one bit. Because he was not at fault in any way. He did what any car owner would do under similar circumstances: He got things together so he could keep racing, then came and picked me up.

But it hurt my feelings, because I was under the assumption things would be different. Me and Bob were friends...I stayed at his house and we worked together and had lunch together every day. But you see, I wasn't Bob Trostle's son. We weren't blood relatives. I was his driver; nothing more, nothing less. And I didn't understand that's the way the world worked. It ain't all peaches and cream every day. Tough things happen and everybody deals with it and moves on.

We stayed in Florida for another week or so, and I was all messed up. My arm was in a sling, and it was hurting. They gave me some medication for the pain, and unfortunately the medication constipated me, of all things. After a couple of days I went off the medication and suddenly I was, how shall I say this, un-constipated. But because my arm was all messed up, it was very difficult to wipe myself. I just couldn't get organized to do it. This was a very difficult situation. Luckily, a friend of Bob's, Jerry Payton, helped me out some. Now that's a friend, there. Definitely.

Eventually I got better, and things settled down. The Florida races finished up and we headed back to Des Moines and concentrated on getting ready for the 1977 season.

It would be a season that would be like no other, a season that literally shaped the future of all sprint-car racing. We had no idea, but we were about to turn the sport up on its ear.

8

Yes, You Can Put a Sprint Car on a Diet

Bob Trostle and I had now been together for a full season, and had done very well together, but we weren't satisfied. I think both of us wanted to win more races, have more success, and so forth. You always strive to be all you can be, and that's where we were. Winning 21 races in 1976 was great, but for 1977 we wanted to win…well, more than 21. Naturally, that's how all racers think.

Our first season together had taken me to many new tracks, and we had raced against arguably the best drivers and best cars in the country. It was a valuable learning experience, because I noticed other cars, and saw what other people were doing with engines, setup, wheels, and so forth. Everybody was searching for an advantage, like it's always been.

I'm the driver, so naturally the first thing I'm wanting is more horsepower. Gotta have more power, Bob. One thing I distinctly remember is hearing the engine in Karl Kinser's car, with Dick Gaines at the wheel. Boy, that motor breathed fire. You could hear it, and you could see it. It was obvious that other guys were getting ahead of us in terms of horsepower. Very obvious.

I knew Karl was getting some of his engine stuff from Earl Gaerte, an engine builder from Rochester, Ind. Earl wasn't well known at this time, although his sprint car engines would eventually make him famous from coast-to-coast. I told Bob he ought to have Earl Gaerte build us one of those kick-ass engines, and we'd probably go better.

But Bob was the car owner, and he paid the bills. It wasn't just a matter of getting more horsepower; it was a matter of getting something we could afford. Big horsepower was going to cost big money, and we couldn't afford what it would take for an engine like that.

So buying a hot new motor was out. We were back to the drawing board.

Somehow in our conversations we got to kicking around the idea that if we couldn't buy more horsepower, then maybe we ought to build a car that was lighter, because the most amount of power pulling the least amount of weight would go from Point A to Point B faster. If we had the same power as last year, but pulling less weight, we'd be faster, right?

That conversation was the genesis of our kick-ass 1977 season. Right there. Almost by default; we didn't have the funds to buy a new engine, so we did the next best thing: we lightened the race car.

It was already late February, so we had to get rolling on it pretty quickly. We decided to look at every single component on the car, from top to bottom, front to back. You weren't going to downsize any one piece and make it happen. We started at the front bumper and went to the rear, from the top of the roll cage to the belly pan and suspension. Our goal was to look at every single element of the car and use a lighter piece that would still do the job.

We studied the rear end, the driveline, the in/out box, the engine, the radiator, fuel lines, filters, everything. We tried to make it as simple and light as we could. For example, everybody had been using steel wheels; we found some spun aluminum wheels and made them work. Nobody had aluminum cylinder heads, but we got some aluminum heads from Brodix that had been used in other types of racing and made them work on our sprint car.

It wasn't any one thing. We tried to look at the big picture, and do a little bit on everything. Of course since Bob built the cars, one of our advantages was that we could build a lighter frame ourselves, a frame nobody else had. I know Bob struggled with the idea that it might be all right for some, but not all right for everybody. He hadn't built anything like this yet. So it wasn't like we just started drilling holes in everything. We tried to be more scientific.

Believe me, the scientific approach of 1977 was nothing like the scientific approach of 2007. For example, metallurgy was not nearly as advanced, because people had not yet developed the exotic lightweight metals available today. We were using pieces and parts that didn't cost much more than the traditional parts, whereas today they'll spend $5,000 to save eight pounds. We were barely into aluminum and magnesium, and there was no titanium. If there was, we didn't know about it.

We had weighed our 1976 car when we started the project, and we would use that number to gauge how much progress we made with our new car. We weighed the old car with tires and wheels and 20 gallons of fuel, and all the fluids, just like we would race it. It tipped the scales at 1,920 pounds, ready to race.

We continued to make progress with the new car. We got the frame together, and slowly but steadily began installing the new pieces and parts. Soon we dropped in the engine, got everything plumbed, chased the niggling little things to finish up, and bolted on our new aluminum wheels. We poured 20 gallons of fuel in the tank, added the proper amount of fluids, filled the radiator, and put the cap in place. We wiped down the finished product with a cloth and pushed the car to the scales.

The car was rolled into place and we stared at the gauge. The number said 1,480.

We were stunned. We had shaved nearly 500 pounds—almost 25 percent of the mass—from the car.

It was an amazing thing. What we were able to do, with limited knowledge and certainly limited funds, was mind-boggling. Our approach was antique, and simple. Actually, our way—antique, simple—was just us; we didn't know any other way to approach it. We did the best we could with what we had.

The whole project was not a top-secret ordeal. We just built it quick. I don't think anybody knew what we were up to, but not because we kept it a secret. Maybe Bob did, I don't know. But I don't remember anything being hush-hush, and us being worried somebody might find out. We honestly didn't think it was a big deal, but then again I know we didn't expect to cut 500 pounds. No way were we that optimistic.

Our first race was at Bloomington, Ind., on a Sunday afternoon. The car had just been finished, and hadn't even been painted yet. We arrived late because we forgot about the time zone difference, and missed qualifying. We started last in the B-main and transferred, then started last in the feature and got to fifth or something like that. Even though it was dry-slick, we were going forward. It was actually pretty encouraging. Not spectacular, but all right.

We discovered that we didn't have the proper amount of gusseting in the rear torsion tubes, and both tubes broke out during the course of the race. We got back home and fixed that problem, and painted the car. We then traveled to Lincoln, Neb., where we won. A week later we won the opener at Knoxville. Things were definitely starting out the way we hoped.

It wasn't difficult to figure out what we were doing. I mean, Stevie Wonder could have seen it: Our car looked different than any other car. We had aluminum torsion arms and stops, and we had a lightweight front axle. You could see these things; no big secret. We used Ford 5-degree spindles with home-made aluminum steering arms, while they were using big, heavy International steering arms and those spindles weighed much more. We had aluminum hubs instead of steel hubs. Instead of steel rear bearing carriers, steel arms, steel radius rods, steel nerf bars, everything was aluminum. Today all this is common, but ours was the first car that had aluminum arms.

I'm sure people believed it wasn't safe. I didn't think much about it, but then again I had already convinced myself years earlier that I was willing to die in order to win. That's stupid, isn't it? I wasn't trying to do anything reckless, but I was willing to take the risk in order to gain the advantage.

Actually, Bob took a great deal of time and effort to understand how to make things as strong—and safe—as possible. He discovered that there are several kinds of aluminum, for example. What type you could bend, what type you could weld, what you couldn't, what was the stiffest, the hardest, the strongest, and so forth. Most of the things we built on that car, they eventually made much lighter. As we—I'm saying "we" as the entire sport, not just Bob and I—learned more, we applied it and continued to progress.

But we were definitely overkill with that first car, compared to what everybody else was running.

How quickly did they react? I don't really know. Bob was the car builder, so he would probably know more than I would.

But suddenly we were winning everything. Everything! I know everybody else certainly noticed that.

Probably the guy who figured it out quickest was Karl Kinser. In no time he had a light car, too. Hey, he was a helluva thinker. You had to get up damned early in the morning to get an advantage over Karl. And he had Dick Gaines, a helluva driver. They were a force to contend with, anywhere they went.

But the lightweight concept was not without its faults. In the summer of 1977 Gaines was badly hurt at Champaign, Ill. in their lightweight car, which pretty much ended his career. I've wondered sometimes if what happened to Dick at Champaign was the same thing that happened to me many times that summer.

See, the lightweight car was real tippy, especially early in the night when the track was tacky. It was stuck real hard, all the time. Stuck down like a nail. This was something we hadn't experienced before. But if you think about it, it made sense. If you're Paul Bunyon, standing in the infield with a fishing line hooked to a race car, and you're slinging it down the straightaway, then through the corner and back to the other straightaway, which car will slide out farther? The heavier car or the lighter car? The heavier car, of course. But we didn't understand the basics. This car accelerated faster, stopped quicker, and didn't slide out as much in the corners. It was instantly stuck down harder on the race track.

Yet, we ran our setup like everybody else: Wheels in, and rear axles narrowed up. We didn't understand, not right away. They're much wider today, but at the time we were using 50, 51-inch rear axles, and 47, 48-inch front axles. Our wheels and tires were narrower, too. When the track was sticky, I'd go into the corner and the car would just stick like glue, lift the inside tires, and roll over. Just like that. This happened to me probably seven or eight times that year. Big time. At first we didn't know what was causing it. And I was still a young kid, and I didn't understand that if I would just calm down I could win against almost any competition, from 24th starting spot in the feature. That's how much faster we were. Plus, the track conditions worked to our advantage; as the night went on, it went from being tacky to being slick. The heavier cars pushed like a pig when it got slick, because you're trying to turn that much more mass. It's just basic physics, really. All I had to do was wait, because when it got slick, God, we had them handled. When they slid out I would just turn to the inside and pass 'em, because my car was stuck while theirs slid out. I'd drive right by 'em.

But I was a kid, and I wanted to win everything, including hot laps. Not on lap three, either; I'm thinking more like before we take the green flag.

I didn't have the knowledge yet to understand what to do when the track was tacky, and the car wanted to tip over. See, I knew something wasn't cool. Listen, when you whistle down into the corner on some big half-mile and the left rear gets up and you start to tip over, that gets your attention real damned quick. I remember being scared to absolute death at Devil's Bowl Speedway in Texas one night, because that track was tackier than most anyplace else. We ran 50 laps, and I think my left rear was three feet off the ground for 50 consecutive laps. I didn't turn over, but Lord, I was close.

If I could just be patient, and hang around until the feature, we were in good shape. It took me a long time to understand this. I didn't know why, but I knew the car felt a lot more comfortable when the track slicked off a little. When it got slick our car just went forward, every time.

When we tallied up the numbers at the end of the year, we had raced 90 times, and won 45, including my first Knoxville Nationals in August. That's an incredible season, one that the sport had never before seen. No team had ever won 45 main events against national competition.

And you know what? I hardly remember any of it. I can't really explain it, other than to say it makes me sad that I can't remember. Of all those races we won, I have almost no recall. I can look at a detailed list, and our wins are just a list of dates and tracks, that's all. I just don't remember, not even Knoxville.

See, things were happening real fast, and I think it messed with my mind. Remember, I thought all this was just a tune-up for getting to Indianapolis. I really did. I figured by winning all those races, that surely would get me to Indy. So I didn't think much in the moment, but rather was thinking of the next step, the next challenge.

At the same time, just to show you how touched I am, I won the Knoxville Nationals and 44 other races that I don't remember, but I distinctly remember four races—or at least four laps from four different races—from that season, remember them vividly in Technicolor with sound effects and all the bells and whistles. Why those four races? Because I got my ass beat, that's why.

In every one of those races, we were coming down for the checkered flag and I'm leading, but somebody passed me and I got beat.

Three days after Knoxville, we're racing at Granite City, Ill. It was the day Elvis Presley died; August 16, 1977. Little Joe Saldana, in the M.A. Brown No. 44 was racing me for the lead. This was a great, stout car, and many top racers—Sammy Swindell, Bubby Jones, Chuck Amati—had each won a bunch of races in that car. Billy Anderson was their mechanic at this time. We didn't have the high side panels then, and I could look over to my right and see Joe alongside me. Joe beat me off turn four, and to this day I can still see the tiny lettering that was stamped into the little wing nut that held the front wheel on: Halibrand Engineering. I kid you not, it's like a bad dream. Over and over I see that little wing nut and those damned letters, like they're in slow motion. We probably weren't going 30 mph off the corner, but I spun my tires and Joe got traction and he beat my ass. Boy, did that make me sick to my stomach.

I don't think this race paid $500 to win, and three days earlier I had won the Knoxville Nationals. Yet I remember this race vividly, and can't remember winning Knoxville. Sad, ain't it? I remember that little guy beatin' me, forever. It must have made an impression, because 30 years later it's like it just happened yesterday.

Two other races I vividly remember were at North Star Speedway in Minnesota, when Bob Geldner had the nerve—*the nerve*—to beat me off the last corner, not once, but TWICE! Actually, when I was growing up around Jackson Speedway, Bob was as good as there was in our area, driving for Loren Woodke. But the fact that he was very good didn't put any salve on the idea of losing two different races in the last corner.

That's the kind of thing that stays with you, haunts you and dogs you and makes your stomach hurt. It could drive a guy to drink, but I wasn't much of a drinker.

Bob Trostle and I won 45 races in 1977, and 21 races the year previous. That's 66 wins in two years. Incredible.

And then what happened? Why, I quit him, of course. Nothing in racing—not winning, not success, not failure, not anything—is forever. A guy named Speedy Bill Smith was going to get me to Indy, and that was still the plan. Remember "The Plan?" Yes, I wanted Indy. More than anything, I wanted Indy. Enough to say goodbye to the man who had been my best friend, who had put me on the map. Nobody had heard of Doug Wolfgang before I sat in the seat of Bob Trostle's sprint car. But they had damned sure heard of me now.

9

Speedy Bill

When I was a kid, one of the biggest races each year was at the old Sioux Empire Fairgrounds, a race called Cheater's Day. It attracted many of the top cars and drivers from around the Midwest, and as a young boy I sat in the grandstand watching those loud, rowdy race cars and drooled.

One car stands out in my memory, although today I'm not exactly sure why this particular car fascinated me. It was the No. 4x Speedway Motors car, and Lloyd Beckman was at the wheel. I watched that car lap after lap, and before long I had made a vow: Someday I was going to drive that race car.

For some guys it's a souped-up '55 Chevy; for others it's a mansion on the hill. For me, it was that 4x sprint car. That was something I aspired to while still in my early teens.

In late 1977 I had just finished two sensational seasons with Bob Trostle. He was my good friend, a father figure to me. We had great success, great chemistry, and a great relationship. But I got a call in November from Bill Smith, the guy from Lincoln, Neb. who owned Speedway Motors—and that famous 4x sprint car. A few years earlier I had pestered him about driving his car, but at the time I was a nobody, a kid with nothing more than starry eyes and dreams. Smith didn't hire starry-eyed kids and dreamers; he hired winners. By November 1977 I had earned a reputation as a winner.

Bill called me from Las Vegas. He was attending the SEMA show (that's Specialty Equipment Market Assn., an organization Bill helped put together many years earlier), and his pitch to hire me blasted me right out of my seat.

He wanted me to drive his sprint car—the famous 4x—but he also said he'd do everything he could to help me gain enough sponsorship to get an Indy-car ride.

Wow!

What should I do? What would *you* do? Bob Trostle and I had experienced tremendous success together, but no way did Bob have the resources to get me to Indy. But Smith, now that's a different story. Bill was a very successful businessman, and he seemed to know everybody in the entire world. When a guy like that says he'll help get you to Indy, that's something you've got to listen to.

It was kind of hard to go tell Bob I was leaving him. But the truth is I hardly thought anything about it. I was so focused on getting to Indianapolis, nothing else mattered. If Smith would have told me I had to live in Las Vegas and never go home again in order to run Indy, I probably would have done it.

I don't remember much about the conversation with Bob, but I know he wasn't happy. Remember, these two guys were rivals; in the Midwest, Trostle's No. 20 and Smith's No. 4x were two of the best cars going. They loved to race against each other, and each relished beating the other. It wasn't a mean rivalry; they were actually very friendly. Still, it was probably a bitter pill for Bob to swallow, me leaving to drive the 4x after the two seasons we had together.

Bill flew me out to Vegas for the SEMA show, figuring we could get started walking the floor, meeting people and talking to prospective sponsors. God, I was such a cowboy hick, I was completely out of my element. Later on I got a little better in terms of talking to people and presenting a little more polished image, but at that moment I might as well have walked around with a jacket that had big letters on the back, "HICK!" I was green through and through, and I'm sure it showed.

If I had met somebody important in Indy-car racing I wouldn't have had any idea, because I knew nothin' about that deal. It was actually kind of comical, now that I look back. If you had told me to go out on the SEMA exhibit floor and find Roger Penske and trip his trigger to get an Indy-car ride, I wouldn't have even known who Roger Penske was, or where his trigger was to trip. That's how dumb I was.

But it was amazing to find myself walking around with Bill Smith. It had only been a few years earlier that I had strolled into his office with a six-pack of Michelob beer—the best beer you could buy in 1974—and told him that if he was smart, he'd hire me to drive his sprint car. Well, he wasn't that smart yet. But I had done exactly what he told me to do: I went out and got some experience. Now he had hired me. It was like everything was coming together.

There was a downside to all this success: It was changing me as a person. I didn't realize it at the time—or understand it— but my sudden success had given me a taste of winning, and I liked it. Now Indy seemed possible. *Real*. So I devoted every ounce of my energy toward winning more. More! MORE!

It had all happened fast, probably too fast. In 1975 I won zero races in 80-some starts in 12 or 13 different race cars; so many cars I literally can't remember them all. Then I won 21 races in 1976, which was a great season, then 45 races in 1977. In a span of just three years, I was going as good as—or better than—anybody in the entire country. It started messing with my mind...I felt like I was *supposed* to win all those races. Like it was pre-ordained. Like I'm God.

You become very unrealistic in that situation. You lose touch with reality, and the fact that there are a bunch of tough, talented guys racing against you. But you don't think they're tough; not really. You think they're just all right, but you're *God*. You're supposed to win.

There were times, and I'm not kidding you, where I'm running fifth on the final lap, and I'm sure something is going to happen and I'm still going to win the race. I'm bound and determined that somehow, some way, I've got to win. Maybe the whole field will blow up on the final corner and I'll win. And that actually happened once at West Memphis, a year or two later when I was driving for Doug Howells. I'm running fifth, and I look across the infield on the backstretch and the starter is waving the white flag; I've got no chance in hell to win this race. West Memphis ain't but maybe 10 seconds a lap, and I take the white flag and get to turn one and the four guys running in front of me have all spun or flipped upside down. I won $5,000.

But that's supposed to happen, because I'm supposed to win. That's how I'd explain four guys all crashing in front of me on the final lap.

That stuff plays with you, boy. Messes up your head. Makes you become a real pain in the ass.

* * * * *

We didn't have any luck landing any Indy sponsors at SEMA, so that project kind of went on the back burner. In the meantime we had to get ready to go sprint-car racing.

Bill had been racing sprint cars for a lot of years, and just two years earlier had won one of the most important sprint-car races in history, the 1976 Tony Hulman Classic, with Jan Opperman beating the best in USAC. But Bill had been in and out of sprint cars for a little while in the year that followed, so we were in a regrouping mode for 1978.

Although our Indy sponsorship search hadn't yielded any results, we did land a sponsor for our sprint car. In fact, to the best of my knowledge we had the very first corporate sponsor on a World of Outlaws-level sprint car. Bill and I traveled down to Dewitt, Neb.—about 40 miles south and west of Lincoln—to the Vice-Grip Corp., and those people agreed to put their name on our race car.

This was a pretty significant thing. This meant a national company saw the value in sprint-car racing to help market its product. It didn't exactly open the floodgates, of course, but it was another indication of how the sport was changing.

The Vice-Grip money was fairly significant, for the times. They agreed to pay us $2,000 per month, for a total of $24,000 for the entire season.

As far as the race car itself, the situation with Bill was very different from my experience with Bob Trostle. Bill had Speedway Motors to run, and the sprint car was something on the side. He spent his time concentrating on his business, and expected me to take care of the sprint car. He provided the equipment and resources, and it was up to me to make it happen. He was not hands-on with the car at all.

We hired Tommy Sanders as my mechanic, and Tommy came to Lincoln to help me build cars and get ready. At this point I was getting to know a lot of people in the sprint-car world and had met Tommy somewhere along the line. I knew he was a firecracker of a guy who really wanted to win, not as a driver but as a mechanic. He had a ton of desire and was exactly the type of guy I was looking for: Somebody who wanted to win as much as I did.

In the beginning we were friends. Aren't you always friends, at least in the beginning? I always thought so. In fact, I wanted to be friends with everybody. But I was still learning. It was later I realized it's not possible all the time. Tommy and I started out as friends, but as the season progressed we started getting on each other's nerves.

Most of that was probably my fault. I had become a very demanding person when it came to the race car, because inside of me I had this powerful sense we were supposed to win every goddam race we ran. If we didn't win, I was pissed, and I wanted to know *why* we didn't win.

Well, you ain't gonna win every race. Not against the type of competition we were up against. But I didn't want to hear that. All I knew is that I won 21 races in 1976 and 45 races in 1977, and by God I had better win more than 45 races in 1978 or I'm figuring we had a rotten-ass season. And I'm certain I made everybody around me miserable when I acted like that. At the moment I didn't give a damn what anybody else thought.

Still, Tommy and I had a lot of good times together. Jeri and the girls often traveled with us, and Tommy had met a girl from Memphis and they were together a lot. In fact, in the springtime they decided to get married at the courthouse in Lincoln, and Jeri and I stood up with them at their wedding. It was a very nice thing and I was proud to stand there with him.

Tommy had grown up in Hanover, Pa., and he was a sprint-car junkie, a lot like me. He had hung around Bobby Allen's shop, and Tommy just became a fireball when it came to racing. He'd work on those cars day and night; it was like he liked it. It wasn't really work for him.

By the time we worked together, Tommy had already been around the horn, even though he was only in his early 20s. He had gone racing with Bobby Allen, Jan Opperman, Sammy Swindell, some great racers. When he came to work with me, he was a definite asset. He was young and ready to go and had his mind right.

We started real well, and won the Florida Winternationals at East Bay in February. But as the season went on, we were only doing all right, and that started to eat at me. Hey, I think we won 26 races that season, but after winning 45 you feel like 26 is nothing. A dismal failure.

Plus, it was the same old story: We just wore each other out. We worked on the car together from eight in the morning till 10 at night, we'd go eat together, we both had young kids and we tried to ride in the same vehicle all those miles to the races, and it was just too much. Even if you're friends, it's too much.

It's a lot like a marriage, only harder. When you marry a girl, you like everything about her in the early going. Then you spend all that time together—weeks, months, years—and you find out if you *really* like her. Because you'll see her bad habits, her faults, her warts, and she gets on your nerves. And you get on her nerves. But you can stick it out if you really love each other.

Well, you don't love your mechanic. In fact, you might not even *like* the SOB. But you're around him 18 hours a day, day in and day out, driving down the highway or slaving in the shop. Pretty soon every little thing he does gets under your skin. Then when you're not running good…

Smith likes to tell the story of Tommy and me, along with Jeri and Tommy's girlfriend, piling into the truck and waving goodbye as we headed out of Lincoln to go racing for several weeks without a break. We were all smiling, happy, the best of friends. A month later, we pull into the shop and park the tow rig, and Smith is there. Tommy and I are standing in the alley screaming at each other and calling each other names, and the two girls are yelling at each other, too. One helluva fight, right there in front of God and Bill Smith and everybody.

That's a true story. Oh, Tommy and I didn't box or anything—he probably would have whipped me if we had—but we were awful close. Just a lot of screaming and name-calling. And all it was, really, was that we were just sick of each other. Pure and simple.

This was all part of my learning curve, and I was too green to understand what was happening. I hadn't yet learned that in order to survive, you've got to have some space. Even then it's hard, but without some space it's hopeless. I don't care who you are, it ain't gonna work if you're spending every minute together. Just ain't gonna work.

It all came to a head at Knoxville, early that summer. We were running all right, but not going nearly as good as I figured we should be. I was constantly pissed off, and after the Knoxville race I just snapped. I wish I could tell you some big, important reason, but there was no one single thing. It was a bunch of little things and the fact that two guys were totally and completely sick of each other.

I told Tommy it wasn't working out, and that he'd have to find something else to do. For a minute he kind of digested that, and then he realized that I meant he was fired, right *here* and right *now*.

We were a long way from Lincoln, and I was putting him out right there on the spot. He asked me how he was supposed to get home, and I told him he'd better find a ride with somebody, because he wasn't going back with me.

That's what a ruthless son-of-a-bitch I had become. Put the guy out 250 miles from home, leaving him to fend for himself. All because I was unhappy about something, tired, irritable, and thinking we ought to be winning more races.

I think Tommy was dumbfounded. He looked at me for a minute, then got his stuff and walked away, asking other guys in the pit area if he could catch a ride back to Lincoln, or somewhere.

There are things you do in your life that you're not proud of, and this was one of those moments. I'm not proud that I would leave Tommy high and dry like that. In fact, it embarrasses me to this day that I was capable of doing it. It was wrong, but I was so consumed with winning, so self-centered, so cold, that I couldn't see it.

But you know what? At the moment I didn't give a shit. My blood pressure was up, the veins in my neck were sticking out, so I fired him and didn't think twice about it. I went on down the road, headed for the next race. I figured I could hire another mechanic somewhere, and I'd be back on track.

The next day I called Smith, and I explained that it hadn't been working out, that we weren't going good enough, and that I had fired Tommy. After we talked for a minute or two, Bill realized I hadn't just fired Tommy, but actually left him there in Knoxville to find his own way back to Lincoln. Bill was outraged, and rightly so. He had no problem with me firing Tommy; that happens in business. But to leave him there, that's another thing altogether. That's not how Bill Smith does business. We then had a heated and strained conversation on the telephone because Bill recognized that Tommy had been treated poorly, and that's not Speedy Bill's way.

Again, I didn't give a shit. We hung up the phone and as far as I was concerned, it wasn't my problem. I didn't care. I was totally focused on getting another mechanic, and winning some goddam races. That's all I cared about. In the meantime Bill tracked Tommy down and tried to make sure he got back home and settled up in the proper way.

Through the course of the 1978 season I had several other guys helping as my mechanic. Terry Otero worked for us for a while, and later Gary Swenson, who had been the mechanic on a car in which Ray Lee Goodwin won the Knoxville Nationals in 1968. Gary was also from Lincoln, so that made it convenient.

In time, I guess Tommy forgave me for what happened at Knoxville. We went on with our lives, and continued to learn. He had a great career as a mechanic, and later was a key person at the Gambler Chassis Co. We still speak every now and again on the telephone, the most recent time was probably a year or two ago when we talked for 45 minutes about different stuff.

It's so much easier to see things today that I couldn't see then. Inexperience, ignorance, whatever you want to call it, but I like to think I'm a different person today. In fact, I *know* I'm a different person. I wouldn't even think of doing something like leaving a guy on his own today. Just wouldn't do it. Because today I recognize that it's not cool to treat people that way. But I didn't understand it then.

Plus, today I could recognize that when two guys are working together under intense circumstances, like when you're on the road racing together, you've got to let things go and not let it bother you. We were just different people, and there wasn't anything wrong with either of us. Whatever it was that bothered me at the time, he probably outgrew. Just like I probably outgrew the stuff that irritated him.

I could probably be friends with anybody. Anybody! I think I'm a friendly guy, respectful, and not so weird that people don't want to be around me. But when you're stuck in a situation where you're spending every waking minute with somebody, it's different. It's hard to get along with that guy, because you wear each other out.

Later in the year we hired John Singer, and I was very excited. John was from Tipton, Mo., and was totally into sprint cars. He was an excellent engine builder, and was absolutely fussy about making the engine run right. John was probably, up to that point, the very best engine guy I had ever worked with. He was kind of the opposite of Bob Trostle; Bob was totally into the chassis, and didn't really care about the engine. In fact, if we could have used electric motors that you plug into an extension cord, Bob would have loved that. Singer was the opposite. He wasn't nearly as much into the chassis—although at the time he worked hard to make sure the car handled well—but he was absolutely tuned in to those engines.

John was a little older than me, and very set in his ways. He had raced for several years, and had worked with many different drivers. Tom Corbin, Jan Opperman, Bubby Jones, Jay Woodside, Eddie Leavitt, and Ray Lee Goodwin, to name a few. John had a helluva resume.

Guys like John were becoming more important in sprint-car racing. We were entering into a time when you had to have a strong motor and you had to know how to "love it up" a little bit. John had built a lot of engines, tried many different combinations, and knew what would work and what wouldn't, and why. He was very fussy with how the engine idled, how the injectors were set, and how the valves were set. He kept the oil and air filters clean, and was very meticulous.

We ran a ton of races in 1978, which maybe was influenced by the brand new World of Outlaws series. I wasn't interested in running all the WoO races, but we definitely stayed busy, and kept the tow rig going up and down the road, running close to 100 races. We really used up Smith's stuff, motors and chassis and spares, although we did all right and won the Knoxville Nationals in August, and also the Super Dirt Cup up at Skagit Speedway in Washington.

It was a fair amount of effort to keep things patched up as the season started winding down, and we were all worn out. We had a long, long ride out west to run the Western World at Manzanita in October, then on to Ascot and the Pacific Coast Nationals. We had already been out West once before with the Outlaws, so we were buzzing the odometer on the tow rig.

Maybe it was all those road miles out West, or maybe it was just that Singer and I were getting tired of each other. John can be a cantankerous guy, and he was pissed that our engines were kind of pieced together, and stuff was worn out and wasn't as strong as it should be.

Bill Smith is a savvy guy, and he didn't get to be a wealthy man by throwing his money away. The sport was beginning to change, though, and it was going to take a lot more money to be competitive, much more than even two years earlier. It's the classic scenario between racers and car owners: Racers don't care how much it costs, they want it. They feel like they've got to have equal equipment in order to be competitive, matter of fact how about if we spend even more and have superior equipment? That won't hurt. The racer doesn't spend one second wondering if it makes sense to spend this much or that much, because they don't care. Just buy it.

Bill was smarter than that. For several years he had ran arguably the premier car in the country, and had put it all together in a way that made financial sense. He wasn't just throwing money at it; he was more thoughtful. He had learned how to spend his money wisely, and still be competitive.

For example, he didn't buy high-dollar motors. Really, up to that point there wasn't such a thing as a high-dollar motor. In Speedy Bill's case, his friend John Miller taught engine mechanics at the local vocational school. John would make a class project out of the Speedway Motors 4x engine, and I'm guessing Bill provided all the parts and machine work. This was a great setup, because the kids got hands-on education with something that really excited them, and Bill got his motors for much less than he might have spent otherwise.

But these kids weren't building engines like those John Singer had figured out. And that's definitely no cut on John Miller and his setup, it's just that Singer was thinking about sprint-car engines 24/7, and that enabled him to advance many new ideas on these things. It wasn't 1968 any more. Sprint-car racing was beginning to get serious, and that meant everybody was looking for more horsepower.

Plus, we were running more and more with wings, which really put a strain on the engine. When you put the wing on you load down the tires and make more traction, and you need more power to make it go.

By the time we made Phoenix in October, Singer was really grumbling about our engine situation. Our stuff was pieced together and that rankled him, because he knew a better way. The better way cost lots of money; but he knew it was a better way. So it chafed at him, because we could be doing better, winning more, if we just had better motors. And I can't say that I blamed him, because I had to admit it was getting kind of irritating to have to deal with piecing stuff together.

Then again, John wasn't hired to tell us how bad our engine setup was. He was hired to get the best out of what we had, and let me do the rest. I don't know if it was us wearing each other out or if I was just tired of hearing him complain—I mean, on a good day John could be cantankerous—but by the time we got to Phoenix I was ready to jump out of a goddam moving vehicle.

But this time I didn't fire John on the spot (boy, wouldn't that have been a helluva deal…leaving a guy high and dry clear out on the West Coast!). I simply called Smith from a pay phone, and told him I'd had it. I was so fed up with this deal that he'd better get his ass out here to California and figure out something, because I couldn't handle it any more.

Bill caught a plane to Phoenix, and got me calmed down. We ran sixth in the Western World, then went out to Ascot Park in Gardena, Calif., for the Pacific Coast Nationals. We ran seventh there, then loaded everything up and headed back to Lincoln. We finished up the season at a $10,000-to-win race at Eldora, where we ran third.

So now what? To be honest, I don't remember exactly what happened next. Did I quit, or did Bill quit? Either way, I think we were both tired of the grind, tired of the challenge, just plain tired. Bill's stuff was all used up, and so was I.

If Bill wanted to quit, I can't say I'd blame him. He was the guy spending all the money, and then had to babysit the driver and mechanic, hearing me complain about Singer and Singer complain about the motors not being right. I'd call Bill on the phone and bitch about this or that, and he was always working to keep us together, keep us going. Maybe he decided that after 25-or-whatever years of doing it, the whole thing wasn't nearly so much fun any more. Hell, Smith had plenty of other things to worry about, and if he decided he didn't want to mess with the sprint car any more, I could understand that.

This wasn't all me, either. Not me, or John Singer, or the race car, or any of the guys who were helping us. I think it was a bunch of things that built up over a period of years, and Bill was tired of the whole deal. He had been worn out before; Lloyd Beckman wore him out and Jan Opperman wore him out and I wore him out. I wore him out pretty good, in fact. Maybe he met his match with me, I don't know. But then again maybe I wasn't that damn bad.

But we weren't sore at each other, not at all. Well, I don't *think* he was sore at me, and I know I wasn't sore at him. I liked him a lot, and, like Trostle, Bill had become an important person in my life. He treated me with kindness and respect and he was a mentor, giving me good, solid advice and treating my family well.

I had grumbled about my mechanics, and had even fired Tommy. But you know what? There wasn't anything wrong with our mechanics. They were all good, real good. They were all fine mechanics. It was the same old story: Going up and down the road, racing a hundred times a year, wears out everything, the people and the tow rig and the race parts and every little bolt on the car.

But when we got back to Lincoln from Eldora, I backed the hauler into the shop, shut off the ignition, and said so long to Singer, who got in his vehicle and headed for Missouri. Jeri and I got our stuff and drove to our house there in Lincoln, and that was that.

Wolfie was back on the market. Jeri and I took a few days of vacation, and tried to relax and unwind and forget about these damn sprint cars. But it was only for a few days. I know that, because I know how I was thinking during that period of my life. In no time at all I would have been pacing the floor, wondering, worrying, trying to figure out where I'm supposed to go from here. As it turns out, I went right back to where I was before: Bob Trostle was waiting.

10

Soap Opera

You know those old melodramas on television, with all kinds of intrigue and stuff going on, and after each show the announcer says in this intense voice, "Will Rhett leave Scarlett? Will Ken and Barbie get back together? Tune in tomorrow, because you never know what will happen next!"

Well, that was pretty much the story of my 1979 season. Lots of drama, lots of characters, lots of things going on, and, I have to say today, it was all pretty damned funny.

Now it's funny. Not then.

At the end of the 1978 season I didn't know what was going on. Bill Smith was burned out, and it looked like he wasn't going to field a race car in 1979. John Singer was back home in Missouri, and he wasn't sure what he was going to do.

I didn't know what I was going to do, either. But I knew I had to do something, because racing season was coming up pretty quick, and I'd look pretty silly running around the track on foot. I had to find a car to drive.

It was simple, really. Why not go see Bob Trostle? Bob had hired Shane Carson to replace me in 1978, and they had a pretty good year. But during the winter of 1978 Bob and I hooked back up, and we were ready to go racing for 1979. I'm not sure how I accomplished this, but I brought the Vice-Grip money with me; I think it was because Bill wasn't certain he was going to race that season. Jeri and I decided we'd continue living in Lincoln, and I'd travel to Des Moines to Bob's shop when needed.

We got started pretty well by winning the Florida Winternationals at East Bay Raceway again. There was something about going to Florida in February that agreed with me, because I always did all right down there.

Just to make things interesting, early in the year Smith decided he wanted to continue racing after all, so Singer got their equipment together and they were ready. Who did they hire? Shane Carson, of course.

So now you've got the two rival cars, the Trostle 20 and the Speedway Motors 4x, trading drivers.

Shane is a good friend, and we had no problem with each other. I had no problem with anybody, in fact. John Singer was still my friend, and so was Bill Smith. In Bill's case, from that first time I drove for him in 1978, our relationship quickly grew beyond just driver and car owner.

Shane and I kidded each other sometimes about trading rides. And it was funny, because as the season wore on Shane bent their car a few times, and I'd see Singer at the track and right off he's complaining. He's got this Missouri twang, and when he gets excited he talks really fast and you can hardly understand him. He always called Shane "Shorty," and I'd come strolling up to Singer and he'd arch his eyebrows and his eyes would bug out and away he'd go.

"That damned Shorty's got our shit tore all to hell, Wolf!"

What wasn't funny was that Trostle and I were not going nearly as well as I figured we would. We were all right, but not winning enough races. We won a couple of World of Outlaws races at Champaign, Ill., but we were discovering very quickly that our motors were getting worn out in a hurry.

Some of this was because we were running with wings more and more. Wings were kind of a spreading phenomenon, because years earlier we would see them only in certain areas. They always ran wings in Pennsylvania and throughout much of Ohio, but when you got into Indiana and most places West we didn't run them.

The fact is, there were certain guys who you knew were very hard to beat with the wings, and vice versa. For example, I was very familiar with guys from out East such as Steve Smith, Bobby Allen, and Rick Ferkel. When you went to a track that ran wings, you knew those were the guys you were going to have to deal with. So when they showed up, let's hope the track decided to take the wings off. Because if they took the wings off, you took a little bit of their advantage away.

See, it was the track's call. Local rules prevailed, so to speak.

Wings were nothing new as far as I was concerned. Even as a kid reading about the Indianapolis 500 back in Beloit, I could see that the cars were using wings, and it was really helping their speed. Even in 1972, with the modified I was driving back at Sioux Falls, we read about Al Hamilton's sprint car wing in a magazine article. We ran right out and bought a 4x8 sheet of plywood, cut it in half and fashioned side panels, using these little angle bracket things to put it together. We weren't smart enough to know how to make it work, but we knew something was up.

Another issue for Bob and me was that we were still trying to build a lighter car. In the process we were figuring something out: You can definitely built a car *too* light. Our "lighter" car for 1979 wouldn't handle well at all. You could put 10 turns of right rear weight in the car, and you couldn't even feel the difference. Plus, the integrity of the chassis wouldn't hold up under the abuse of the race tracks, with the tubes on the frame and suspension bending too much.

We put together a second chassis that was actually heavier, and that car worked much better. So the accidental discovery of "lighter is better" had its limits.

By May and June we were going a lot better, and we again made the long haul out to Washington to win the Super Dirt Cup at Skagit.

Our growing motor troubles were causing friction between Bob and me. With the Vice-Grip sponsorship, I felt like we ought to have better motors than we had. In fact, we had even gotten a motor from Earl Gaerte, but we blew that up, too. These wings were putting the hurt on motors, I'll tell you.

Bob was kind of stubborn, and he insisted what we had was going to be fine, even though we probably blew up three motors before we went out West.

I was wanting more. Whatever "more" was, I wanted it. More wins and fewer struggles. Definitely fewer blown-up motors.

After Skagit we traveled back to the Plains in late June, to Houston and Dallas and Lawton, Okla., then Wichita, Kan., and on to Belleville. It was getting hot, like the kind of hot you can only experience at places like Wichita and Belleville in the summer, where the sun cooks you and the wind comes at you at 30 mph and you can't even breathe.

We raced at Wichita, and blew up another motor. God, I was frustrated. Jeri and I checked in at the local Holiday Inn and went to bed.

The next morning I got up around 8 a.m. and opened the shades. The sun was already blazing, and it's going to be 100 degrees in the shade, maybe 105. We were staying on the second floor, and down below in the parking lot I could see our trailer. Bob and the two kids helping him had two or three motors all in pieces, spread out in front of them. Three blocks, two or three crankshafts, two or three sets of rods and pistons, and a mish-mash of bolts and various other stuff.

I knew what they were doing: They were sorting through everything to find enough decent pieces to put one motor together to run Belleville that night. God, of all places; Belleville is a big, fast, high-banked monster of a half-mile that's going to take as much motor as you can stand.

I guess I was a little cocky by the time I reached that morning in July, 1979. I had won two or three Florida Winternationals in a row, two straight Knoxville Nationals, a couple of Super Dirt Cups, and a few World of Outlaws features. I could already smell that I probably wasn't going to get to Indianapolis—call it a hunch, I guess—and I had figured out that my sprint-car career was going to be important to me after all. The point is, I was cocky enough to know I could win a race or two, and I knew in my mind that running 10th or 12th or 15th or blowing up a motor at Belleville was not something I was very much interested in on this day when it's 9,000 degrees in Kansas.

So I got dressed and moseyed down to talk to Bob, just kind of hung out for a couple of minutes. He was as irritable as I was, and I know he wasn't having any fun on the hot blacktop of that parking lot.

I finally said, "You know, Bob, what we ought to do is load this stuff up, take it home, take the rest of the week off, and regroup. We can get some good motors together, maybe even go to Earl Gaerte's and see if we can make a deal. Let's do something different, because what we're doing with these patched-up motors isn't working."

Well, he told me in so many words that he wasn't interested in my idea. In fact, he was going to put a motor together, and we're going to run Belleville. Period.

By then I'm pretty grumpy, too.

"Well, I don't know if I want to drive the damned thing."

He looked up and basically told me that, by God, he was going to Belleville, and somebody was going to drive his race car. Might not be me, but he was going to be there and somebody was going to drive his car. If I wasn't there, that's fine with him.

You know, like a couple of squabbling kids: "Fine!" "Fine!"

I said, "Okay, Bob!" Then I walked upstairs and told Jeri to get the kids up and ready, because we were going home. I think I used the phrase, "lost cause" more than once in the conversation.

To get to Lincoln, Neb., from Wichita you head north on U.S. Hwy. 81, and you eventually pass right by Belleville. We're tooling along in our van, the kids playing in the back seat, Jeri riding alongside me.

I started to rethink my position. Maybe Bob was right…maybe he'd get a good motor together, and we'd go all right. I'm beginning to talk myself into the idea, and by the time we got to the little town of Belleville I turned off the highway and headed for the race track.

By this time it's 1:30 in the afternoon, and it was so hot I didn't even want to get out of the van. I pulled right up to the edge of the race track in turn four, and poked the nose of the van all the way out where I could get a good look at the track. They're watering the Billy-hell out of the thing, dumping water on like no tomorrow. That instantly told me one thing: Tonight's track is gonna be a heavy, rough, motor-eatin' deal.

I threw the van in reverse and drove out of town like the law was chasing me. I had my foot down full-bore on the pedal, because I didn't want there to be any chance at all that I might change my mind. This deal was not for me!

Sure enough, Bob got a motor together, and that afternoon he rolled into Belleville. He doesn't see good ol' Wolfie anywhere around, does he? So now he's looking for a driver.

You'll never guess who he put in the car: That's right, Shane Carson. Couldn't have been more perfect! See, Shane and Singer and Speedy Bill had used up all their stuff, and they were parked for the time being until they figured out what they wanted to do. Shane shows up at Belleville, and lo and behold the Trostle seat is open.

Shane is running about 10th in the feature that night, and sure enough the motor blew up and locked up the rear end. The thing hammered the fence and he flipped it probably 15 times, absolutely tore the car in half. Luckily, he wasn't hurt other than being badly shaken up.

I didn't know about this immediately, because I'm back home in Lincoln, cooling my jets.

Early the next morning my phone rings. It's Speedy Bill. If you've ever talked to Bill, you know he's got this distinctive high-pitched voice, and when he calls you on the phone he doesn't even need to say who it is. You know instantly.

"Well, my driver killed your car last night at Belleville," he began.

"Oh, really?"

"Yeah, all our stuff is torn up and Singer is pissed off and we ain't racing. He's taking a couple of weeks to get some stuff put back together.

"Last night Trostle went down there to Belleville and your motor blew up (suddenly it's "my" motor) and it flipped the car upside down after it locked up the rear tires. And nothing was left of the race car, and the steering collar was holding the front of the cage on. You know, knocked the thing clean in half.

"So, you want to come drive my car for a while?"

This conversation sure made things happen in a hurry.

"Aw, I don't know," I said. The whole thing really was a soap opera by this point.

I told Bill I didn't even know what all this meant yet, because I haven't even quit Bob. But you know what? It chapped my ass that he put Shane in the car. Never mind that I wasn't there; it still burned my ass. Only a racer has a mind so messed up he can think like that.

I told Bill I'd think about it, and we hung up. Then I got to thinking that maybe I'd mess with Trostle a little bit.

I called him right away. I figured he'd be back to Des Moines by now, and he'd be in the right frame of mind when you consider that after sweating all day in the hot parking lot building a motor and watching the motor blow up and his car get destroyed, then driving through the night to get back home, he'd have a real fine attitude.

I got Bob on the phone, and acted as innocent and pure as the driven snow.

"So, Bob, when are we gonna get those new motors together, and by the way, when's the next race we're going to?"

Bob kind of hem-hawed for a minute, and said something like, "Aw, well, it's not just the motors…the race car's crashed, too. So it's gonna take a little longer. We put Shane in it and the motor blew up and he crashed the car, you know."

So I got on his ass and said something like, "Well, why don't you put Shane back in the son-of-a-bitch when you get it put back together!"

Bang. End of conversation.

Me and Bob are friends and always will be. But I think we were mad at each other that day. Matter of fact, I know we were.

So it was time to drive for Speedy Bill again. Singer thought that would be okay, so he's back in Missouri, getting ready. We decided our first race together would be July 13, at Sedalia, Mo., which made sense because Sedalia isn't far from John's shop. I would meet John there and we'd get going.

As if my life didn't already have enough drama, in the meantime we had endured an IRS tax audit, and Jeri and I decided we'd move back to Sioux Falls. We were going to use the few days off to return to South Dakota and get started looking for a house.

The Sedalia races went real well for us. They ran one race with wings, and one race without, and we won 'em both. Pretty damn good start. In fact, we got on a hot streak and won six or seven in a row, right out of the blocks.

We went on to win maybe 14 or 15 main events through the second half of the year. However, we didn't do very well at the Knoxville Nationals. Ron Shuman won it, and I ran 17th. John wanted the car set up a certain way, and I didn't, and he won the argument. The car was an absolute nightmare, so bad I actually spun out all by myself. I threw a fit after the race, but it was too late then.

The night after the Nationals we went to a World of Outlaws race at North Star Speedway, the last Outlaws race ever held at that track. I drove away from everybody and won, where one night earlier I looked like a goofball. It was nice to win at North Star, but boy, it bugged me that we squandered a chance to run well at Knoxville.

Naturally, since I was back in the Speedway Motors car, Shane got back together with Trostle. The soap opera continued. I definitely wasn't sore at Bob. He's such a good guy, I don't think anyone could stay mad at him. Particularly me, because we had developed such a strong friendship over the past few years.

But it was interesting for the fans, because they'd probably show up at the track and try to figure out which one of us was in which car!

I mentioned earlier that by this time I had begun to realize that Indianapolis was probably not going to happen for me. I guess you'd call it a reality check. Even Bill Smith couldn't get me to Indianapolis. This was 1979, after all, and by this time they had been running rear-engine cars for 15 years. What I was learning—front-engine sprint cars on dirt—had nothing to do with what they were doing down there.

In the days of A.J. Foyt, Parnelli Jones, and Mario Andretti, they learned on a dirt track, but when they went to Indy the cars were still four-bar torsion cars and not all that different. They were lay-down Offenhauser engines, offset cars, whatever, but the cars were still of a similar design. But by 1979 the cars had evolved into something totally unlike what most American drivers were learning on.

So I was pretty much out of luck.

I wasn't angry, and certainly had no resentment toward Speedy Bill. It's just the way it was.

Was it time for a new plan? I probably didn't think in those terms in 1979. I had become a sprint-car racer, through and through. So I spent zero time thinking about where I might ultimately be going. I only thought about the here and now, and maybe just forward enough to think about the next race. I was thinking like a sprint-car driver. It was a permanent affliction, after all.

11

The Darkest Night

July 7, 1979. The date is etched in my mind, one of those terrible memories you can't shake no matter how much time passes.

It was the night one of my heroes died. And you never forget a night like that.

My friendship with Darryl Dawley was kind of complicated. In the beginning he was my hero and mentor, because as a young kid I idolized Darryl. When you're a kid, and you meet somebody and you want to grow up to be just like him, it's a powerful thing. You overlook their faults and stuff, and they become larger than life.

On the other hand, as my own racing career began to get going, Darryl and I had a very difficult period where we weren't even speaking. He was stubborn, and I can be pretty hardheaded myself, so we kept our distance for almost three years.

All the while, he was still my hero. Even though my racing career had taken off and had actually surpassed Darryl in terms of my range of success, I looked at him in a special way. In my heart, it didn't matter if I won 10,000 races, I was never gonna see myself as better than him.

In my younger years Darryl was good to me, and helped me a bunch. He was also a crusty guy, and could be difficult. He was hard-nosed and he wasn't in the habit of compromising.

In early 1976 Darryl and I had a huge argument. I'm not exactly sure what started it, but it got very ugly. You see, Darryl was dating a girl whom I didn't think was good for him, and in the heat of the moment, while he and I were arguing, Darryl said something that really hurt my feelings. I came back by telling him this girl was no good and he ought to get away from her. I wasn't polite with how

I said it. Obviously, that comment didn't sit well at all. It was out of line and Darryl got really angry.

I don't blame him. Here is this younger guy, telling him what to do with his personal life. It was none of my business and I was wrong for saying it. But it was the heat of the moment for both of us and things were said that weren't very nice. I don't know why we let it get to that point, but we did.

For the next couple of years, I pretended it didn't bother me. You know, my career was going great, wasn't it? I didn't need a guy like Darryl any more, did I? Who the hell cares what he thinks. Let him stay mad, the big dummy!

That's what I'd say to myself to rationalize the hurt churning in my guts when I thought about our big argument. See, that whole thing hurt me very much. Darryl was a really important person in my life, and I thought the world of him. His approval of me, and my career, meant a lot. Knowing he was mad at me— he might have even said he hated me—broke my heart.

All those angry words, those words I would have given anything to be able to take back and make them never be said, they haunted me for a long time.

For his part, Darryl apparently also regretted the situation. I found out later he was following my career through the racing papers, and when the *Speed Sport* came each week Darryl would look it over real quick and say real loud to the guys in the shop, "That little sumbitch won another big race last weekend! God, he's good!" He was kind of like my dad in that he'd never tell me something like that personally, but then he'd brag me up to others when I wasn't around.

But did we pick up the phone and call each other to patch things over? We did not. Two dumb stubborn men allowing a stupid argument to rob us of three years of friendship, three years I would desperately love to have back.

My telephone rang one day in June 1979, and I was shocked to hear Darryl's voice on the line. For a moment it was kind of awkward, but only for a moment. Right away we were happy to hear each other's voice and we talked on the phone for a long time about lots of different things.

It was great, and it made me feel good.

We talked a lot about racing, and Darryl told me about the new sprint car he had purchased from Lloyd Shores of Danville,

Ind. It was a good car, but Darryl couldn't make it work for him. He was totally out to lunch.

He was asking me for advice on how to make his car better. Which amazed me for a moment, but then again it made sense. I had been learning at a different level for the past couple of years, racing multiple times nearly every week. Darryl's situation was different than mine; he was a transmission man who also raced, while all I did was race. So I had learned a lot since we had been together.

When Darryl told me about his setup on the new car, frankly I was amazed he could even drive it, because it was so far off. Based on what he was telling me, God himself couldn't have driven that car. So I told him some things to help him get the balance back in the car. Things I thought might work. We probably spent 90 minutes on the phone. We talked a lot about his new car and how to get it right.

When we finally hung up, I felt as if a huge weight had been lifted off my shoulders. I was grateful he took the initiative. That's a big man who could do that. The way I understand it Darryl was proud he called me, based on what he told a couple of our friends.

Lo and behold, he goes out and wins the feature at Knoxville the next week. Boom! It was the first race he'd won at Knoxville in five years. All of a sudden he's right in the hunt again. He called me back and laughed, all pumped up, telling me how good the car felt. I laughed too. It was cool to think that the long-haired hang-around kid who used to sweep his shop floor actually gave him some decent setup advice!

The 1979 season was one in which I was bouncing between Bob Trostle and Bill Smith's cars. I was spending a lot of time in Lincoln, and during the summer my tax return was audited. I was informed that because Nebraska authorities believed Lincoln was my principal residence, I owed $8,000 in state taxes from my 1978 return. I argued that my principal residence was still Sioux Falls, but it fell on deaf ears. Never mind that I didn't race one lap in the damned state; they wanted their money.

I paid it, of course, but immediately Jeri and I decided to move back to Sioux Falls and make sure this deal didn't happen again. South Dakota was looking mighty good at that point.

I had been driving for Trostle, but we decided to split up for a while. I wasn't sure what I was going to do but eventually decided to go back to driving for Bill Smith. John Singer was taking care of

Bill's cars, and we were going to get started with our renewed relationship the following week at Sedalia, Missouri.

Jeri and I decided to take a few days to go to Sioux Falls and look for a house. That's when Darryl called me back to tell me about winning at Knoxville. I explained our plans to go back home, and then I got an idea.

"Hey, how about if I hold off until Saturday, and we'll go to Knoxville first and then on up to Sioux Falls from there," I said. "I can come to Knoxville and help you with your car. Then we'll still have a few days to look around Sioux Falls."

"Yeah, that would be great," he said.

Saturday Jeri and I headed for Knoxville, and hooked up with Darryl. It was great seeing him again, along with Danny Everett and Rich Giodonni, a couple of guys from Sioux Falls, who helped him with his car.

Darryl was fifth-quick in qualifying, and the track was very fast. Eddie Leavitt was quick time, and second-quick was Steve Hainline, driving a car owned by Kermit Schafer, who lived just up the road in Newton. During his heat race Steve caught a rock on the elbow and chipped a bone. A very painful deal. They hauled him to the hospital for X-rays and it was immediately obvious he wouldn't be back in time to run the feature. Kerm was standing there, probably trying to figure out a replacement driver for the feature, when he happened to look over in Darryl's pit and spotted me.

"Say," he said, brightening up, "how'd you like to drive my car in the feature?"

Naturally, my helmet bag was in my van. Kerm's car was built by Trostle, and it sure wasn't a stretch at the time to say I was comfortable driving a Trostle car. This was the night's second-fastest qualifier, and I might make some money...might even win the race!

"Sure," I said, knowing I'm gonna start something like the third or fourth row. "Let me get dressed!"

I crawled into the car, and got ready to race. One of the officials hurried over and said I'd have to start last—in a 22-car field—because we changed drivers. I was kind of grumpy, but that was the rule. So they pushed me off and I fell to the back.

Darryl was starting sixth, with Roger Larson starting third. Roger was a very good racer from Madison, S.D., not far from Sioux Falls. Two South Dakota guys, starting toward the front.

It was a tense, ragged start, and it was called back. Everybody settled down to try again, but it was still too ragged and it was called back a second time. When that happens everybody's nerves get more frazzled with each attempt.

We came rumbling down the backstretch, and everybody hammered it for the third time. Third time's the charm, right? Not this time. Not by a long shot.

From my vantage point in the back, I could see that all hell had broken loose at the front. At least two cars were flipping end-over-end...it seemed like *bunches* of cars were flipping. Just a terrible accident. I dropped to the inside and got on the brakes, trying to get slowed down and not get caught up in the wreck.

I got my car stopped just short of the flag stand, and unbuckled. I could see wrecked cars and parts lying all over the place. Across the way I saw Darryl's car, on its wheels, turned around and facing the fourth turn. I could see immediately that his roll cage was bent down toward the front of the car. He must have had one helluva hit.

I jumped out of my car and ran toward Darryl's car. He was slumped over in the cockpit, far forward, almost half out of the car. I ran around to the left side of his car, which would have been the grandstand side of the track.

His left arm was outside the cockpit, and I could see his hand was lying on the hot exhaust pipe. Instinctively I reached for his arm to lift it away from the burning pipe.

As I grasped his uniform to lift his arm, I realized his left hand was severed at the wrist. But there was no blood; not one drop. I knew instantly he was dead. There was only one explanation for no blood; his heart had stopped beating before his hand was severed.

To this day I sometimes have bad dreams when I flash back to that moment.

I'm not sure how I was able to think so clearly, but I knew he had a broken neck. I knew it. I gently lowered his arm and let go, and stepped back from the car.

In a moment Rich and Danny came running up to the car. Rich was yelling, "Oh, God! Darryl! He must be hurt! We've gotta get him out of the car, Wolfie! We've got to get him out! We've gotta help him!"

I tried to calm Rich down.

"Rich, he don't need to get out of the car right now," I said, trying to get Rich to walk away from the car with me, just get him away from there.

"But I gotta get in there and help him!"

"No, Richie, you don't need to help him."

"Yeah I do! He's my friend!"

I was trying to get him to look at me, and not keep looking at Darryl.

"Richie, listen to me: Darryl is dead."

"No he ain't! Damn it, don't say that! He ain't dead!"

"Yes he is, Richie. He don't need us around here right now. They'll handle this deal."

Richie started to calm down, but I think he was going into shock. I was, too. The whole thing seemed surreal, like it couldn't really be happening.

In a moment a bunch of people were there, and it was chaos. Somebody was getting Rich calmed down, and kind of helping him and Danny, and I looked over toward Roger Larson's car.

They had Roger out of the car and he was lying on the ground on his back. I walked over to check on him, and saw Dale Drotz—everybody called him Hopper—trying to help Roger. There was a connection there; Hopper worked with Bob Trostle for a long time, and Roger had been their driver for a good while. Hopper was really a Roger Larson fan, and a good friend.

Hopper was kneeling beside Roger. As I walked up, Hopper looked up at me with one of those helpless, hopeless looks of desperation.

"Help me, Wolfie," he pleaded. "He can't breathe, and I can't get his helmet off. The strap...it's too tight, and he can't breathe. Help me get his helmet off, please?"

I knelt down and tried to get my fingers under his helmet. I knew exactly how to undo the strap, because I'd done it with my own helmet a thousand times. I found the little buckle and tugged it loose and got the strap undone. I could hear Roger making a gurgling sound, like he was trying to breathe, and I was trying to hurry.

"There we go," I said. We gripped Roger's helmet and real carefully slipped it off his head.

I knew he was in trouble. He was bleeding from every orifice; his nose, his ears, his mouth. Not profusely, but there was blood. His head immediately swelled up, and his chest was swelling up. In a moment they had him in the ambulance and were rushing him to the hospital.

The whole thing was like a blur. I looked around and could see steaming, broken race cars, people walking around in a daze, like a war zone. They hauled four guys away; Eddie Leavitt hurt his back, and Chris Maurer broke his collarbone. It took a while to get everybody hauled off in ambulances and get the wreckage cleared.

So then what did I do? When the time came to restart the race, I walked over to Kerm's car, pulled down my belts, and hammered that sumbitch for all it was worth. I restarted 19th, and at the finish I was fourth. John Stevenson, a very good racer from St. Paul, Minn., won the race. But if I would have had a few more laps I think I could have won it.

I have no idea why they went ahead and raced that night. I mean, it was a really bad deal. But that's what we did; somebody gets killed, you look the other way and go on.

When I got out of the car, I pulled my helmet off and saw Hopper walking toward me. He shook his head.

"Roger didn't make it."

"What? What did you say?"

"Roger didn't make it...he died."

I felt like the world was spinning out of control, all over again.

Through the years I've thought a lot about that night. I have many questions, things I ask myself from time to time. How could I get back into a race car after watching two of my friends get killed? I looked at it like it was simply my job; I was supposed to look past that stuff and do the best job I could in the race car. And I'm certain that in spite of my grief and shock, I was pissed I didn't win the race. I'd be lying if I said that wasn't going through my mind.

I do know this: At that moment, I knew this was a night I would never forget, even if I lived another 100 years. Almost 30 years have passed now, but so many of the memories from that night are vivid in my mind. The night air, the cold chills, my heart pounding, the feeling I got when I lifted Darryl's arm, listening to Roger choking for breath, the overwhelming shock of it all; they all give me bad shivers sometimes.

I don't know why, but I changed into my street clothes real quick and Jeri and I drove over to the hospital. Rich and Danny were there, and we were trying to figure out what we needed to do. They had already called Larry Nagel, one of our friends in Sioux Falls, who built Darryl's motors, to break the news to him. Larry had the hard job of going to inform Darryl's parents and his brothers, there in town.

Then Rich called Darryl's wife, Mary, who was in Rapid City.

Rich and Danny said they were taking the car back to Sioux Falls, and it was probably 2:30 a.m. when we left the hospital.

I had made the trip to Knoxville dozens of times, and my routine was always the same. No matter how hard I tried, I could never get an hour out of town before I had to pull over and get some sleep. But on this night, I was wide awake. Jeri and I sat and talked all the way back to Sioux Falls—350 miles— remembering the happy things about Darryl and Roger and trying to grasp what had happened. We drove right along through the sunrise until we got back home.

We had come here to look for a house, but we didn't get much looking done. Instead, we got up the next morning and went clothes shopping. We had two funerals to attend.

One of the things that still goes around in my mind is this: What if Darryl hadn't called me, and he'd have gone to his death without us first patching things up? That would have weighed on my mind for the rest of my life. As it was, we were both happy that we repaired our friendship, and I'm very proud I helped him get his final win.

What if the officials hadn't made me start the race at the back? I would have been right in the middle of that accident. That thought has played through my mind many times over, believe me.

In spite of anything else that might ever happen to me, no matter how difficult or painful, the darkness of that night will be with me forever. I don't understand why such bad stuff happens. I really don't. But it does, and we deal with it, however we can.

Darryl was a big part of my life, and my career. I'll never forget him. He was an all-right guy.

12

Birth of the Outlaws

Let's talk about the world of sprint-car racing, circa 1977. For many years, USAC had been the premier sprint-car series. Bob Sweikert, Pat O'Connor, A.J. Foyt, Parnelli Jones, Jim Hurtubise, those were the guys in the 1950s and '60s who became relatively famous in USAC sprint cars.

In the Plains states, IMCA sprint-car racing was very popular, but most people viewed them as secondary to USAC. There were also several other series around the country, such as URC in the East and CRA in California.

As the 1970s came, something was happening within the sport. "Outlaw" racing—that's the word used to describe racing outside USAC's sanction—was growing. There was a new generation coming up, maybe a little bit rebellious, who didn't relish life under the tight USAC confines.

To us—and I'll include myself in this group—USAC was all about rules. Yes, it might help you get to Indianapolis, but you traded off a lot of freedom to get there. It restricted you from running sprint car races outside of its own series, and stuff like that. Well, a lot of guys looked at that and said, "No, thanks." No way was a group of race officials going to tell us where we could or couldn't race.

I figured I could get to Indy anyway, without USAC. Jan Opperman got to Indy, not because he ran USAC, but maybe because he won the Knoxville Nationals. Joe Saldana also got to Indy, and he won the Nationals, too. Yes, both those guys raced with USAC later on, but their real fame came at the Marion County Fairgrounds in Iowa, or in Opperman's case, also in Pennsylvania at places like Williams Grove and Selinsgrove.

But "outlaw" racing wasn't organized. It was just...there. You'd look at *National Speed Sport News* and see which races were paying good money, and that's where you'd go. Maybe it was an hour away, maybe it was eight hours away. Didn't matter. Fuel was cheap and your time was free.

Pretty soon some of the promoters realized that if they put up a bigger purse, they'd get the cars. *Better* cars. Plus, some of the guys began to develop a following. Rick Ferkel, Bubby Jones, Chuck Amati, Bobby Allen, and myself, people had heard of us. For example, I won 45 races in 1977, and people had seen my name a lot in *Speed Sport*, yet none of those races were with USAC.

A race that paid $1,000 to win was considered a big race. Pretty soon it was $1,200. Then $1,500. Then it kind of settled on a new magic number: $2,000. If a race paid $2,000 to win, that was considered big. You'd see $2,000 in the ad, and you were gonna race against the big dogs. Well, me and Bob Trostle—this is 1977 I'm talking about—figured we could beat those big dogs. So we'd load up and get on the road.

Sometimes we didn't have to travel far; some of the local races paid pretty good money. Knoxville, I think, was paying $1,000 at that time for a regular Saturday night show. Williams Grove was also paying pretty well, I believe. I didn't race out there much but I knew it was pretty good pay.

Sometime in 1977 I heard guys talking about a man named Ted Johnson, who was promoting some big races, one of which was at Boot Hill Speedway in Shreveport, La. I loved racing at Boot Hill, and Bob and I wanted to go down and run it.

We didn't win that race, but something happened that I thought was pretty unusual. It was the first time in my career I received a check at a race track that was no good. Bounced. I wasn't sure why or who or whatever, but all I knew is that this Johnson fellow gave us a bad check.

But talk kept coming up that Ted was going to form a new series for Outlaw racing. Nobody knew much about Ted; word was he was actually a pots-and-pans salesman, but as far as having a big, long history in the sport, nobody seemed to be aware of his background. He just kind of showed up, and the next thing you know he's organizing this thing.

That made me kind of squeamish, because of the bad check thing. And I wasn't sure if the deal even needed somebody like Ted. Sure, it was a loose deal, but why wouldn't that work?

But Ted was a guy who knew how to work the telephone, and a calculator, and in 1978 he announced that every race that paid $2,000-to-win was an official "World of Outlaws" race. I have no idea where he got the name, but that was it.

Sometimes there might be three such races on the same night, at various parts of the country. Didn't matter; all of 'em paid WoO points.

So now we actually had a series. In 1978 when I began running for Bill Smith, we ran a lot of those races. We weren't running for points; in fact, at the time I don't think anybody even knew if there would be a point fund. The whole "Outlaws championship" was an afterthought, at least as far as I was concerned. You ran those $2,000-to-win races not for points, but because each race offered a nice payout.

Pretty soon there was the same group of guys running most of the races, nearly all of whom I had met over the previous couple of years. Steve Kinser, I met him at Knoxville in 1976 or '77, I think. Sammy Swindell I had seen racing several years earlier, when he was still a boy with a snotty nose and peach fuzz on his face.

Rick Ferkel from Ohio, Bobby Marshall from Texas, Jimmy Sills and Jimmy Boyd from California (Boyd was in Kenny Woodruff's car, and I had known Kenny from when I went to work for Trostle two years earlier), Bubby Jones from Illinois. Bobby Allen and Steve Smith from Pennsylvania.

See, if you did this deal very long, you figured out who the real players were, the guys you were gonna have to deal with before the night was over. A lot of it was a matter of region. If you went to Pennsylvania, where they ran wings, Allen and Smith were real good. If you were out West, without the wing, Dean Thompson and Jimmy Oskie—and later on Bubby Jones— were the guys you had to beat.

After you're around this deal for a little while, pretty soon you know everybody. And in defense of myself, I had won a couple of races by this time. If I didn't know them, they damn sure wanted to know who I was, although I didn't quite grasp this at the time. I didn't understand how anybody could look upon me as being well-known. Couldn't figure that out. I was this long-haired guy with big black glasses, and those guys probably wondered, "Where in the hell did *he* come from?"

That first year, I didn't have any desire to run all the races. Some of the guys did; Steve Kinser, Ferkel, Sammy (I think), and several others. But not me.

Some of the reason was that I still didn't understand who this guy Ted Johnson was, even though I'd see him at the races and talk to him pretty often. It looked like what he was trying to do was working, because interest seemed to be on the increase. He had more promoters wanting dates, we were getting some publicity, and the thing was starting to catch on.

But I couldn't put it out of my mind that he had cut me a bad check. This is nothing against him, really, but it stuck with me and I couldn't quite get past it. I was proud to race against that bunch of guys, because they were the best. But I never considered myself a died-in-the-wool "World of Outlaws racer."

I never treated Ted bad, or anything like that. But deep down, I always felt like I needed to keep my distance.

Here's where I'm coming from: Throughout my entire career, I only got four bad checks. All four were signed by the same guy. Yes, Ted Johnson. This spanned many years, of course. It didn't all happen at any one time.

Now, if you race for somebody and they give you a bad check once, that's their fault. But anything beyond that, it's your fault. You ought to know better. But despite the initial bad check from the Shreveport race, I kept coming back. Stupid? Naïve? Maybe a little of both. But in fairness to me, it was evident almost right away that Ted was gonna be the main man in outlaw sprint-car racing. So, if you had a problem with him, you were in a tough spot. You could be hard-line and say you ain't racing for him, but where did that leave you? You'd miss out on a lot of big races.

So you hold your nose and toss the bad check in a drawer and write it off. That's what I did.

That's why I always felt something like an outsider. I was never close to Ted. We were friendly, but at the same time I didn't trust him, not completely.

There was another reason I didn't want to run for points and be obligated to only running for Ted. Even though the money was good at the WoO races, they certainly didn't have all the big races. Plus, the difference in payout between "big" Outlaws races and other non-sanctioned races often wasn't that great.

For example, we might load up in Lincoln, Neb., and tow to Eldora to race for $2,000 to win. But in doing so we'd drive right past three $1,000-to-win races that were much closer to home. How did that make sense? So lots of times we would pick and choose, and ultimately it worked out better that way.

Granted, winning the WoO races got your name in the paper in a little bit larger type. But I didn't care about that. Name in the paper? Don't matter. What'd we make? Now, *that* mattered. I'm not sure I'm exactly right on this, but when I was racing a lot of non-sanctioned races during that early stage, I believe I was the top money earner for several of those years and didn't even finish in the top five in WoO points. I won enough big races that when it came right down to it, I won more money than the Outlaws champion.

The first couple of years it was interesting to watch the evolution of the World of Outlaws. Ted and his officials were learning things on the fly. Most of those guys didn't have any experience running a series, so much of this was new to them.

One of the first changes, which came after the 1978 season, was that instead of paying points to any race paying $2,000 to the winner, Ted developed the concept of one single touring series of racers. That was a more salable product anyway, and it was probably inevitable that it would come to that.

At first the whole deal was supposed to "bring us all together," as Ted said, meaning Ted and the racers, as one group. Later it was Ted, us, and the promoters. "We're all in this together," you know. Well, it never ended up being that way. In our sport, it never does. Everybody had their own self-interests and it's impossible to get everybody to work together for the common good, whatever that means.

Before long Ted wanted to have some meetings to promote the idea that this was some kind of democracy. About every other month or so, we'd be off in the middle of the Midwest, maybe Michigan, Ohio, Indiana, wherever. Most of us stayed at the same motel, and word would circulate that in room 230 at two o'clock in the afternoon we're going to have a meeting to discuss something and to get something squared away on a rule or procedure or whatever.

The first time I went to one of those meetings, I could see the writing on the wall. Karl Kinser was one of the most vocal guys in the room, and very strong-willed. No matter what everybody else might have thought, Karl would lobby long and hard to get something the way he wanted it. Karl is definitely a "my way or the highway" kind of guy.

This is no knock on Karl; he was taking care of business. The fact is, he had very strong feelings about things, while the rest of us were much more laid-back. We didn't much care one way or another on a lot of those issues, but boy, Karl had an opinion and, by God, that's the way we needed to do it!

I figured out pretty quickly: Why do I need to sit in these meetings when nothing I say or do matters? They were gonna do what they wanted, so it didn't do me any good to argue or get upset about anything. It was better to just not go to the meetings and not get all worked up about things.

Besides, what if I didn't like how they were doing something? What was I gonna do, quit and go home? That was the option, right? So it didn't make any sense to worry about it.

You know what's funny? None of it mattered anyways. There would be this meeting and lots of arguing and yelling and somehow after three hours we'd all come to some kind of an agreement. Then three days later one of the officials did it differently anyway, and we'd all grumble and gripe and go right on down the highway.

All of this leads me to the biggest problem with Ted: He was never firm with anything.

See, Ted's biggest problem was that he wanted to be friends with everybody. And when you run a racing series, that's impossible. Ted was a habitual nice guy, trying to make everybody happy, and in the process all he did was piss everybody off. He would tell you what you wanted to hear, because he wanted to be friends, but then when you weren't around he would change his mind and everything he told you yesterday evaporated into thin air.

Guys figured him out very quickly. When Ted was standing there telling you great stuff and all the things you wanted to hear, you might as well walk away because none of it was true. You were wasting your time.

I'm a long way from being an expert at running a racing series. Hell, I wouldn't know where to begin in terms of what to do and not do. But I've got enough experience to know that the only way it works is that whoever is calling the shots has got to be firm.

Ted was never firm with anything. It would go down like this: "All right, boys, we're wasting too much time waiting on people to change a tire. So tonight, if you blow a tire you're goin' to the infield. Now, don't argue with me, goddam it, if you cause a yellow you're going to the infield and that's final."

Three heat races later a guy would get a flat, pull to the apron, argue with the officials, jack up the car, change the tire, and not only not go to the infield, but he'd get his original starting spot back!

And of course we'd all bitch and Ted would say, "Well, yeah, but that boy has had some hard luck lately, and I wanted to give him a break, and…" It was always the same.

There is no doubt in my mind that Ted didn't intend for it to be like that. But he could never separate himself emotionally from what was happening on the race track. He couldn't bear to see a guy have hard luck, so he'd bend the rules to help him out. In the process whatever confidence we had in him making a fair, unbiased call went out the window.

That's probably the root of all the problems, like cutting me a bad check. I don't think for a minute Ted did it on purpose. But he'd over-promise, then have trouble getting everything in place to cover his commitments, and next thing you know—boom!—bounced checks.

See, what he was doing was really difficult. It's one thing to envision the concept of the series, and getting it started; it's an entirely different matter of actually running a full-fledged series. Ted had the first part figured out completely, and he defied all the critics and got the series off the ground. But it's my opinion he would have been much better off if he'd had some partners after he got it started, and brought in people with more experience in how to successfully run a growing business.

But I've got to hand it to Ted: In no time at all, he had the whole thing wrapped up. The World of Outlaws was official, it was successful, and he owned it. End of story.

He could see what it could be, and he made it work. Got to give him all the credit in the world for that.

Change was already in the wind for sprint car racing by late 1977, and the birth of the World of Outlaws accelerated the evolution of an entire sport.

To understand these changes, you've got to look back prior to 1977. The sport was much more laid-back, far less serious. You had a race car, and you'd roll it up on a little single-axle trailer and hitch it to the back of a Cadillac, and drive to the track. When you got there you'd roll the car off the trailer, and maybe rub some Turtle Wax on the hood to spiff it up. You'd go out and qualify and then wipe the dust off the car, and wait to race the feature. When you finished you'd roll the car back on the trailer and drive home, but after you had a couple of beers with your friends, because you knew almost every single person in the pit area.

It was a hobby, like going fishing at the lake, or camping. You were having fun…this was your gig and everybody else's gig in the pit area. It was a day at the fair, and you did it mostly because it was fun.

By the late 1970s, it wasn't like that any more, at least in most places.

In 1977 when Bob Trostle and I built the lightweight car, that was a big change right there. I mean, that car had…*aluminum cylinder heads*! Can you imagine that?

Now, I'm not trying to give all the credit—or the blame—to Bob and me because we built that car. It's just that much of the change seemed to be triggered right at that time. All of a sudden guys were focusing far more attention and effort and energy on the race car itself. It was like somebody turned the light on where you could see the intricate workings of the car, and now everybody pored over the car, searching for ways to make it lighter, faster, better.

Guys used to run one gear for all half-mile tracks. "What gear did you put in?" "I don't know, it was the half-mile gear." They'd run the same pills in their injector all year long. Once they got the motor to run, they didn't touch the injectors. It didn't matter if you were in California, New York, or Denver at 5,000 feet. It didn't matter if it was 35 degrees outside, or 105 degrees, and it didn't matter if the humidity was 10 percent or 100 percent. That's simply how you did it.

You ran the same magneto for 10 years. The same fuel pump for five or 10 years. You didn't even know they actually rebuilt the pumps on a regular basis; you ran it till it quit. You had no idea how much pressure the pumps put out.

Guys had an idea of how you were supposed to do things, and that idea was chiseled in stone. You didn't dare try anything different. It was definitely like that when I got involved in 1974, and my guess is that it had been that way for a while.

Most of the issue was that we knew so little. But in a short time, everybody started exploring the technical issues with the car and we all learned a lot. And the *approach* was different; before, what you brought to the race track, you raced. But all of a sudden guys started looking at how to tweak and change and improve the car, *at the race track*. Now, that was different. That meant spares and things, and it also meant the cars themselves had to change in order to be more adjustable and serviceable.

For example, remember me telling you about how we couldn't figure out in 1977 why our first lightweight car was so tippy early in the night when the track was wet and tacky? Well, we were behind the 8-ball on two counts: one was grasping why it was happening, and the second was knowing how to adjust the car. We didn't have the knowledge to understand the dynamics of the suspension well enough to address an issue like that. Today racers have 15 or 20 torsion bars among their spares and 30 different shock packages. Guys have the knowledge to criss-cross the weight and wedge it here and tilt it there and all that kind of stuff. Hell, we had no idea about any of that.

It didn't all come overnight, of course, but it came quick. The technical side of sprint-car racing was suddenly far more sophisticated.

When I started driving for Trostle we had dirt track tires. That's simply what they were called; cross-groove double-diamond tread pattern, and they were hard as a rock. It was amazing how hard they were. Then tires started getting bigger; all of a sudden somebody bought a set of Drag 500 tires off a dragster, took a grooving iron and cut cross grooves in them and darned if they don't work pretty good. They've got floppy sidewalls, and we discovered that the less air pressure you ran, the better they stick. Now they're working *really* good. But at low pressure they popped off the wheels, so we put screws through the wheel into the bead of the tire. Then somebody came up with bead locks, and you were off to the races.

But our 1977 car—along with some things several other guys were doing—focused attention on the weight of the car. That car taught us a lot. Everybody was paying attention, and before long everybody had a light car. In fact, it got so bad there for a while that nobody cared if the car handled or not, they wanted the lightest car and the best possible motor because they figured as long as you can accelerate like balls-out on the straightaway, who cares if it doesn't handle. We hadn't learned yet how to find the right balance between lighter weight and a chassis that actually worked.

In so many ways this was the beginning of the end for sprint-car racing, particularly from the cost standpoint. The advent of the lightweight car made just about every car out there obsolete, and quickly. Suddenly a new market cropped up for aluminum cylinder heads, spun aluminum wheels, radius rods, aluminum bumpers, lightweight engine parts, and so on.

All this meant money. At first, the lighter components didn't carry that big of a price tag, because we were into aluminum, and aluminum wasn't that expensive. But over time guys started messing with titanium, and that was serious money.

But our first noticeable change was engines. Just a few years earlier a $2,000 engine was good enough to run anywhere in the country. All of a sudden engines were nudging at a $5,000 price tag, because guys were messing with the heads and machining the block and that cost money. Then it was $6,000. Then $7,500...

It was other things, too. Those old cast magnesium wheels were strong, and you could run them forever. The new aluminum wheels, however, weren't nearly as tough, and if you banged wheels with somebody they were junk. We went away from those rock-hard double-diamond tires, which could be run for a month, to the drag tires that wore out in one night.

All of a sudden this deal was adding up to be serious money.

I'm just the driver, so the financial implications didn't register with me. Hey, it wasn't *my* money. I just knew that if other guys had this stuff, I needed it too. You look at your car owner and say, "We *need* this stuff! Let's rock, boy! Let's get rolling! If you want to play ball, let's play ball!"

This was very hard for a lot of car owners who had been at this deal for a while, because this throwaway culture was foreign to them. For example, Bill Smith did not become a wealthy man by throwing money away. And that's exactly what we were doing. By going to pieces and parts and tires that had a lifespan of minutes instead of weeks or months, we were throwing money away.

Another element that was foreign to all of us involved the travel. Ted's concept was simple: Build a schedule of big races across the country, one after another, following a loosely planned map. You didn't go home after each race, not even after each weekend. You just went farther away, on to the next race.

This was new and different. We had all been brought up on the concept of operating from our home base, traveling to the race, and coming home again. With Ted's schedule, you left home, and stayed gone for two weeks. Or four weeks. Or eight weeks. Or three months.

That idea was not so cool. But you know what? We were a bunch of eager young bastards and we didn't even object. We kind of nodded and said, "Well, this is what you need to make more money and get more success, so this is what we'll do." I'm sure we griped and groaned, but beyond some minor complaints there was very little said out loud.

In the beginning the guys from the Midwest had a distinct advantage, because the majority of the races were held in their area. The first couple of summers the deal was like the Indiana and Ohio Traveling Show. It seemed like every other Saturday night we were at Eldora Speedway or another track in Ohio or Indiana. Which is cool if you live there, but Eldora is 15 hours from South Dakota. And guys like Gary Stanton or Ron Shuman really had it tough, because they were from Phoenix.

Actually, now that I think about it, the concept of the long, far-flung schedule didn't come about until 1980, '81, maybe '82. You see, for the first couple of years everyone traveled in pickup trucks and vans, and you could only survive for a limited amount of time before you had to go home. We weren't quite tuned in yet to having motor homes, or staying in Indiana at someone's house. It was instinctive at the end of the weekend that you were supposed to go home, so most of the time we did.

The first guy I recall moving to a motorhome was Shuman. He had a neat little mini-home, and it was cool. I remember everybody looking at that and saying something like, "Say, now that's a cool idea! Maybe we need one of those!" Jeri and I finally got one in 1982, and by that time we had already worn out a couple of vans.

The travel was far and away the most difficult aspect of this new world we were entering into. I don't care who you are, you get sick of it after a while. Sick of it! And in truth, that was a key element in determining how much you really wanted to do this.

If you're willing to live on the road, then maybe this deal is for you.

By the end of 1978, the die had been cast: Ted Johnson had forever altered the course of sprint-car racing. Our world had changed. Now it was up to us to change right along with it, and we did. Every last one of us worn out, burned out, cynical, broke, tired Outlaws.

13

A Little Dust and Pigeon Shit Never Hurt Anything

Racing with John Singer was an adventure. He was a bunch of fire in a small package, probably five-foot-six or something like that, with a real deep voice. He didn't say much, but when he got going, he was a banty rooster, boy. If he had something on his mind he'd definitely let you know about it.

With John, the way you went about things was pretty simple: His way or the highway. He had a distinct idea of right and wrong, and there ain't anything wrong with that. Whether I agreed or not didn't matter; you weren't going to change John's mind. But he was meticulous with the race car and was an excellent mechanic.

Some days John would wake up and if he didn't feel like getting in a hurry, you might not go to the races at all. You just didn't make it, tough shit. That didn't sit well with me sometimes. But I still liked John, and respected his knowledge.

We got a good start on the 1980 season, and by the middle of April we were leading the World of Outlaws points. We won our third straight Florida Winternationals at East Bay Raceway in February, and also won at Big H in Houston. We were going good, but soon started having motor troubles. Again.

We were still using an open trailer at this time, but our trailer had a big enclosed box on the front in which you could carry a couple of spare engines. The front of the trailer had a boom that swung out, allowing you push the car alongside the trailer and change engines right there on the spot. For its time it was a trick little deal.

We won two at the Devil's Bowl in Texas in March, and won at Topeka, Kan., on April 17. A couple of nights later we traveled to Lakeside Speedway in Kansas City on a Friday night, and I rolled out to qualify. The car was good—really good—and I set quick time on our first lap. But midway through the second lap the engine "expired," as they say.

I got the car back to our pit, and Singer was pissed. He'd just about had it with our motor trouble, and was fit to be tied. Luckily, we had plenty of time to change motors, and probably wouldn't even miss our heat. Even if we did, we were still in good shape, because we'd transfer to the feature through the B-main and get our time back.

But Singer crossed his arms and said we weren't going to change the motor. He was disgusted and said we'd load the car and worry about changing the motor tomorrow.

Boy, that really set me off. I mean, sooner or later we've got to change it, right? Why not do it right now, and still get a chance to race tonight? Why would you have a spare engine in the trailer if you're not going to change it? But he refused, because he was mad. At first he was just disgusted, and when I tried to tell him we needed to change it and race, he got stubborn and that was that. He put the car on the trailer and left.

The next morning I called Bill Smith and complained. We were supposed to run the Knoxville season opener that night, but I wasn't sure what Singer was going to do. I was irritated and perturbed and I probably vented a little bit to Bill.

I suppose it was the build-up of a lot of frustrations, but right then and there Speedy Bill said he'd had enough. He didn't want to do this any more. All the money, the worry, the complaining, the babysitting, he decided it wasn't worth it any more. So he said it as simple as you could: "We're done."

And we *were* done. There would be no going back, either. That night at Kansas City was the very last time I drove the Speedway Motors No. 4x. We'd reached the end of the line, the close of an important chapter in my career.

I hung up the phone and figured I'd do what I had always done in this situation: Go look for another ride.

I bounced around for a few weeks, eventually running a few races for Bob Trostle, winning at Lernerville, Pa., in May. My friend Dick Morris from Sioux City let me take his car to the races a couple of times, although I ended up destroying the thing at Knoxville. Actually, I didn't crash the car, but Danny Smith flipped and came down on top of me and tore Dick's car all to hell. That was a shame, because Dick always had nice stuff, all shined and polished. But when I brought the car back to him it was complete junk.

Through the past couple of years I had driven on occasion for Doug and Joanne Howells, a couple out of Hunter, N.D. This was primarily at unsanctioned races where Singer didn't want to run. Doug and Joanne had raced with Don Mack as their driver for quite a while, and had done very well. They even won the Little 500 on pavement at Anderson, Ind. in 1978.

Mack was a very successful farmer from up around their area, in East Grand Forks, Minn. Don missed some races in the sprint and fall when he was in the fields, and that's when Doug asked if I would run the car a few times.

Right along the same time Bill Smith decided he'd park his sprint car, Mack's elderly parents were killed in a car accident. As they began to settle the estate and take care of all the difficult things related to such a loss, Don decided he needed to cut back his racing in order to focus on his family's farming business.

Doug had wanted to go racing full-time, but Don's farming schedule had kept him somewhat close to home. When Don decided to retire, Doug was looking for a driver who could go on the road, because this was his opportunity to finally go full-time sprint-car racing.

The timing was good for both of us. It seemed natural that we hooked up, and as soon as I got in Doug's car we went pretty good. We weren't killers, but we were all right. I must say, they had a fine motor program with Loren Woodke of Lakefield, Minn.

Doug and Joanne were old enough to be our parents, and actually had a daughter about the same age as Jeri and me. But they were definitely racy. And they seemed to like us—Jeri and me and our girls—which made it very nice.

As a couple, Doug and Joanne were as different as night and day. I'm telling you, it was amazing once I got to know them, that two people so different could be together. He was very quiet, while she was outspoken and assertive. Is assertive the polite way of saying bossy? Joanne was definitely bossy.

The whole deal suited me pretty well. The car ran good, and I sat in it real nice. Comfortable. It wasn't a spit-shined car, by any means. It had cow shit on it from North Dakota and pigeon shit from sitting out in the barn, a barn that had a dirt floor. But I loved that kind of stuff. I don't know why, but I did. I had begun to realize that most of the cars I drove that had chrome all over 'em were show-n-go cars, and didn't do much. But every car I got into that didn't have chrome all over it, ran damned good. Well, Doug's car didn't have any chrome on it. It hardly had paint, and it ran strong.

We started out by running all of the World of Outlaws races, and anything else that fit. At that time the Outlaws went to California a couple of times a year, which meant a helluva lot of seat time in the hauler.

I didn't yet have a motorhome, so I either rode with Doug and Joanne in the tow rig or followed them in our van. Sometimes Jeri and the girls and I rode with Doug and Joanne, which made it a bit cozy but we managed.

John Singer had built Doug's car, and toward the middle of the summer we decided we wanted something a little lighter, so we drove down to Bob Trostle's shop in Des Moines and built a new chassis. We also went completely through the old car, updating some things, so now we had a backup.

We kept getting a little better in 1980, and as we got later into the summer I was thinking about Knoxville a little bit. The Nationals in August had become a real goal for me, after winning it in 1977 and '78. It was a nice payday and a real barometer of your season, because you're racing against the best of the best. You always hope you peak for that race.

But our luck was no good at Knoxville in 1980, at least for the Nationals. On my qualifying night we sheared the pin on our oil pump, an old tri-drive unit that was pretty much out of date at this time. I didn't even make the A-main, and on Saturday night crashed in one of the preliminary races and our weekend was over.

We were still pretty good through the rest of the year, though, winning a couple at Eldora in late August.

Want to spend some time in the tow rig? Here's a schedule for you: Race in Houston on Sept. 10, then at Riverside Speedway in West Memphis, Ark., on Sept. 15. Four days later it's Capital Speedway in Sacramento, then the Gold Cup in Chico, Calif., on Sept. 26 and 27. Load your gear and drive all the way to Syracuse, N.Y., for an Oct. 11 race, then go back to Eldora for

Oct. 18 and 19. Now it's time to drive all the way back to Phoenix to run the Western World Championship at Manzanita on Oct. 25. Then on to Ascot, up to Corona, and back to Texas for the Devil's Bowl Winternationals in early November.

Whew!

I'm not complaining, because we won some of those races. That makes the miles seem much shorter, believe me. When you're struggling and unhappy, those trips riding across the country seem much longer.

I actually closed out my year running a midget at the USAC Turkey Night Grand Prix at Ascot on Thanksgiving. I didn't do very well, and maybe some of that was making the transition to the smaller cars. I didn't run them often, and while I did win some races, they were definitely an adjustment for me. When you're accustomed to running 600-horsepower cars, getting into a 200-horsepower car was different.

Some guys said midgets were twitchy and darty, but I thought they were fun to drive. And for me the element of fun was important, because I only drove those cars to have fun. I could drive the wheels off of 'em. And that was my problem: I'd drive so hard, they'd blow up after 20 laps. You had to baby them a little bit, and I didn't know that. It was wide open, all the time.

But I had good experiences in those cars, for the few times I drove 'em, maybe 10 races. Many of those times I drove for an Illinois owner, Nick Gomjeric, and those guys knew how to have fun, boy.

I met Nick through Kenny Schrader. We had an early-spring Outlaws race at Knoxville in 1982, a two-night Friday-and-Saturday affair. On Saturday afternoon they were running USAC midgets at the Iowa State Fairgrounds, maybe an hour from Knoxville. Kenny was supposed to run Nick's car up there—this was before Kenny went South to join NASCAR, and he was still a USAC regular—but some kind of conflict had come up. Kenny called me early in the week and said, "Doug, I can't make that race, and I know you're running at Knoxville on Saturday, but could you get up there and run that car?"

"Is it a good car?"

"Aw, it's a *great* car!"

"Well, yeah, I'll run it!"

So I hustle up to Des Moines on Saturday morning and find Nick, and introduce myself. I'm all hot-to-trot, thinking I've got these boys covered. I asked Nick, "Say, how many times has Kenny won in this car?"

"He ain't never won in it. We ain't never won a feature anywhere. Not yet, anyway."

So Schrader is telling me this is a great car, and he ain't never won in it. Well, he wasn't kidding; it *was* a great car.

Nick let me go around the car and adjust it like I wanted, which when you think about it made no sense because I had no idea what those cars liked. But I figured since it was dirt, you put right rear weight in it, because those cars go real good up on the cushion. Boy, it was fast. And fun, too. I think it was a 40-lap feature, and I lapped all the way up to second place. Just killed 'em.

One of the guys I met that weekend was Kevin Olson, who actually finished second to me in the race. Now, *there* is a character. I got to interact with him a little bit, and realized very quickly that this boy wasn't right. Off-the-wall not right. But he and all those guys knew how to party and have fun, which was cool.

For me to go race with USAC was kind of like culture shock. It's like it wasn't my brand, you know? Our brand—outlaw sprint-car racing on dirt—I liked better and it paid more, so why would I go over there very much? I was comfortable in my world, and their world was different. But I did enjoy running with them some. I raced the midget a few times, and ran a few of the Silver Crown races, which in those early days were still called Champ Dirt cars.

In the sprint cars I actually won a USAC race in July 1978 at Lakeside Speedway in the Speedway Motors car. I raced on what is known as a Temporary Permit—everybody referred to them as a "TP"—which allows you to race with USAC without purchasing a full license. Well, it's cool when a guy running on a TP beats the USAC regulars. It's a point of pride as an "outsider" that you've beaten their best.

Life with Doug and Joanne was interesting. I mentioned earlier that they were as different as night and day, and that translated to this: Doug was exceptionally easy to get along with, and Joanne was, well, opposite.

Doug rarely said anything, especially anything critical. If things didn't go our way he'd shrug his shoulders and we'd go on down the road.

Not Joanne. She had an opinion on just about everything, and by God you were going to hear it. Loudly. And if somebody screwed up, oh my God, there was no mercy. Now, don't get me wrong: She was a fine lady, a very nice person. But her personality was that she cackled about things and let you hear about it.

It was funny, riding with them in the tow rig. Doug would sit there, not saying a word, and Joanne was jabbering 24/7, complaining about this, telling Doug what he's doing wrong, speed up, slow down, yadda, yadda, yadda. And Doug wouldn't even flinch.

Except one time. Which makes me laugh when I'm sitting here thinking about it.

We had raced somewhere in Ohio, and we're driving back home (during this period, "home" was a loosely defined area of Sioux Falls, or Hunter, or maybe Loren Woodke's engine shop in Minnesota). We hit Chicago around 5:30 a.m., maybe six. It's just cracking light, and the big tollway is starting to get busy.

Doug would drive that tow rig one speed, and one speed only: Wide-ass open, 90 mph. I mean, his cruise control was planting the accelerator pedal flat on the floor. I'm sitting in the passenger seat of the truck, with my hat pulled down, about half asleep. Joanne is sitting in the back seat, leaning forward, with her arms crossed and resting on the back of the front seat. She was cackling at Doug, and it kept getting louder and more persistent.

"Doug, you better slow this sumbitch down, it's getting busy...Doug, slow your ass down. You're gonna kill us in this goddam truck, because look at all those cars...I mean it, Doug, slow this sumbitch down. You'll kill our ass, right here. And goddam it, I gotta pee, Doug. Pull this sumbitch over and let me go pee...Right now, Doug! I've gotta pee, bad! Slow this truck down, Doug...You're gonna kill us, you big dumb-ass!"

All of a sudden Doug had heard enough. He takes both hands off the wheel, and turns his whole body around to face Joanne in the back seat. Keep in mind; we really are going 90 mph.

"I'll tell you what, young lady," he began. "I've heard about all the cackling I want to hear from you. When was the last time I killed you in a car wreck? You shut up with the cackling and by God we'll stop when I say so."

For the first time ever, Joanne is speechless, and wide-eyed. Now, I don't know if it's because Doug actually spoke back to her, or the fact that we're going down the crowded Tri-State

Tollway at 90 mph and nobody has their hands on the wheel (that fact had my undivided attention as well).

Doug slowly turned his body back around in the seat, puts his hands back on the wheel, and doesn't say another word. The cackling stops, and Joanne is sitting there in silence.

Now, remember how Joanne said she had to pee, really bad? Well, guess when Doug stopped to let her go to the bathroom? That's right, when we pulled into Loren Woodke's shop at Lakefield, Minn. Something like 6 hours later, and I'm not kidding. I have no idea how she held it. Hey, by the time we got to Lakefield, I had to piss so badly that I literally had tears rolling down my face. I had a death grip on myself, to keep from wetting my pants. And I never said a word, never asked Doug to stop on my account. To tell you the truth, I wanted to see how far we'd go before Joanne exploded in the back seat. Somehow she must have held it, because we rolled into Lakefield and nobody said a word, just piled out of that truck and went about our business.

We had driven all night, and Doug did some quick engine work there at Loren's shop and we jumped back in the truck to haul to Fairmont, Minn. Hoosier Tire had given me a brand-new white racing uniform, and I wore it for the first time that night. I climbed into the car for warm-ups and I didn't even make a straightaway before everything went up in a cloud of oil smoke. I pulled back into the pits, drenched from head-to-toe in oil, ruining that new uniform.

I climbed out of the car, shrugged my shoulders, and Joanne runs over and says to me, "Well, you just destroyed our goddam motor!"

Doug never said a word, just pulled the hood off to take a look. The left side valve cover had come completely off, and was laying on the right side of the engine, just about to fall onto the race track. That's all that was wrong; they had neglected to tighten the valve cover and it fell off. In fairness to Doug, he had raced the night before, driven through the night, gone without sleep, worked on the engine, towed on down the road, and in the process the valve cover bolts had simply been overlooked.

Doug was bolting on the valve cover, with Joanne flitting around the area, huffing.

"That just shows what you dumb-asses know about engines. I'll tell you what, you sorry sumbitches couldn't even get a valve cover on right..."

We got it put back together, and I won that night. Jeri had traveled to the track to meet me, and she and the girls were going to travel on with me in our own vehicle. As Doug and Joanne were pulling out of the pit area that night, you could look through the window of the truck and see Joanne already cackling in Doug's ear, and him staring through the windshield with no expression.

I looked over at Jeri and said, "I sure hope she's got her bladder all stretched out, because right now I don't think Doug would stop between here and Alaska for a pee break."

Doug and Joanne were neat people. Both came from the Red River Valley of North Dakota, and Hunter was their native home town. Both came from prominent farming families, and between the two of them they had inherited thousands of acres of prime farm ground, which easily sold for $5,000 per acre. They were so loaded, they couldn't have spent all their money if they tried.

Yet, both were tighter than a dry can of WD-40 oil. They lived like they were only 48 hours from being completely destitute. Doug owned about three pairs of blue jeans, one pair of shoes, and three racing shirts that people gave him. He'd wear a racing shirt out, boy, and I mean wear it out. Just wash it over and over until that thing was absolutely yellow, and couldn't be bleached any further. Then somebody would finally give him a new shirt, and he was good to go for another year.

Doug somehow put a 300-gallon fuel tank in his tow rig (that baby had range, I'll tell you), and he'd drive 200 country miles out of his way to save two cents per gallon on fuel. But you know, when they hired me, Joanne took me aside, and said, "If you need anything, you let me know. I'll make sure we get it taken care of."

And I didn't really mind Joanne and her cackling. We mostly ignored it, partly because she was older than Jeri and me and to be honest she was kind of the mother figure, and her cackling seemed natural. We just let it go. Plus, Joanne was all right, a very nice person. It's just that her bark was much worse than her bite. Good thing; she barked a lot.

I would ultimately spend two-and-a-half years with Doug and Joanne, including a great year in 1981. We won the Florida Winternationals in February, the Devil's Bowl Winternationals, the Eldora Sprint Nationals, and the Syracuse Supernationals, plus a bunch of races with the World of Outlaws. A pretty good season, really. We also ran third behind Steve Kinser and Sammy Swindell at the Knoxville Nationals.

That season we made a serious effort at winning the World of Outlaws title. We ran up and down the road with everybody else, wearing ourselves—and our stuff—out. We started the year with a new car and ran that thing through the entire year, something like 106 starts. I ran into enough people through the course of the season (sprint car wrecks almost always start at the front of the car, near the axle) that the front torsion tubes were finally bent so badly they were junk. We improvised a quick-fix at somebody's shop on the road, where I laid a couple of new tubes on top of the old ones, cut the head off a 3/8-inch bolt to use as a spacer, and welded the new tubes to the old ones.

This completely changed the handling of the car, because the location of the tubes was now a good couple of inches higher. However, the car actually worked better, and we went out and won something like six straight races! That wasn't what we were looking for, but it turned out to be a bonus. Funny story: It was such a speed secret that Bob Trostle had several customers bring their cars back to him, asking him to weld a set of torsion tubes on top of the old ones!

These days, of course, guys use several different chassis through the course of the season. We weren't quite there yet. In fact, the concept of bringing a brand new car to Knoxville was still very foreign.

We won 20 Outlaws features that year, but finished second to Sammy Swindell by 230 points. Man, I was bummed out. We had tried as hard as we could, and we still fell short. I'm sure my line of thinking was, "What's a guy got to do to win this thing?"

That season Sammy drove for LaVern Nance, and their approach was different. They were chasing the objective with an all-out assault, sparing no effort or expense. They had different cars at their disposal, and fresh Gaerte Engines. That's not why they beat me, though. I figured they just whipped our asses. No excuses.

But this was the way it was going to be from now on. You could no longer look at sprint car racing in the same light. Running the same car all year? That wouldn't get it done any longer. Come to Knoxville with older stuff? Wasn't good enough, you had to have fresh stuff.

And it wasn't that Doug Howells was lacking for money. We had good stuff, and in fact I felt our stuff was as good as anybody in the country. If we needed something, Doug went and got it. But the approach to the sport was changing. Doug didn't mind spending money on things, but we didn't realize that having fresh stuff and plenty of spares would make that much of a difference. I suppose there were times that year when we finished second because maybe we weren't fresh, but at the time we wouldn't have realized that's *why* we finished second.

The competition had escalated. Doug Howells, like every other car owner out there, probably had a set amount of money he was willing to spend to do this. Within that level, money was no object. Lose $10,000 a year? $50,000? Maybe that would have been tolerable. Actually, our car made money, but if we had been buying fresh chassis and engines and spares, it wouldn't be long and you couldn't win enough to cover your costs. Once we reached a certain point Doug would have probably gone home, just like every other owner out there. But right along that time the dollar figure had stepped up several notches. Today it's so far beyond anything we could have contemplated, it's amazing. But for today's generation of car owners it seems reasonable because that's what it takes so let's get to it, boy!

Just to be clear, I don't blame Sammy for the rising costs. It wasn't his fault. He's just one of the early guys to understand how spending money on key things will give you an advantage. Every segment of racing has now figured this out. It's nobody's fault, it's just the nature of the beast.

In 1982 we started out strong with several wins, but things were starting to come unraveled. Not on the race track; we were still winning races, but we were about to wear each other out.

In fact, we had a stretch where we won something like seven races in a row, really had it going. At our next race I was running good, and moved up to second place, right behind Steve Kinser. I had taken my time getting to second, and there wasn't any doubt in my mind that I'm going to win this race. I pull alongside Steve, and at the flag stand he's about a foot ahead of me.

We came up on a lapped car, and we split it, with Steve on the inside and me on the outside. I steered to the outside and I was going to take both of them off the corner, and take the lead.

Well, this boy getting lapped reacted to Steve on his left, flinched, and moved to the outside.

We weren't running nerf bars because we were so weight conscious, so this boy's wheels tangled with mine and it put me right on my head. I didn't crash all that hard, it just folded up the top wing and bent the car. But I'm laying there in the car, upside down, hearing the sound of that wing getting flattened, and I just shook my head and said, "Shhhhhhhit!"

I crawled out of the car, and I could see that while the car wasn't totally wrecked, we weren't going to do any more racing tonight. The wrecker driver hooked it up to haul it back to the pits, and the guy says, "Hop in, and show me which trailer is yours." I pointed to the white trailer back there and said, "That one."

"Ain't you gonna ride back?"

"No, I'm gonna ride with this guy in the other wrecker."

I climb into the other guy's cab, and we get to the pit entrance, and I say, "Just stop and let me out here."

I walked along the fence line, completely out of sight, back to our pit. Where I change clothes is on the far end of the trailer, so I slipped into the side door, quickly changed clothes, and I'm about to make a clean getaway when Joanne spotted me.

I knew this was going to happen. She comes running up to me, very upset.

"Who the hell ever called you a race driver??!!" she yelled.

Keep in mind; I had won seven straight races. I guess it's true that you're only as good as your last race, and in Joanne's mind at that moment I wasn't very damned good.

The end for us came in late June, 1982. I can't say it was any one thing that led to it; it was lots of little things. I believe I can say with good authority, however, that Joanne wasn't a piece of cake to be around all the time. I'm not saying that to be mean, it's just fact. She was very intense and sometimes would say things that got on our nerves. But hey, nobody can spend that much time together without getting on each other's nerves. It's really the same old story of people just wearing each other out.

She began telling Jeri and me that we weren't raising our kids right. They shouldn't be going to the races every day, this and that, whatever.

Now, you can tell a dad that his kid is a piece of shit, and it's not big deal, because the dad will ignore you. But you can't say that to a mom. And when Joanne started telling Jeri that we weren't very good parents, it really worked on her emotionally.

For me, I was always looking at what I needed to win. That was all that mattered. I was a ruthless son-of-a-bitch. But in a way, I had to be. I had to make a house payment on Monday. I had kids, and was traveling with my family, long before Steve or Sammy or any of the other guys had families with them. My first responsibility was to myself as a human being, but right behind that was my responsibility to my family. I took that totally seriously.

So I could rationalize and ignore things—like Joanne telling us we're not raising our kids right—because if we were winning that was first and foremost. Winning was not a big thing; it was almost *every*thing.

Besides, I wanted everybody to be happy. I wanted to be friends with my car owners and never have any conflicts. In the beginning, that's easy. But inevitably time works against you.

Every car I got in, almost from the very beginning I said to myself, "Man, this is great…I'll probably retire in this car." In the beginning everything is peachy. Wonderful. But in six months you ain't saying that any more. Things change, and people wear each other out. And that's what happened with Doug and Joanne and me.

It was Wichita, and it was 103 degrees when we took the green flag that night. Their tow rig broke a timing chain, so they were having a bad day anyways. Joanne was pissy, and it was not a good situation. Jeri and I were desperate to get home. We hadn't been home for several weeks and we were tired too.

The plan was after this race we would all go home, and Doug and Joanne would pick up a new car that was ready. So it wasn't like we were running terrible, or our outlook was bad; on the contrary, things on the race track were going pretty good. But everything else had worn us out.

We got in our mini-home, and Jeri sat up with me for a while as I drove north. I was wired; all emotional and wound up. I told Jeri to go ahead and sleep, because I was wide awake and I'd drive a while and we'd be that much closer to home.

In my mind, I was running through a lot of things. Something was wrong, and I knew it. We had reached the point, however painful it was to realize it, where we had to make a change.

I still remember pulling into the rest stop near Sioux City and walking to the pay phone. I dialed their motel number and woke Joanne up. It was just cracking light, maybe 5:30 in the morning.

"Joanne, this isn't fun for me at the moment and I need to make a change," I said. "You guys need to get another driver."

"But we don't have anything lined up!"

"I know that. But you'd better get busy and start looking."

When I quit them, I think Joanne was pissed at me for a long time. She was so intense, so competitive, she took it personally, you know? But it wasn't a big deal, because as time went on we naturally began seeing less of each other. Eventually they cut back on their racing; actually, they raced less and less with their own car, while Doug took care of the USAC Silver Crown car in which Mike Bliss won the championship in 1993. We all kind of went our separate ways and that was it. There were definitely no hard feelings on my part. I still liked Doug and Joanne, very much. We had a great run together and some very good times.

It's important to not let the ending of the relationship overshadow all the good times you had together. Every racing relationship has an ending, and most of the time it's a little rocky. But that doesn't mean you can't still be friends.

A couple of years ago when I heard that Joanne had passed on from cancer, I called Doug right away and told him how sorry I was to hear the news. Jeri and I drove up for the funeral, and it was good to see Doug again, even it if was under difficult circumstances.

Doug and Joanne. Boy, what a couple of interesting people.

14

The Gambler

It's a quiet November afternoon in my shop here in Sioux Falls, and it seems that every tiny noise echoes in here. Sunlight streams through the windows, and I'm here working all alone. Cody Toupal, a motocross suspension expert who rents a corner of my shop, is off running errands, and my pal Jack Trigg hasn't stopped by yet today.

I'm busy hanging the bodywork on one of my WolfWeld race cars, getting it ready for the powder coaters. This car belongs to Butch Hansen, a friend of mine who runs in our area. Butch won a championship last year in a WolfWeld car, and I'm glad to have him for a customer.

The sunshine keeps my mood light, but it's only about 25 degrees outside. Across the street I can see a flag snapping sharply in the wind, which means when you step out the door the cold will immediately gnaw at your face and ears. That's November in South Dakota.

It's like this a lot here at my shop; me working alone, lost in my work and my thoughts, pausing occasionally to answer the phone throughout the day.

In the corner we have a radio, tuned to country music. I stopped working just a moment ago, and listened: It was a Kenny Rogers song.

All of a sudden, my mind wandered back to 1983. It was a difficult chapter in my career, but I still smile a little bit when I think of my turn in the famous Gambler sprint car. I can sum the whole thing up like this: great expectations that never did pan out. Still makes me shake my head, because I don't understand it.

Not long after the World of Outlaws were created at the start of the 1978 season, a fellow from Nashville by the name of C.K. Spurlock became interested in sprint-car racing. C.K. was the concert promoter for several big country music stars, and he was a flamboyant, outgoing guy who, like all good promoters, had a penchant for doing things in a big, splashy way. C.K. was particularly tight with one of his clients, Kenny Rogers. I don't know anything about the nature of his finances, but it was obvious C.K. had some money behind him.

When C.K. got into sprint-car racing, he did it in a big way. First he created a company—Gambler Chassis Co.—to build sprint cars, locating the shop in Hendersonville, Tenn. He also put a car out on the World of Outlaws circuit, with prominent sponsorship from Kenny Rogers. This car immediately became known as the Gambler "house car."

This was a new way of doing things in sprint-car racing. A "factory" team? Unheard of. Immediately the team had a high profile, and in 1982 wound up on the cover of a brand new magazine called *Open Wheel*.

Probably every driver in sprint-car racing lusted for that car. Who wouldn't? It was glamorous, they had what appeared to be an unlimited budget, and you could rub shoulders with a famous musician and movie star, Kenny Rogers. What could be better?

In the latter part of the 1982 season I got a call from C.K. He wanted to hire me to drive their car! I liked C.K.; he wined-and-dined me, flying me to Nashville to tour their place and meet with him. He told me I was great and how if I'd drive their car, boy, we'd have fabulous success. He said they had Kenny Woodruff as their mechanic, who was really good, and with me as the driver the sky was the limit. Of course, he was telling me all the things I wanted to hear, stroking my ego, but I didn't see this at the moment.

Looking back, it's obvious that C.K. was far smarter and savvier than I was. I viewed him as being "slick," but he was slick in a way that I didn't recognize at the time. Not a dishonest kind of slick, but just...*slick*. He was a lot more experienced at business than I was, and any time you're dealing with someone that much more experienced or smarter than you, you're at a disadvantage. I'm not throwing bricks at C.K., he was all right to me and I've got no kick with him. But now I see how you ought to do your homework when dealing with someone so experienced, because you're out of your league. I was definitely out of my league with C.K., but I wasn't smart enough to realize it.

At first I turned C.K. down. I wasn't ready to drive his car. I'm not sure why, but that's what I told him. I needed some time to think it over, I guess. I was driving for Gary Stanton at the time, and we were goin' pretty good. We won our qualifying night at the Knoxville Nationals, then ran second to Steve Kinser in the championship race. We also won the Gold Cup out at Chico in September, so we were all right.

But 1982 drew to a close and during the off-season C.K. and I talked again. This time I was more receptive. All of a sudden everything pointed to this deal as the killer of all killer deals, the deal of a lifetime. Doug Wolfgang in the Gambler house car for the 1983 season. That had a nice ring to it.

This was probably like getting hired today to drive for Rick Hendrick in Nextel Cup, or by Roger Penske to drive his car at Indianapolis. The pinnacle, so to speak. When you're hired into a situation like that, your instincts tell you this deal is gonna be A-number-one and everything is going to be great. A no-brainer.

But I hadn't quite figured everything out yet. I still wasn't very smart. At the time I probably felt like I had lived every possible scenario—fighting with Tommy Sanders and firing him at Knoxville; working with John Singer, who was cantankerous beyond words; being driven crazy by Joanne Howells—even though I knew a lot about the things that cause a team to come apart, I still thought the Gambler deal was a no-brainer. I thought working with Kenny Woodruff would be easy, and I thought we'd be super-successful.

God, I *knew* we would be great. I *knew* it. We had to be great, because all the pieces were in place. Kenny was very talented, and had the knowledge to do chassis, engines, whatever. The team had the best engines you could buy. They had spares, and plenty of help. They had the backing of the most prominent car builder in the sport. Why, we couldn't help but be successful, right?

In fact, I'm not so sure that in January 1983 I wasn't actually feeling a little sorry for those other boys out there, because they didn't have a chance in hell. We were going to slaughter 'em.

To say I went into 1983 as a very confident race driver would be a big understatement. Confident? Hell, Jeri and the kids probably didn't recognize me, with my head swelled up so big.

This deal was going to be like printing money. When do we get started?

By the way, there was just one small detail. When C.K. hired me he made it very clear that they expected two things from me and the team: They expected to win the Knoxville Nationals, and they expected to win the World of Outlaws championship.

No problem, I said.

My education began on the very first night. We were opening the season in Jacksonville, Fla., and I climbed into the car for hot laps. Kenny had the car ready, along with Floyd Bailey, who also helped wrench the car.

They had a new-fangled setup with the steering wheel, which allowed it to be easily removed so the driver could slip in and out of the seat easier. I had never seen one of these before. I'm not a big guy, so removing the steering wheel was never an issue for me; I just squeezed my legs under the wheel and had no problem.

I'm humming down the backstretch on the first lap, and the steering wheel came off in my hands. I'm a passenger at this point, and the car spun around and bounced off the fence, knocking the front axle out from under it.

The wrecker tows us back to our pit, and Kenny walks out to look at the car.

Kenny looks at me and grunts, "Huh…what happened, bud?"

"The steering wheel came off."

"Huh…why didn't you put the locking pin in it before you started?"

Now, keep in mind: This was the very first quick-release steering wheel I had ever seen. I had no idea of any locking pins or stuff like that. I just shrugged my shoulders, not knowing exactly what I'm supposed to say.

Kenny grunts again, obviously disgusted, and says something like, "Who the hell ever called you a race driver, anyways?"

The race car was sitting there, pointed straight at my motorhome, parked across the way. At that moment I made my first mistake with the Gambler team: I should have walked right across to my motor home, climbed in, and driven that sumbitch straight back to Sioux Falls. Because I could see right away that this deal wasn't gonna be the cakewalk I thought it was.

Call it a gut feeling, whatever, but all of a sudden, all those great expectations were replaced with a powerful intuition that we were in trouble.

And that's pretty much how it was. It seemed that these guys didn't think very much of Doug Wolfgang, no matter how good we did.

At the time I was put off by Kenny's gruffness. But in time, as years have passed, I realize it was just Kenny being Kenny. He isn't a bad guy, by any means. He's actually a *good* guy. He's just gruff, and that's his nature, his personality. He'll tell you exactly what's on his mind at any moment. Plus, he's a mechanic. About 90 percent of mechanics out there believe in their heart that they could drive better than their driver can. At *least* 90 percent. They're impatient, because "goddam it I'm giving you a fantastic car and you still can't win! What's wrong with you?"

Many years later Kenny teamed with Dave Blaney, and they had great success together. But he cussed Dave, too. They won the Knoxville Nationals together and the World of Outlaws title, but I'm pretty sure Kenny still thought Dave was a dumb-ass driver. He sure thought *I* was. He thought we *all* were.

Kenny's philosophy is very simple: "I want my driver to drive this sumbitch as hard as I work on it." And you could never question his workmanship. His cars are put together properly, and stuff didn't fall off. He makes the car nice and it's put together right.

But I'll tell you, that Gambler deal was a pain in the ass. From the get-go. Lots of drama, every day. I don't know why, but that's how it was.

Today I can pinpoint the problem: It wasn't a team effort. We never gelled, never made the personal connection all great teams have. Those guys did things their way, and I was supposed to drive it my way.

I was just another driver. Here today and gone tomorrow.

We had a fair amount of success, but we also had many disappointing days. I'm not saying that simply from my perspective; I'm certain that Kenny and Floyd and C.K. were disappointed, too.

The Gambler program was the first corporate deal I encountered in racing, certainly the first one I was directly involved in. It's easy to wish that more companies would come into the sport and drop wads of money, but the downside is that in doing so, they have demands and expectations.

This deal was no different. There were expectations, one of which was that every piece on the car would be an official Gambler Chassis-approved piece. Whether it was the right piece or not didn't matter; it had to be the "official" piece.

I've always used a lot of brake in my car, and prefer a lot of pedal. Not so much for stopping power, but to help feel the car through the corner. I used the brakes to help turn the car. Well, that was a problem with this car because the Gambler brake setup wasn't very good. Their engine program was great, but their brakes didn't suit me at all.

We went to Pennsylvania in March, and ran an afternoon show at Port Royal. We finished second, even though I was growing more frustrated with our brakes. I was getting a little bit aggravated.

After the race I went to the Tobias part truck. I knew Stanton—they were a competitor of Gambler at the time—had a very good brake setup. I used my own money to buy a Stanton master cylinder and Kenny and I bolted it on our car. It immediately solved our brake problems. Now I had plenty of pedal!

I went out that night and won at Selinsgrove. Life is good, right?

Not quite. Here's what happened: Kenny took the car back to Hendersonville to prepare for our next race, and the Gambler guys immediately spotted that Stanton master cylinder. They took it off and put their piece back on.

Now, I know what you're thinking: It's only right that the Gambler car has *only* Gambler parts and pieces. Yes, that's reasonable, but from my perspective, just the ol' race driver who needs to drive the thing, their brake piece wasn't worth a damn.

Didn't matter. Stanton piece off, Gambler piece on. Shut up, boy, and drive the damned car.

Maybe part of my discomfort with this team was that for the first time in my career, they didn't want me messing with the car. They had Kenny and Floyd on the road, and they handled stuff there. On the occasions when we visited the Gambler shop back in Tennessee, they had their own guys there and didn't need me making suggestions or helping them make stuff.

We didn't go down there much, anyway. Maybe during the course of 1983 season I was there three or four times.

I did get to meet Kenny Rogers a couple of times. To be honest, it was kind of a letdown. He was distant, not the warm, fuzzy kind of guy he projects on television. I got the impression that everything was strictly business, that the bottom-line dollar was the key element in everything.

Maybe that's not fair. I was just the race driver, and it wasn't like Kenny Rogers and I went out and had a beer together. I didn't get to know him well at all, and he might be the type of guy who takes some time to get to know, to figure out. He might have been all right, I don't know.

In early June promoter Paul Kuhl paid appearance money to Sammy Swindell and me to run an unsanctioned race at Flemington Speedway. Flemington was always a tough track for newcomers to master because it was kind of a square-oval, but I took to it right away and won in Gary Stanton's USAC Champ Dirt car the previous year. This time I was back with the Gambler machine.

I was chasing Sammy in the feature, trying to get under him, and I clipped the inside fence going into turn one. It upset the car and turned me to the right, where I shot across the track at very high speed and slammed into the outside wall.

It was a massive, massive impact, one that literally stung every part of my body. The car finally stopped and I sat there for a moment, trying to shake off the cobwebs, and the medical people got there quickly and began to examine me.

They said I had no broken bones, and I didn't feel like I needed to go to the hospital. But boy, I was hurting. I managed to get back to our pit, where I lay down on the floor of the trailer.

As the minutes passed, it felt like the pain was growing more intense. Not any one particular area, but my body hurt from my toes to my fingertips to my scalp. A strong, aching pain.

The longer I lay there the more I began to wonder if maybe something serious was wrong with me. We got an insurance slip from the promoter and Jeri drove me to the hospital, located just across the street.

We went into the emergency room and they took me back to a small room where the doctor would see me. Jeri stayed in the waiting area with the girls, and I lay on an examination table, waiting to see the doctor. I could hardly move, because every muscle and joint ached.

Suddenly the doors flew open and they wheeled in a guy on a gurney. A dozen doctors and nurses were working on this guy, and it was obvious he was in cardiac arrest. I'm sitting there, not eight feet away, but all those people were oblivious to me. They were completely focused on trying to save this guy.

They're barking orders and clamoring around, and all of a sudden somebody yells, "Clear!" They shot the electricity to the guy, and his legs jumped three feet in the air. They're calling for this injection, that medication, clearly trying desperate measures. Then they shot him with electricity again.

After about 10 minutes the doctor in charge steps back from the gurney and says, "He's gone...there's nothing more we can do." Slowly the doctors and nurses began to filter away from the room, and soon there is just the patient, the doctor, and maybe a couple of other medical people in the room. I don't think anybody even noticed that I was sitting there.

"Well, I've got to go tell them," the doctor says, and he walked out of the room back into the hallway. The patient had apparently been accompanied to the hospital by a bunch of family members. A few moments after the doctor walked out the door, I could hear this loud, outpouring cry of grief and anguish from the man's family. They were crying and weeping and it was a sad, powerful moment.

By now there is only me and the dead guy in the room. I looked over at his body, covered by a sheet, and I felt this enormous sadness sweeping over me. I had just watched this poor guy die.

I shook my head and said to myself, "Sonny, there ain't anything wrong with you."

I climbed down from the examination table, put my shoes back on, found my jacket, and walked back to the waiting room, where Jeri and the girls were sitting. Jeri was surprised to see me so quickly.

"Did you see the doctor?" she asked. "Is everything okay?"

"I ain't hurt," I said. "Let's get out of here."

By early summer I could feel a growing tension with everybody on the Gambler team, probably because we weren't dominating like we all thought we should be. Yes, we were all right, and had won some races, but when you think back to the start of the season, we thought we'd be so special that Jesus might make his second coming just to watch us. And our performance wasn't anything special.

We followed the World of Outlaws swing up into New York and Pennsylvania, and our car was getting worse, almost to the point where I couldn't drive the thing. It was the same every night: The car would go into the corner, lay over hard on the right side, and damn near burn my elbow off rubbing it on the right rear tire. It would slide like a bitch, put the left front wheel up in the air about a foot, and even a super-stud couldn't have driven it like that.

I kept trying to tell Kenny Woodruff that something was wrong.

"Kenny, crack some right rear weight in this thing," I begged. "I'm telling you, somethin' ain't right!"

Kenny would kind of grunt and shake his head, telling me it had plenty of right rear weight. Basically, I must be driving it wrong.

We had a string of five straight nights of racing, and unloaded at Canandaigua, N.Y., and prepared to hot lap the car. Canandaigua is like riding around a professional baseball field, only very bumpy and rough. Well, our car was so dreadful I couldn't take it any more.

I took two hot laps, and headed back to the pit area. Kenny had walked out to the edge of the track to watch, and it took him a minute to get back to our pit. I jumped out of the car, threw my helmet in my bag, threw the bag over my shoulder, and was walking away when Kenny got to the pit.

"Where you goin', Bud?"

I was completely pissed. I turned and looked at Kenny and said, "I've got a $5 bet with my wife on a ball game on television, and by God that's going to pay me more money tonight than driving this race car. So I'm gonna go watch the goddam ball game."

He just looked at me as I walked away. I got to my motorhome and threw my bag off to the side, and sagged into a chair to sit there and pout.

In terms of gauging Wolfgang, I was only semi-seriously upset. If I had been *really* upset, I would have fired up the motorhome and driven back to Sioux Falls. But since I was only moderately upset, I just sat there feeling sorry for myself, complaining to Jeri, but not yet taking my uniform off. Finally after a few minutes I had cooled off enough to walk back to the race car.

Just as I got there Kenny was pulling the torsion bars from the front end. A new type of bar had been introduced that year, a design that called for the bar to be hollow. I'll never forget this: As Kenny slid that bar out, it fell apart. It had broken in half.

So we essentially had *no* right rear weight in the car. But it had taken us four, maybe five nights to discover it! I was so disgusted I could've puked right there on the spot. Listen, I had been around the block a few times by then, and I knew what it took for a team to be successful: good chemistry, and a willingness to work together. But in this deal, the driver was just somebody to sit and steer, and you didn't need to listen when he tried to tell you what was wrong with the car. God, I was disgusted.

We immediately began running better, but I think everyone was still pretty steamed. At each other, at the situation, at the world in general. We rode west to Lernerville, Pa., and the plan was to go from there to Eldora, after which we had a week off.

We raced at Lernerville and finished fifth. Jeri and I drove to nearby Butler, where everyone stayed. Most of the racers stayed at the same two or three places, which afforded space out back to park tow rigs and motorhomes.

Late that night I was awakened by some loud voices. I lay there a moment, getting my bearings, remembering where we were. Soon the voices were louder. It was several guys, loud and boisterous, drinking beer out in the hallway.

All of a sudden I could recognize one of the voices. It was K.C. Spurlock, C.K.'s son. He was evidently hanging out with some of his buddies and they were just now getting back to the hotel.

I could hear K.C. clearly, and he was very loud and rude. He was telling his friends that Wolfgang is such a piece of shit and a good-for-nothing driver, really badmouthing me. I sat up in bed, now wide awake.

It hurt my feelings, hearing him say those things. Right at that moment I said to myself, "I don't need this...I'm out of here." We got up the next morning and went home. It was another of those spur-of-the-moment decisions, where I decided things weren't my cup of tea and just said goodbye. I didn't waste much time making up my mind. Time to move on.

Frankly, it wasn't so much what K.C. said that bugged me. See, he rarely came around; he was usually off doing whatever, and we rarely saw him. So he probably didn't know much of what was going on anyway. But for him to say those things, I figured he probably heard them from others within the team. That, to me, was a revealing look at how the team felt about me.

Was quitting the right thing to do? I don't know. All I know is that it felt like it at the time. Besides, there are other cars out there. That's something you have to believe when you're a race driver: No matter what happens, when you no longer believe in what you're doing or who you're driving for, there is always something else waiting around the corner.

Might be better, might be worse. But it's different. And I was ready for something different.

15

Good News Does Not Travel by Registered Letter

From the very beginning, I liked Gary Stanton. I've known him now for 30 years, and through all kinds of situations we've never stopped being friends. I've driven Gary's race cars off and on through different periods, and even when we'd fuss and argue, we were always all right with each other.

Stanton was from Phoenix and had been building sprint cars for about 10 years when the World of Outlaws got going. He built a good car and to me it was obvious Gary was a smart guy who could figure things out.

Pretty soon you started seeing the Stanton "house car," usually No. 75, out on the road. Like the Gambler deal, this car was primarily out there because if it did well and won races, it would generate interest in Stanton's chassis and other products.

Stanton was a car builder, not a racer. And there is a difference. Bob Trostle was a car builder, but he was also a racer. Bob was very interested in getting on the road and winning races. Gary, however, did not like being out on the road.

See, Gary was a different kind of person than the rest of us. Most of us were so consumed with this deal, we lived it 24/7. Even when it made us sick, because of the hours and the hassles and whatever, we couldn't help ourselves. Sprint cars were all we knew, to the point where it crowded out any other distractions in our life. Families, hobbies, whatever; there wasn't much time for that stuff. In my case I made it work primarily by bringing my family along with me, and that helped a little bit.

But Stanley—that was my nickname for Gary—was different, and you could see it. Maybe it's because he is so intelligent, but I always figured him for having the sense to see that life is supposed to be a lot more balanced than the way sprint-car racers lived it. Gary always tried to keep some sort of a normal life going, while at the same time making his living by building cars and parts.

He wanted to race some and promote his product, but he wasn't blood-and-guts addicted like the rest of us. He had other interests in his life, which is good.

In 1982 when I quit Doug and Joanne Howells, I drove for Stanton through the balance of the year. We did all right, and had a pretty good finish to the season, winning some prominent races. But when C.K. Spurlock called and offered me the Gambler seat, it was kind of a no-brainer to take it.

I don't know if that upset Gary; he never let on that it did. Gary and I are somewhat alike in one way, and that's in how we deal with stuff. Try not to get mad and stay mad, and hold a grudge; just let things flow and maybe it will work out again later.

So there was always an easy manner to our friendship, and our relationship as driver and car owner. Never real formal, but easy and simple. I quit Doug and Joanne; then maybe it's, "Hey, Wolfgang, how about driving my car?" Or maybe, "Hey, Stanton, I'm looking for a ride…can I drive your car for a while?" No problem. If the timing is right, we'll go racing together. When the deal dries up and it's time to make a change—either I quit him or he quits me—hey, that's no problem, either.

When I quit Gambler in June of 1983, it wasn't but a few days before I hooked up with Stanton once again. And we got going pretty good, too. Won at Jackson, Minn., and won a couple at Knoxville.

But we had motor troubles. Not blowing up, but just getting them to run. They weren't right, and we were all quite frustrated. We swapped engines a couple of times and the damn things *still* wouldn't run.

We were racing in eastern Ohio—probably Sharon Speedway—and our car wouldn't run, so we changed engines.

The new engine was still doing the same thing, obviously down on horsepower.

When I said Stanton and I are kind of alike, I wasn't kidding. Like me, when he's unhappy or frustrated it doesn't take him long to make up his mind to make some changes.

That night in Ohio was the last straw for Stanton. He said to me, "Wolfgang, I'll tell you what...how about if you and Jeri and the girls drive this tow rig back to Phoenix, and I'll pick up your airfare back to Sioux Falls. Because right this minute, I'm done. I'm goin' to the airport and I'm goin' home. I quit."

Well, I can be a little hot-tempered, too.

"No, Stanton, I'll tell *you* what...we'll drive this thing back to Sioux Falls, and then you had better get somebody out there to drive it the rest of the way back to Phoenix and get it to hell off my property right *now*!"

He nodded his head and said that would be *just fine*. He and our mechanic collected their stuff and drove off in a rental car, headed for the airport. We're officially done.

Jeri and I and the girls loaded up everything and started driving home. The next day or so we're rolling across Wisconsin, and I'm staring through the windshield. Boy, it bugged me that those motors wouldn't run. I couldn't understand why they wouldn't. We had good stuff and they were put together right and, damn it, they *ought* to run. How come they wouldn't?

I looked over at Jeri and said, "You know, when we get up into Minnesota I think I'll swing by Lakefield and see Loren Woodke. Maybe Loren can take a look at our engine and tell me why it won't run. At least then we could tell Stanton what was causing the problem."

Now, remember, I'm fired. But not really; I knew Stanton was just blowing off steam and he'd be fine after a few days. Yes, I would go drive for somebody else for the time being, but I knew we were a long way from finished. We had a friendship we both could count on, and we'd be back together at some point. And I was genuinely curious about what was causing the trouble. Plus I figured it would help Gary later on if he knew what was wrong. He knew he'd probably be back racing in a couple of weeks. He'd simply had a belly full of it and needed a break.

I explained the symptoms to Loren, and he started poking around on the engine. He discovered that the ignition points in the magneto were set incorrectly, and did some adjusting. We fired it up and it was like night and day, boy, that thing would run now. Obviously, the ignition was the problem. I thanked Loren and we rolled the car onto the trailer and headed for Sioux Falls.

"At least now Stanton knows what the problem is," I told Jeri as we swung onto I-90.

It's now about noon on a Saturday, and we've got a local station on the radio. Suddenly a commercial grabbed our attention.

"*Tonight!* VFW Speedway in Jackson, Minnesota, it's the Mid-Season Championship! $1,500 to win!"

I looked over at Jeri.

"Say, that ain't bad," I said, nodding my head. "Maybe we should stop off and run the thing…at least we'd see if we've got the engine trouble sorted out!"

Next thing you know, we're wheeling into the pit area. It was just me and Jeri and the girls, and we picked up a couple of local friends in the pit area to help us carry fuel and mount tires and push the car up in line.

We wound up winning the race, and won $1,500. Not a bad deal for somebody who was fired, I must say.

The next morning I called Gary on the phone. First I asked if he had somebody to fly up and get the truck and trailer, because I couldn't leave it parked in front of my house for more than a day or two. He said he had it handled.

"Oh, by the way, Stanley," I said. "I've got some good news and bad news. Which do you want first?"

He paused for only a heartbeat.

"Did you wreck my trailer?"

"No, I didn't wreck your trailer…which do you want, bad news or good news?"

"Well…give me the good news first."

"We got your engine trouble figured out. I stopped by Loren Woodke's and he found that the points were set wrong, and that thing runs like a blistered dog now."

"Really? That's great! But what's the bad news?"

"Well, we stopped off last night at VFW Speedway and won the Jackson Nationals!"

The phone was quiet for a second.

"That ain't bad news," he finally said.

"Sure it is," I said. "It paid $1,500, and I'm keepin' the money!"

Well, he laughed.

Now, some people might not feel that's right, since it was his car. And I would have never raced anyone else's car without them, and certainly wouldn't have kept the money. But Stanton and I had the kind of relationship where this was a fun way to get one over on him, kind of like getting your buddy to pick up the dinner tab and then having a good laugh afterward.

Boy, I like Gary Stanton. Ol' Stanley is still one of my favorite people of all time.

When I got back to Sioux Falls, I spoke again with C.K. Spurlock, and we patched things up a little bit. It wasn't too late, he said, to salvage a great season. Let's try it, we both agreed. So I was back in the famed Gambler sprint car.

Actually, money was on my mind a little bit. This was still a very good car, capable of winning big races, and if we could get things figured out the potential was very good. No matter what, if I kept my head down and raced hard, maybe we could both make some money while we were trying to figure it all out.

We traveled to Knoxville in August, where we faced the first of our objectives for 1983: winning the Nationals. We were close; we had a pretty good week, but ultimately ran second to Sammy Swindell in the Saturday-night finale.

We had come up one spot short. We were all disappointed, but we just loaded up our stuff and tried to keep our focus on doing the best we could with what remained of our season.

We pressed on toward season's end and were actually running real well. Things stretched into October, and there were only a couple of races remaining on our schedule.

I was thinking a little bit about the next year, but something in my gut told me I was going to get fired from the Gambler car. Intuition, I guess. It didn't change my approach; I still wanted to win as many races as possible before the end of the year, and I tried my hardest at every outing.

We went east and won the Syracuse Supernationals, which paid $17,375 to the winner. That was actually more money than the Knoxville Nationals paid at the time ($15,000). The win was also memorable because Keith Kauffman was there in Al Hamilton's car, running a top-of-the-line Gambler chassis with a monster 504-inch big block engine, and we beat 'em.

Then we came back to Missouri in late October, and won the Jerry Weld Memorial at I-70 Speedway, picking up another $10,000.

The race had been scheduled for Saturday night, but was rained out. They then moved it to Sunday night, and because of the wet conditions things ran a little bit long. Plus, when you win you tend to hang around the pit area for a while afterward, and it was probably well past midnight when we climbed into our motorhome for the drive back to Sioux Falls.

Jeri and I put the girls to bed in our little motorhome, and we drove on through the night. When we were on the outskirts of Sioux Falls Jeri woke the girls, got their faces washed and got them ready for school. We swung by their school and dropped them off, then drove home to get some sleep.

We heard a knock on the door about 10 a.m. and I rolled out of bed. It was the postman, with a registered letter. I rubbed the sleep out of my eyes and signed for the letter and closed the door.

The letter was from the Gambler Chassis Company, informing me that my services would not be needed for the 1984 season.

Over the past two weeks we had won two of the biggest races of the year, and I'm fired. What I thought was interesting is that C.K. Spurlock must have mailed the letter the previous week, even though we were scheduled to run I-70 that weekend.

Was I shocked? Not really. Hey, they hired me to win the Knoxville Nationals and the World of Outlaws point championship, and we didn't get those two things done. We were second at Knoxville and second in the Outlaws points. Maybe if I hadn't quit for a while in the summer, we would have won the title, so I can't blame anyone else.

But I would have lost a bet on the whole experience. Never did I foresee how it eventually played out. I figured we were such a sure-fire winner, I couldn't imagine any other outcome.

I definitely had no hard feelings over the deal. They gave me plenty of time to find a ride for 1984. I wasn't sore at C.K., or Kenny Woodruff, nobody. C.K. was pretty good to me and he treated my wife and kids nice. And Kenny could be cross and gruff sometimes, but it wasn't personal. Maybe I felt like it at the time, but today I realize that's the nature of the beast in racing.

You know what? Now that I look back some 24 years later, I see things that probably hindered our performance, things I didn't see at the time. For example, during this period one of the characteristics of the Gambler cars was that they were stuck down on the race track all the time, like they wanted to roll up on top of themselves. The engine was too high in the car or something.

It suited Steve Kinser just fine; he went great in those cars. But it never felt right to me. Not my cup of tea.

But I do know this: Without question, it's very important that the driver be confident in whatever combination you're using. He's the one sitting in that thing, and he's got to feel it. In my mind, I wasn't confident with the Gambler chassis in 1983.

Things haven't changed much in sprint-car racing in that regard, and today that issue is a challenge for me on the car-building side. I don't build an Eagle or Maxim chassis, and some guys believe in their mind that if it isn't an Eagle or Maxim, it won't work as well. That's exactly the way I used to think.

I tell guys today, "Are you kidding me? These cars are all the same. It's just steel tubing, welded together." But if the guy in the seat doesn't believe that, it affects his performance. There is no doubt in my mind. If he's confident it will work, it will probably work. If he's not confident, it's probably not going to work.

The registered letter from C.K. meant I was once again a free agent. Luckily it was late in the year, and I had time to begin lining something up for 1984.

My phone rang pretty quickly, and it was a longtime friend of mine, Mark Todd. Mark was originally from Bloomington, Ind., and had spent some time wrenching various sprint cars. We got to know each other out on the circuit and struck up a friendship.

During the previous couple of years Mark had worked with Bill Smith and Speedway Motors. Speedy Bill had decided to resurrect the No. 4x sprint car now and again, and with Mark as the mechanic they hired Ron Shuman. And of course they occasionally ran Shane Carson because…well, just because. I like to kid Speedy Bill and Shane that they could never quite get rid of each other. If Speedy Bill puts a car together for the 2079 season, Shane will probably be driving it.

During his time with the Speedway Motors car, Mark had Larry Nagel, who is from here in Sioux Falls and was a good friend to Darryl Dawley, doing some engine work on the car. Mark would sometimes drive up to Larry's shop, and would often stay overnight at our house. We were buddies.

By late 1983 Mark had left the Speedway Motors car and was now working for LaVern Nance in Wichita, Kan. The Nance name has quite a history in sprint car and supermodified racing, and Sammy Swindell had great success in their car in the early 1980s.

"Listen, we're looking for a driver," Mark said. "Why don't you come down and drive for us in 1984?"

Frankly, I had reservations. I had driven the Nance chassis a couple of times, and it didn't suit me very well. Now, I realize Sammy did very well in them, so it wasn't that their stuff wasn't any good. It was more like the car didn't suit me as well.

And I wondered if they hadn't fallen behind in the sport a little bit. See, sprint-car racing was still in the midst of great change, and a lot of progress was being made on chassis, engines, and so forth. If you're not up on those things, you fall behind very quickly. I wondered if the guys at Nance had stayed on top of things.

I explained my concerns to Mark, but he didn't give up. He talked with LaVern, who agreed to let me do what I wanted with the chassis, make whatever changes we needed to be competitive. And they wanted me; that was key, and just what I wanted to hear. I needed to feel like I was wanted. See, if they *wanted* me, they'd tend to listen and respect what I had to say, which would go a long way toward building the chemistry that had been lacking with me in the Gambler car.

Mark suggested I come with them out to the new Firebird Raceway near Phoenix over Thanksgiving weekend, to run an unsanctioned sprint-car race. This would give us a chance to gauge what was needed for the off season, and we'd be that much further ahead for 1984. That idea made a lot of sense to me.

Jeri and I rode with the Nance guys to Phoenix. This wasn't a big race, and I couldn't even tell you what it paid. This wasn't the World of Outlaws, but just a local race. The level of competition was not anything like you would see with the Outlaws, in fact.

Well, that's when the worst thing possible happened: I won the race, using their stuff from earlier in the season. The Nance guys—not Mark, but the guys in the shop who built everything—immediately thought, "Well, our stuff must be all right *just like it is*, because he went right out and won the damned race!"

I knew what would happen, as sure as anything. And I was right. When we went to Florida in February, nothing had been changed on the Nance cars. Nothing. Even though I had outlined some things I wanted done, everything was still the same.

We didn't run well the first night, and the following day in the motel parking lot we looked at the car and started talking. I kind of pleaded my case and convinced them that we really did need some changes, and they reluctantly agreed to listen.

One issue was that they located the engine too high in the car. That day we shimmed the motor a little bit and got it lowered in the chassis some, and it immediately improved the handling. We won three or four races in a row, and I felt a little better. That was encouraging. There were still issues; for example, they didn't want to make the move to aluminum blocks for their engines, even though that's what virtually everybody else with the Outlaws was running. But at least we were making progress.

Shortly after that, Mark suddenly left the team. I guess he had worn out his welcome and...*g'bye!* That's the way it always works in this business; things might be great one day, but they always end up stopping at some point. Always. This was Mark's time, and he left the team and went on down the road.

LaVern decided he'd come out on the road with the car, along with a couple of kids who would help him. LaVern was quite a bit older by this time, and in my mind I could sense that the business—Nance Speed Equipment—was slowly, steadily winding down. Sometimes it doesn't happen overnight; you see a business that quietly begins to fade away, and that was my intuition of what was happening with the Nance business in 1984. Listen, nobody stays on top forever. Nobody.

LaVern and I got along all right, and never had any trouble. We were not running very well, but there was no friction between us. Our girls were still in school back home, so I didn't bring my motorhome out, and I traveled in the tow rig with LaVern and his guys. Still, we got along all right.

Rumors are always floating around the pit area in racing; they're as much a part of the scene as tires and fuel. Seems like you can't have a race without 'em. I began to hear rumblings that LaVern was getting ready to quit.

I was missing Jeri and the girls, but the good news was that the girls were almost finished with their school year. We decided as soon as school was out I would fly to Chicago, and Jeri would drive down in the motorhome to pick me up. Then we'd all ride back to Pennsylvania and hook back up with the Nance car. But I didn't want to buy my plane ticket until I talked to LaVern. I wanted to find out if there was anything to these rumors floating around.

I asked LaVern if we could sit quietly and talk for a couple of minutes, and we did.

"You know, LaVern, I realize things aren't going so good right now," I told him. "I've had different times like this in my career, but if I hang in there I've had a lot of wins in between. The important thing is that I need to know if you're committed to sticking with this thing.

"I'd like to fly to Chicago to hook up with Jeri and the girls, but I don't want to go through all the trouble if we're not going to be out here."

He assured me that everything was all right.

"You're sure everything is cool?" I asked again.

He said everything was cool.

A few days later I flew to Chicago and met the girls. We hurried back to Pennsylvania and life was all right.

Two days later at Williams Grove LaVern comes to me.

"Doug, I'm sorry to do this, but we're going home," he said. "We're not running well enough to justify being out here, and it's time to quit. Sorry."

Well, *shit*. I wasn't mad at LaVern; hey, I understand things change and sometimes you aren't sure of what you're doing, in spite of what you say. LaVern was a little older, and I understood he wasn't having any fun. Listen, Speedy Bill Smith had this Outlaws deal pegged years earlier when he observed, "It's tough out here."

But still…now we've got to turn right around and drive all the way back to Sioux Falls.

A few days later I reunited with Doug Howells. Doug had a new Osborne chassis, and the seat was open, although Doug wasn't interested in going on the road and following the Outlaws. At this stage he preferred to race closer to home. I can't blame him, but it's hard to make any money as a full-time racer if you're running locally.

But the car was pretty good, and we won our first night out at Hawkeye Downs in Cedar Rapids, Iowa. That felt pretty good, but within a few weeks I realized this deal wasn't going to work out for very long. We were competitive on a local basis, but against the Outlaws we were probably a sixth-through-10th-place car. That's no knock on Doug, by any means; by this time the teams following the Outlaws were getting some damn good equipment and they were hard to handle.

I finally sat down and told Doug where I stood. I explained that I enjoyed racing with him, but I needed to keep my eye open for a car I thought could win a big race. Doug understood; it wasn't that he *couldn't* put a car together to win big races, but he didn't want to travel and run the big races much any more.

We stuck together through the early summer, and won a few races here and there. That was okay; hey, it's always great to win. But honestly I would have traded several of those smaller race wins for a big one. It wasn't just the money. There is pride involved, because at the big races you know you're beating the best out there.

It was somewhat of a depressing period for me. I felt a little bit lost and frustrated. As much as I enjoyed racing with Doug, I knew this wasn't the program I needed in order to win big races and ultimately keep my career going. But here I was, floating along.

16

The Beefmobile

A long about the middle part of the 1984 season—say July or so—if I would have paused to take stock of my career, this is what I would have seen: I was coming up on my 32nd birthday, making a living as a sprint-car driver, supporting my wife and two children. My past few seasons had been all right but not wildly successful. I had been fired at the conclusion of the previous season by the most high-profile team in the country because I failed to win the two things they hired me to win: the Knoxville Nationals and the World of Outlaws championship. The team I started the season with had disbanded partly because we didn't win enough races.

The truth is, it had been six years since I had an honest-to-God kick-ass season. And I had a growing suspicion—call it fear if you want—that maybe my peak had come and gone.

See, in 1975 I jumped right out of the blocks and within one year was a force to be reckoned with. In 1977 I had the most successful season in all of sprint-car racing. In three short years I had become a storm, a towering black cloud of whip-ass that rumbled across the prairie and made everybody seek shelter. That's what a really big storm does; it scares you, makes you look over your shoulder, wondering if this thing is going to swallow you up and bury you. I liked being that storm.

But my thunder wasn't so loud in 1978, or '79, or the years that followed. Oh, I was all right; every year I had a respectable season. But I didn't care about respectable. I wanted thunder. And lightning. I wanted to be a rolling F-5, Class 1, big black thunderhead that turned everything dark and dangerous and got everybody's attention. However, if I were honest with myself on a July morning in 1984 I felt like a small windstorm, capable of light damage only if it hit a building that was already a little bit weak.

In my mind, the mind that stares at the ceiling at night and fills you up with doubt and fear, I was starting to wonder if I was all washed up. I thought my time had passed. I thought my best days as a race driver were behind me.

I didn't tell anybody about this, of course. I didn't let anybody know of my fears, my worries. No, I strutted around like I was still something special, like I was Doug-badass-Wolfgang, a super-stud. But in reality I was fighting very hard to find the level of success I had experienced back in 1977, when I won 45 races. I was also wrestling with the growing problem of self-doubt.

I didn't need to worry. In July I hooked up with a man named Weikert—a pretty big wind in his own right—and along with two great mechanics we finally put the thunder back in my storm.

Bob Weikert was a prominent Pennsylvania beef rancher who had owned a sprint car since the early 1970s. Some great drivers had been with Bob at one time or another, some of whom had great success. Kenny Weld, for example, won the Knoxville Nationals with Bob in 1972 and '73.

Actually, Kenny played a big role in how I ultimately hooked up with Bob. It began about a year earlier, at the 1983 Knoxville Nationals. Bob and Kenny were talking—Kenny was not racing at the time, I don't think—and Bob expressed frustration that the Weikert team had not lately been as successful as he wanted. They had cycled through several drivers—most of whom were very good—but had not been able to win consistently.

By pure chance, the Gambler pit was just a few feet away as Kenny and Bob were talking.

"What you really need, Bob, is to find a good driver who knows what's happening with the car, so he can tell the mechanics what it's doing," Kenny told him. "You need somebody involved, who can also help work on the car."

Kenny suddenly pointed toward the Gambler car, where I was busy helping Kenny Woodruff get the car set up.

"That's the guy you need, right there," Weld said. "Wolfgang will work on it and he'll drive it and you'll win some races. That's who you need to hire."

"You think so?" Bob asked.

"Sure do," said Kenny. "That's just the guy you need to get back on top."

I first heard from Weikert in June 1984, a day or so after LaVern Nance quit. In fact, after driving from Williams Grove to Sioux Falls, the phone was ringing almost when I walked into our house.

Bob asked if I'd be interested in driving his car. He explained that they had gone through a bunch of cars and engines but they were in the process of regrouping. He was going to let Smokey Snellbaker—a very successful and popular Pennsylvania racer—drive it for a few weeks while they replenished their inventory of spares.

I told Bob I didn't think I was interested. See, he was a Pennsylvania car owner; by that I mean he only ran in that region. I had raced those tracks before, but I didn't consider myself a local racer, and sure wasn't interested in only running there every weekend. After all, I was looking to follow the Outlaws.

Bob was persistent, and I finally said, "I'll tell you what…when you get all your stuff totally ready, give me a call. Maybe I'll be interested by then."

One month later he called again. By this time I had been running for Doug Howells, and I was ready for a change.

I knew almost nothing about Weikert's operation. He had a father-son team of mechanics, Davey Brown Sr. and Jr. I knew them only casually, but had never worked with them. I had certainly seen the Weikert Livestock car at many races, but I didn't know much of what the whole deal was all about.

I knew they weren't afraid to get on the road a little bit and run the bigger races, because I had often seen their car at such events. So I felt like maybe it was a bit of a compromise: Yes, it was a local car (which didn't thrill me), but on the other hand I could also run some of the big races.

When Bob called me back, I agreed to give it a try for a couple of weeks. You know the drill: "Let's see how it goes." Kind of a trial relationship.

I ran for Doug Howells at Cedar Lake, Wis., on July 17, then boarded a flight to Youngstown, Ohio, the following day. I caught a ride from the airport to nearby Sharon Speedway, where I hooked up with Davey Sr. and Jr. for the first time. That night's race was paying $4,000 to the winner, sanctioned by the

All Stars, a touring group that wasn't quite as big as the World of Outlaws.

Our "two-week trial" was about to begin.

One of the reasons I wanted to give the deal a try was that just prior to his death in a racing accident in 1978, Dick "Toby" Tobias told me that Davey Sr. was a helluva mechanic. Toby really praised him, and that stuck with me. That's probably what caused me to say yes to Weikert; in the back of my mind I was intrigued with the idea of working with Davey Sr.

The first time you race with somebody new, it's a matter of everybody feeling each other out. There isn't a cast-in-stone "right" way to race; there are lots of ways to go about it, and it's mostly a matter of everybody being comfortable with each other, communicating well, and having some basic chemistry.

Right off the bat, I felt good with these guys. I liked both Browns, and Fred Grenoble, the third crewman who helped with mounting tires and driving the tow rig. We all seemed to match up just right. They had good equipment, for starters. Their motors ran real well. They weren't what I'd call piping powerful motors, but they made me go fast. I like motors that run into a corner hard because I'm more interested in the entry into the corner than anything. Well, these motors ran great into the corner. I liked it.

We set fast time that night, and won our heat. We were going to start sixth in the feature, and after the heats were over I was in the trailer, putting cover-ups on my helmet.

I'll never forget what happened next. It stands out in my mind because it perfectly illustrated what it was going to be like working with these guys, and told me we were going to be all right.

Davey Jr. walks into the trailer. "What do you want us to do with the car for the feature? How do you want us to set it up?"

Naturally, the track was getting more slippery as the night wore on, and Davey wondered if I wanted them to change the setup accordingly.

I hardly looked up from putting the cover-ups on my helmet.

"Oh, I don't know...I guess whatever you guys normally do...as long as it's good enough to run second, that'll suit me."

Davey looked at me kind of funny and walked out of the trailer. Not five minutes later he comes back in.

"We, uh…we don't really understand why you want to finish second."

"No, I don't want to finish second. I didn't say that. You asked me how I wanted this car. I said I just wanted it good enough to run second."

"Oh, okay," he says, and he walks away.

A minute or so later Davey Sr. comes ambling in. Davey Sr. is more relaxed, a little slower-moving than Davey Jr. Davey Sr. ambled; Davey Jr. walked. There's a difference.

"We don't understand," he drawled, "why you don't want to win the race."

I just smiled and said, "You didn't ask me if I wanted to win or lose. You asked me how I wanted the car. So I answered the question: I want it just good enough to run second."

He looked at me with kind of a puzzled expression, but nodded his head and ambled back outside.

Jac Haudenschild was in Bob Hampshire's car that night, and I think he led the first 39-and-a-half laps. But I beat him off the final corner to win it. That felt good, yes, but not as good as the feeling I had from the start of the race, because I knew I was going to get along great with this car and these two guys.

So the car *was* good enough to run second, but I passed the leader on the final lap and won the race.

We climbed into the hauler and turned east, back toward the team's shop in Fairfield, Pa., not far from Gettysburg. It's probably two a.m., and I'm sitting in the back seat of the truck, with Davey Jr. driving and Davey Sr. riding shotgun. I'm about half-asleep when Davey Sr. turns around and looks at me.

"Now I understand," he said slowly.

"Understand what?"

"I understand what you were talking about, about setting up the car."

When he said that, I just grinned. I had found a new home.

Do you know what I meant when I told them to give me a second-place car? Let me explain.

Every team wants to hire the best driver they can get. At the same time, every driver wants the best mechanics *he* can get. Both sides want to be the best, and they'll both try very hard to hold up their end of the deal, to be the one that makes the difference.

I didn't want to tell those guys to make the car a hot-rod, capable of lapping the entire field. Because when you tell a set of mechanics that, they'll try to do it for you. But when you try to make a car killer, killer fast, you can also mess it up to where you can't drive it.

All I wanted was a nice, consistent car over a period of the next 100 races, which is about a year. If you can get that baby capable of finishing second every night, that's all I'm asking. Because in that many races, we'll win 20, 30, 40, because we're close.

If you can get me close, I'll make up the difference. That's what I was telling them. Don't do back-flips trying to give me a killer car; just get me close, and I'll do the rest.

What's really cool was this: On our very first night together, we were already on the same page. Boy, that's tremendous. Tremendous! I felt so good that night, riding down the Pennsylvania turnpike, it was like I had a new lease on life. I was energized and felt really, really good about how all this was going to work out.

Most of the time, you can trust your gut. Seldom does your gut lie to you.

In early 1983 when my steering wheel came off in Florida on my first night with the Gambler team, I immediately had a feeling that we were in trouble. And my gut was right.

Now I had a very different feeling. I knew in my gut that working with the Weikert team was going to be very good. Time would prove out that my gut was absolutely right.

One part of the deal was weird, though, and a bit unsettling. It's something I've never experienced at any other time in my career, and I'll bet not very many other guys have, either.

I was with the Weikert team for three-and-a-half seasons, till the end of 1987. I can divide the deal into two parts: One was what was happening on the race track; that part was great, just fabulously successful and enjoyable. But the second element involved what was happening outside the actual race team. That part, I have to say, was much more difficult.

I never felt like I fit in there in Pennsylvania. Never. For a span of 42 months I raced in that area almost every weekend during the racing season, but it never felt like home. Some of it is me, I know; I'm kind of distant sometimes and it's hard for me to warm up to different people.

But some of it was real, too. See, sprint-car fans in Pennsylvania are like no other. They are as hardcore as you will ever see. Probably the most devout, most fanatical, most emotional, most loyal in all of motorsports. They call their local racers the "Pennsylvania Posse," and there is a powerful "us-versus-them" attitude.

A lot of locals have a very strict idea of who is "good" and who is "bad." If you are not from that area, you're an outsider. It's that simple. There was never any question that many of the local fans viewed me as an outsider. When I first came to the Weikert car, Bob had just fired Smokey Snellbaker, a great Pennsylvania driver who was very popular with the local fans. So from the get-go I'm the guy from South Dakota who took this seat from one of their favorites.

Actually, the thing with Smokey was something of a misunderstanding, at least from my part. When Bob contacted me, I had the distinct impression that Smokey was in the car only temporarily, and it was my ride when I wanted it. However, it seems that Bob neglected to tell that to Smokey, and when I accepted the ride they let Smokey go, and he was naturally upset. Had I known that accepting the ride would have meant Smokey would be fired, I would have flat turned Weikert down. I don't want to be treated that way as a driver, and I don't want to treat others that way either. But I did not know the real situation with Smokey until a couple of weeks after I had already taken the seat, but it didn't matter: A lot of people resented the fact that I "took Smokey's ride," and they let me hear it.

Not everyone, of course, was like this. I met a lot of cool people and made a lot of new friendships, many of which I still enjoy to this day. A lot of people went out of their way to make me feel welcome and comfortable, and I don't want to diminish that. But on the whole I struggled to fit in there in Pennsylvania.

How did I know there was some resentment? Because almost from the very beginning, the fans at the Pennsylvania tracks booed the hell out of me. At Williams Grove, there is an area just outside of turn three that's known as Beer Hill, where fans stand shoulder-to-shoulder every week, putting a few back and watching the races. When I'd walk the track prior to the feature—studying the surface to determine what we needed to do to the race car—I could hear the fans yelling at me, calling me bad names. Pretty soon the beer cans started sailing over the fence, and I'm dodging them. Empty ones and then full ones.

Well, I might be a dumb race driver, but I soon got smart enough not to walk over in that section.

I wasn't a Pennsylvania coal miner, I wasn't a local. I understood that, and it didn't bother me. By this stage of my life I was hardened some, because life does that to you. It makes you understand that not everybody likes you, and as a defense you learn to not let it bother you.

But I'll tell you something funny: One week they'd boo me until their teeth fell out, and the next weekend when the World of Outlaws came to town I'd get the biggest cheer of all. Because those fans absolutely wanted a local car to beat the Outlaws. It's kind of like two brothers: I can pick on him because I'm his brother, but by golly *you* ain't gonna pick on him.

As soon as the Outlaws left town, I'm back to being the bad guy. The next Friday night they're booing like hell and the guys on Beer Hill are pitching the full ones over the fence at me. Crazy.

I'd just snicker when they booed me, because if anything it motivated me further. And of course when somebody is down on you, you kind of dismiss what they're saying because they don't know what they're talking about. Just a bunch of weirdos. However, when I'd get back out to Knoxville or Sioux Falls and the fans cheered, well, obviously these fans understand what's going on and they're smart and educated. Right?

You put up a wall for the boos and you take it down for the cheers. You ignore the boos because at that moment the crowd doesn't matter; but you accept the cheers because you love getting a pat on the back. Racers have rationalized that deal for a long, long time.

Three days after joining the team, we won again at Port Royal Speedway. In the weeks that followed we were all right, but not able to win. I still felt good, though, when we loaded up for the trip to Knoxville and the Nationals.

We finished third on our preliminary night, then took the lead on lap 10 of the finale and led the rest of the way to win my third Nationals.

That was a great, great feeling, because it put aside all my worries and suspicions about being past my prime, over the hill. We lined up against the best in the business and beat 'em, and I don't care who you are, that will boost your confidence.

We didn't win a lot of races through the rest of the year. We won the Williams Grove National Open in September, however, which put our total since July at eight. Not bad, but not great.

Actually, we had a lot of work to do. As soon as our season was over we sat down and talked about what we could do for 1985 that would help us. Just like in 1977, we stepped back and looked at our race car, and kept an open mind about how to make it better.

The typical Pennsylvania sprint car of early 1985 had a massive big-block engine of maybe 500 cubic inches, just an elephant. They made a ton of power, but they were heavy, heavy, heavy. You couldn't even pick up the crankshaft because they were so heavy, and the cast iron block weighed 575 pounds.

To be honest, these cars were tanks. They were reasonably well-suited to the big tracks of the area, because the high speeds generated a lot of downforce from the wing. But when it got slick these cars were hard to drive, because they spun their tires. The Outlaws would come in and consistently beat them with their smaller, dinky-ass engines but lightweight stuff.

But those huge engines made a lot of power. A LOT of power. When I first got into Weikert's car, even their "junk" motors weren't pooches. And their big motors were excellent. They were tailor-made for big race tracks, big corners, lots of ground speed, and they were much better in the spring and fall because the tracks were tackier.

However, everything associated with the engine was heavy. Cast-iron water pumps, and so forth. We got to talking and I said to Davey, "Let's build these big motors, but let's build them a hundred pounds lighter. Build the motor lighter, build the car lighter, and then we'll kick 'em all; not just Pennsylvania, but we'll beat anybody in the country. We'll win *all* the races."

Sometimes it's just a matter of good luck; one of our key strengths happened to be that the engines Davey Sr. built ran well for me. What I'm saying is that their power band perfectly suited my driving style. His engines made power that you could roll into the gas pedal and it didn't light up instantly to where you couldn't drive it. It was pulling hard, but it was pulling all the way down the straightaway.

It was becoming apparent to me that most guys would run down into the corner, get set for the corner, and for whatever reason they would pinch the car down and the engine would bog. So they felt like they needed more bottom-end power in their engine in order to combat this. But many times when you put a lot of bottom-end power in the engine, by the time you get to the flag stand they just want to kind of cruise. That's all there is, you know?

I wasn't smart enough yet to fully understand this, but I knew something was up. Something was wrong with some engines and something was right with other engines, but I couldn't put my finger on what it was. Why or how I couldn't explain, but I knew there was a difference. For example, back when I was in the Gambler car there were engines that to me—sitting behind the wheel—felt like a pooch. But when we put the engine on the dyno it put out impressive numbers. How could that be?

Today I can see it a little more clearly, maybe because I understand it better. It has to do with things like torque ranges and power bands. All these guys were asking for more torque in their engines, and that became the fad. But I wanted more top-end in my engines. They had to pull on the bottom, yes, but I wanted them to accelerate hard down into the corner, four or five lengths longer than anybody else.

Well, Davey's engines did that for me. I don't know *how* he did it, but he did it. He wasn't doing anything different; it just happened that the way he built his engines fit me perfectly.

We weren't afraid to experiment a little bit, either. Our big-block engines were aluminum (instead of cast-iron), and we also had a couple of small blocks that were good. We liked a small block that was punched out to 440-inches, and they ran real good. *Real* good. Yes, we were giving up a little horsepower and torque, but the winner is the guy who is quicker and better at the end, not just the guy with the most horsepower. In addition to the 440s, we also tried some 400-inch aluminum small-blocks, with lightened crankshafts and aluminum heads. We used titanium valves, made a smaller oil tank, stuff like that, streamlining and making things lighter and more efficient.

One of the other changes we made was with our chassis. They had been using Gamblers, but I felt like they were too top-heavy and they didn't work so good for me. I explained this to Davey Sr. and Jr., and they listened. They told me to go ahead and do something different, so I got in touch with Bob Trostle and spent some time that winter in his shop, welding up some race cars for us to use. They were Trostle cars with a few things specific to what I liked.

We spent the rest of the time studying the car, lightening it where we could, and we ultimately built four or five different cars through the season to try some subtle changes for different race tracks.

By opening day of 1985 I felt totally confident in our situation. I felt that we were the best team in the country. We had the best mechanics, the best driver, the best team. I really felt that.

The whole process was enjoyable because nobody was fighting. The Browns were great to work with, just great. They taught me things and I taught them things and the whole deal worked.

From the very beginning, it was easy for all three of us to sit down and talk about something, and between the three of us somebody would come up with something good, almost every time.

Davey Sr. had worked with some great race drivers in his career, and he was very smart. He didn't say much, but when he spoke you needed to listen because what he was saying was probably right. To him words were like gold, and you didn't want to waste any gold. If he felt strongly enough to speak up about something, there was something you needed to listen to, to react to.

Davey Jr. and I really clicked, and became great friends. Some of that was because we were much closer in age; I was friends with Davey Sr., too, but in a different way. I socialized much more with Davey Jr. and we interacted differently than I did with his dad. Davey was our chassis guy and rarely—and I mean rarely—did he miss the setup.

Doing our homework paid off in that winter of 1984-85. The following season we killed 'em, night after night. *Killed* 'em. We won 53 races (I won two races in other cars on off weekends during the course of the season for a personal total of 55), an incredible number. Not just local races, either; we could beat the Outlaws anywhere in the country.

With all that success came a lot of media attention, and I'll tell you right here and now, it got to be a problem and I didn't handle it very well.

Part of it was my fault, because I wasn't very good at keeping my mouth shut. I had dealt with writers and radio/TV people down through the years, but by the mid-1980s there was probably much more media coverage of our kind of racing than there had been just 10 years earlier. Plus, there are a lot more cities and towns in the Pennsylvania region than where I grew up, so naturally that means more newspapers, radio stations, and TV stations and more overall attention.

As we got hot and started winning a lot of races, there were more interviews. I was always the type of person who said things off the cuff, said what was on my mind. I guess I wasn't smart enough to think about things first, and realize what the reactions might be, who might be offended, etc. I said it and that was that.

Plus—and this took me a long time to figure out—you have to understand how it works with most writers. They're looking for something brief, maybe a sentence, because their space is tight. But when they asked me a question I'd go on and on, giving them several paragraphs. Then they lifted the one sentence they needed and ran it, but when you saw only that sentence and not all the other stuff I said, the meaning of that sentence was very different. That drove me nuts. I would have been better off to say only a few words and leave it at that, but I didn't understand how it worked plus that's not my personality.

For example, let's say a guy asked me about a particular track. So off I'd go:

"Well, I like runnin' here because the people are so nice and I've made some good money at this place. It ain't easy to get around here because the corners are real different and you've got to learn how to get your car right down on the bottom so you'll come off good. It gets real dry here on the longer races. I don't know why they don't put more water on, the track gets too dry and I hate it when it gets like that. But it don't matter because it's the same for everybody, and probably it makes for better racing because it slows down some and buddy the traffic here is real tough to get through. But I like coming here."

Then I'd pick up the paper a couple of days later and this is what they used:

"I don't know why they don't put more water on, the track gets too dry and I hate it," said Wolfgang.

People read that and thought, "Huh...that Wolfgang guy must be a real jerk, complaining that the track is too dry."

See how it works? Now, I ain't saying they intentionally tried to make me look bad. That's not it at all. But I wasn't smart enough that when the reporter came up and asked, "How do you like racing here?" to answer, "I like it, it's racy and I've done pretty good here."

There were a couple of episodes where the things I said created problems with our team, or with other racers, so I kind of withdrew from the whole process. I was tired of the hassles, and I didn't want to cause any more problems. It seemed easier that instead of wasting my energy and their time, I just declined interviews. So I stopped talking to the media, pretty much altogether.

In some ways I hated that, because by this time some of these guys—Bob Chorpenning, Bruce Ellis, and several others—were my friends. In many ways we were alike: They were really into racing. But although their job was different than mine, that was their gig and they loved it. And I liked these guys terrifically, only I didn't want them to know that I liked them so I played with them all the time. I messed with them.

But I still cut myself off from the interviews. I wasn't trying to hurt anyone's feelings or cause any trouble, especially with the writers themselves. I wasn't trying to make their life difficult. I know they've got a job to do. But it was still better, I felt, for me to shut up and spare my teammates the aggravation of reading the wrong things in the newspaper.

I did make some exceptions. I remember riding from Port Royal to Selinsgrove with Bruce Ellis in his Camaro, and he taped an interview for *Open Wheel Magazine*. It was a hot day and I was by myself, the girls were back in school and they were back in South Dakota with Jeri. It was one of those weekends where we raced five times in three days, and I had won a bunch of races in a row. I always felt Bruce was all right, and I liked Bruce and his wife Denise. It was an enjoyable ride in the car and I felt okay that Bruce would do the story right.

When I cut myself off from the media, that didn't do my image any good. A lot of writers felt personally insulted, and they weren't too kind to me in their columns and stories. That's their prerogative, I've got no beef with that. But it created some tension, and whenever you've got tension, it's easy for things to get blown out of proportion.

For example, one night at Williams Grove I won the feature, and pulled to the front straightaway for the victory interview and the trophy pictures. There were a lot of people milling around, photographers getting into position for the trophy photo. An older man was there with a little Instamatic camera, and clearly he wasn't a big-time photographer. He got jostled around a little bit and then one of the primary photographers yelled at him, saying something like, "You don't even belong down here!"

That pissed me off, and I said so. "He's got as much right here as you do," I said to the guy. There were a few more things said, and I got mad.

"Well, if he can't take my picture, nobody can."

I stuck the checkered flag in the ground, picked up the trophy, and walked to our pit. Piss on 'em. For several weeks when I won, I granted no interviews or trophy pictures.

So now I'm the bad guy even more. That's fine, but people didn't understand *why* I did what I did.

Eventually we all got through it. I learned some things, and the reporters learned some things, and eventually we figured out how to co-exist. It wasn't easy, and there was a certain tension that never really went away.

But that's life when you're racing in Pennsylvania. It's hardcore, all the way.

17

Pinnacle

Look back with me to sometime in 1985, on a typical race night at Williams Grove Speedway. We're parked in the pit area, getting ready for the Friday-night action.

No matter how good I was going in the Weikert car, the night was going to be difficult. Hey, just look around: A lot of great racers were parked in the pit area, and sooner or later that night you're going to have to deal with all of them.

Keith Kauffman was probably the biggest stud at that time, and had won 32 races in 1984. When I arrived one year earlier, Kauffman was the best threat to win, driving Al Hamilton's car. Donnie Kreitz, Jr. was still young then but he was all right. Bobby Allen was on the road with the Outlaws but not all the time, and if he was around he was tough.

Steve Smith was still racing, and he was good. His son Stevie had just kind of arrived, and everybody knew this kid had talent and he was going to be very, very good.

Bottom line, there were a lot of guys who could beat you on any given night.

But the biggest challenge by far was the race program, and the handicapping. Williams Grove inverted 12 cars each week, based on points. If we've been on the road and missed some shows, I might have to start 18th. That means you've got 25 laps to pass 17 cars; that's the long and the short of it. And none of those cars are likely to be a turd, either.

Even if you've got the best car in the field, even if you figure you're a great driver, winning from 12th—or even 18th—was one helluva challenge. No doubt about it.

Am I complaining? No way, because my experience in Pennsylvania helped me become a much better racer. It taught me a lot about traffic, and dealing with a slower car quickly without taking unnecessary chances, and how to be aggressive but still not abuse my car. You have to learn those things, or you're not going to do well in Pennsylvania.

I could go to a World of Outlaws race and get second- or third-quick time, and start very close to the front every night. Even though all the cars were very good, it's still much easier if you're starting up front like that. You don't have to deal with nearly as much.

It might be simple to think that it's easier to win a weekly show at Williams Grove compared to a World of Outlaws race, because some great cars are with the Outlaws. Sure it's easier to win at Williams Grove; once you get to the front, it's easy, right? All you have to do is pick and choose to pass 17 cars properly. Easy, right?

I don't care if you're way faster than everybody else, when you've only got 25 laps to do this it's very difficult. Some of the guys in the field are younger and they're learning how to race, and they have no clue where they're going on the race track. You might be 30 mph faster, but it ain't easy to clear the field without wrecking yourself.

The Weikert team won 53 races in 1985, which is a big number by anybody's standard. I've never been comfortable talking about things like this, because I feel awkward about anything I consider bragging. It makes me uncomfortable even to watch a football player on TV bragging about himself; there's something inside me that says that ain't right. So I talk about the numbers—53 wins with Weikert in 1985—simply as a matter of fact, and history.

Besides, I didn't need to brag, because Bob Weikert did enough bragging for everybody on the team.

Weikert was maybe the most forceful, assertive, brash, loud guy you could ever imagine. He was probably the best racing promoter in the country, even though that wasn't his job. He was just a car owner. But he'd get on the microphone after the races and get everybody all riled up and I guarantee people bought tickets next week in the hopes that Weikert's team was gonna get their ass beat and they wanted to see it happen.

He would tell everybody that you were King-f***ing—Kong and even if you thought you were just all right, if you'd listen to Bob long enough he'd probably have you believing it, too.

He was that way with everything he did. He didn't do anything small; it had to be big, first-class all the way. In that respect he was a great car owner, because he gave us everything we needed to be successful. Need more money to try some different engine parts? No problem. Need some new tires? No problem.

It wasn't just a blank check; there were expectations that came with that setup. He expected to win. No, he *demanded* to win. I don't imagine he would be much fun to be around if his team had a rough period where they were struggling. I was fortunate that we ran very well during my 42 months with Bob, so I never saw that side of him. But I'm certain he wouldn't be a joy to deal with in that situation.

In late 1985, for example, we won 17 straight races. When we finally lost, Weikert was stomping and cussing, pissed off that we lost. But not *just* pissed off that we lost; he knew that for whatever reason we weren't 100 percent that night, and he felt like there was absolutely no excuse to not be 100 percent.

That's how Weikert operated. He demanded top performance from everybody around him. He provided you every opportunity to be successful and didn't want any excuses if you weren't.

Personally, I never had a problem with Bob. We got along fine, and actually in a funny sort of way kind of built something of a friendship. I didn't go to dinner with him, but I still considered him a friend and I think he would have said the same about me.

The only thing I struggled with was his brash, open bragging. I never, ever felt comfortable with that. Matter of fact, I hated it. I mentioned earlier how people booed me, and I'm sure Weikert's interviews poured fuel on the fire.

I read once where Kenny Weld used to tell Weikert, "You go ahead and brag, and I'll cover your ass." Well, that ain't me. I'm a fly-under-the-radar kind of guy. I like to sneak up on 'em a little bit, and you can't do that if you're yelling how great you are.

I'd stop on the front straightaway after a win, and the announcer would interview me. Bob would hover alongside me, chomping at the bit to get to the microphone. Most of the time

I'd be as brief and quiet as I could, and say, "Why don't you talk to Bob, he'll tell you all about it." He was going to talk anyway, so why not get it over with?

People would boo and he'd grab the microphone and put his fist in the air and yell, "You like that? Next week we'll give him full throttle!"

People were complaining that he was outspending the other teams, and he really thrived on that stuff. "Next week we'll bring three cars if that's what it takes to win!" You know.

A lot of times I'd quietly walk away while all the attention was being focused on Bob. I didn't dig that whole deal. It wasn't a big deal and I didn't let it affect me—maybe it would have been different if I was 21 years old—but I didn't like it. I didn't need anybody pumping me up because I worked on myself. I didn't think it was cool to be like that, bragging and yelling and all.

With Weikert it was no act. That was actually his real personality, boasting and bragging and overbearing and larger than life.

I considered us to be friends, but his definition of friendship was different than most people. Friends ain't like he called me at my house to chat. Friends ain't like when I later got burned in 1992 he sent a card or called to see if there was something he could do. It wasn't like that.

But we respected each other. Some of it, I think, was that Bob dominated just about everybody around him, but I tried to not let that happen. Definitely he was the team owner; but I still tried to keep our relationship about simply being an employer and employee.

For example, one Friday morning we were sitting in the shop, talking about the car and what we needed to do that night at Williams Grove. Suddenly the door flew open and in walked Weikert. He saw us sitting there talking, and he yelled, "What the hell is going on here? I'm not payin' you guys to sit around on your ass! Get busy!"

Davey Sr. and Jr. hurried over to the bench and acted busy. I just stood up and walked over to Bob.

"Say, Bob, I've got a question," I said. I pointed out the window at a cow grazing on a nearby hill. "What's the story on that cow, there? Where'd you get him?"

"Oh, I bought him two months ago at an auction at Sandersburg," he began with enthusiasm. "Yes, that was a great buy, and I expect that herd to make x-dollars per pound when I sell in two weeks. You've got to be sharp, but we'll make good money on that one."

"So you know the cattle business?"

He puffed out his chest.

"I'm one of the top cattle men in the entire country."

"Tell me, Bob, why did you hire me? And Davey Sr. and Jr.?"

"Because you know the racing business."

"That's right...I'll tell you what, Bob: I'll stay the f*** out of your business, if you'll stay the f*** out of mine, how 'bout it?"

He had this shocked look on his face, and didn't say a word. He spun around and stormed out the door, and slammed it so hard it shook the walls. He went tearing out of the parking lot in his Monte Carlo SS, squealing the tires on the road.

Just a few hours later, there he was at Williams Grove, handing us our pit passes. "Nice to see you boys, here you go, it's going to be a great night..."

Bob wanted to win races as badly as any car owner I've ever been associated with. But at the end of the day, he wasn't in the racing business. He was in the cattle business. If he respected you he'd leave you alone and let you do your business.

But you know what? I wasn't driving that car because of Bob Weikert. He wasn't what led me to take the seat. It was Davey Sr. and Jr., and the fact that we had great equipment at our disposal.

Bob's job as car owner was to provide us with the things we needed. You could never kick with him on that issue, because if you could prove to him that this tire worked better, then hey, let's buy 10 of 'em. And his idea wasn't that he liked to spend the extra money, but he reasoned that if we found something unusual that worked, we can buy them all up and even if the other guys catch on there aren't any more left to buy.

The bottom line was that by early 1985 we were not giving up anything to anybody, at any race track in America. In fact, I think we had an advantage. We didn't actually expect it would work out like that, but it did.

Some of it was timing. By this time the World of Outlaws had been going for eight seasons. Guys running all the races would load their stuff and be gone for four, five, six, eight weeks at a time. It's very difficult to keep your stuff fresh when you're doing that. Plus, they didn't have the 40-foot tractor-trailers at that time, and it's tough to keep your personnel fresh, too. Guys would flat wear out in that scenario.

And here we are, running locally much of the time and we're home almost every night. We might only get six hours of sleep, but we're sleeping in our own bed. So when we traveled to the bigger races, there was a sense of excitement and freshness to us, while the other guys were about half worn out.

We had a car we raced on Friday night, a different car for Saturday, a car for Sunday, and a car specific to when we raced with the Outlaws. Plus we were charged up, motivated.

By the time summer came and it got hot and everybody was getting tired, we were just hitting our stride. It also helped me that I had been starting way back every Friday night at Williams Grove, and my reflexes were sharp as a razor. It helped me get through traffic with a lot of confidence.

It's always been argued that you need to be out there with the Outlaws all the time in order to stay sharp, and to keep up with what everybody else is doing. I don't think so in our situation. We had the best of all worlds, the best possible scenario.

The whole thing came together like a perfect storm in 1985. Everything clicked: Our equipment was fresh; we had found some things technically that worked; our driver was very confident; everybody on the team was reading from the same page; and our car owner gave us everything we needed to remain competitive.

However, we had a couple of setbacks, and one very tragic loss.

Ohio Speedweek was paying pretty good money at the time, at least $5,000 to win. It was a cool deal, seven races in seven nights. We won the second round at Buckeye Speedway on June 1, and we were running second—and running down Kenny Jacobs—two nights later at Eldora when a rear axle broke. I hit the fence pretty hard, and they took me to the hospital for X-rays and found I had cracked my shoulder and bruised my rib cage. They taped me up and I was sore as hell, and was down to one arm. I sat out the following night but on June 5 taped my shoulder extra-tight and tugged my uniform on. We won $5,000 that night, and in victory lane the guys were needling me that if I had used both arms, maybe it would have been $10,000!

We had five or six days off following Speedweek, and I healed up and forgot all about my shoulder hurting. Winning always eases the pain, it seems.

But our real heartbreak came in July. All year we had been building a special car to run the $50,000-to-win King's Royal at Eldora, set for July 27. We had slowly worked on that car at various times, using a special part here, special bolts there. We wanted to go to that race with absolutely the best possible car. As July approached we got all psyched up, man, we were at a fever pitch. We knew we were gonna win that 50 grand, just knew it.

But one week before the Kings Royal, Davey Jr. got some alarming news. He and his wife Debbie were expecting their first child, and she had been hospitalized for a blood ailment and all of a sudden it looked like she and the baby were in trouble. Davey hurried home, and the next thing you know she's on a respirator. Things looked grim and they took the baby, but it was very premature. Debbie died on Wednesday, and later on the baby died as well.

It's hard for me to describe how devastating this was. Debbie was a great lady and Jeri and I had grown close to both her and Davey. But now suddenly she was gone and all of us—everybody associated with the team, as well as many of our friends—were in a state of total shock.

Davey stayed home while we went to Eldora, and we ended up winning the Kings Royal. It was an emotional wringer; we were happy to win but obviously losing Debbie took all of the joy out of what should have been a wonderful victory.

We kind of regrouped, and somehow managed to keep our focus on the race car. Actually, it did us good to go racing, because we didn't have time to think about losing Debbie, and how much we missed her. We could go racing and put all of that out of our mind, and it's a testament to both Davey Jr. and Sr. that they could keep their chin up and still put a great race car under me every night.

On the surface things were great; we were the hottest team in the country. But deep down inside we were all hurting, very much. Like many things in life, though, we didn't know what else to do but try to keep going. What else do you do?

Two weeks after the Kings Royal we won the Eldora Nationals, hauling another $10,250 back home. The next big race was the Knoxville Nationals, and we loaded up and headed to Iowa.

We killed 'em at Knoxville. We set fast time and won our preliminary-night feature on Wednesday, scoring a perfect 500 points. We started on the pole Saturday night and led all the way, and the pot of gold at the end of the rainbow was worth $25,000. It was my fourth title as a driver, and Bob Weikert's fourth title as a car owner. It was a very special, cool night.

It's safe to say we were flying high when we came back to Pennsylvania. There were still some big races coming up, and we were wide open, on cruise control.

Then came the streak.

Three days after winning the Knoxville Nationals, we ran a local show at Silver Spring, Md. Even though I probably figured I was a King Stud after winning Knoxville, we couldn't do any better than seventh at Silver Spring.

Talk about a reality check; that was like hero-to-zero in about 15 minutes.

But we went to Hagerstown and swept a two-day show, then towed all night clear out to Jackson, Minn., where we swept both nights and won the $9,000 Jackson Nationals. A week later we won at Williams Grove on August 30. We hauled west to Sharon, Ohio, and won the Sharon Nationals. Then it was back to Pennsylvania, where we won two races on the same day—an afternoon race at Port Royal, and a night race at Selinsgrove.

We had won nine straight races over a 12-day span. Not bad, and we weren't finished.

We had a few days off before we ran again at Port Royal, where we won the Tuscarora 50. The following night we won at Lincoln, collecting $6,000, and capped a weekend sweep by winning Sunday night at Susquehanna. Next up was a $4,000-to-win race on the following Friday night at Hagerstown, where we won our 13th straight race on Friday the 13th. We picked up another $4,000 in victory lane the next night at Selinsgrove, and won the following day at Susquehanna.

Next was the prestigious and lucrative Williams Grove National Open, set for Sept. 20 and 21. We won the Friday night preliminary, making it 14 straight. More importantly, at least to Bob Weikert, that was our 50th win of the season. Bob had been predicting it in victory-lane interviews since June.

The following night we won again, giving me my second National Open win. That was very nice, and our weekend take of $13,315 was nice, too.

We loaded up and hauled to nearby Susquehanna the following night, with 17 straight feature wins under our belt. That's where the streak ended, right there. We weren't right and I finished third, and that's all there is to it.

You know what's funny? I don't remember it being a big deal, winning 17 straight. We just loaded up and raced, and didn't pay much attention to that stuff. Maybe the fans and the media got excited, but we didn't. Hey, don't get me wrong, we were happy to be winning. But we didn't think about "the streak," we just thought about winning the next race. And when we finished third at Susquehanna, we lost because we weren't right that night. The car wasn't right, we weren't right, whatever, but we got beat.

The truth is, and I'm going from memory here, what probably happened is that winning the National Open was a very cool thing, and we celebrated a lot afterward. Not a lot of drinking, not that kind of celebrating. I'm not a beer drinker, so getting drunk didn't interest me. But we hung out a long time after the race at Williams Grove, then went back to our shop and stayed till three or so in the morning, bullshitting with each other, our families, and some fans. We took a different car to Susquehanna and I think that car had our weakest motor in it, and we weren't ready that night. Simple as that.

I remember Weikert being pissed. Now, think about that: We won 17 straight races and he's pissed because we lost the next one. But Bob was right: We showed up at the track not fully prepared, and not ready emotionally or mentally.

We felt a little better a week later when we towed out to Knoxville for a World of Outlaws double-header, and won the Saturday night finale and $15,250. Later in October we closed out the year with two more wins at Selinsgrove and Manzanita to run our total to 53 as a team, plus the two I won in other cars through the course of the season. The Weikert car had grossed a little over $350,000 for the season.

Not a bad year.

When I think about our 1985 season, I'm kind of amazed. Amazed that we won so many races, yeah, but more amazed that we *finished* that many races. See, it's easy to lose a race, because there are so many variables. You can crash, have a flat tire, have electrical trouble, break the driveline, have the wrong setup, and so on. Over the course of the year you're bound to have some bad luck, and cause you to run second or even drop out altogether. But we had very little of that.

Much of it wasn't luck. We had two great mechanics preparing the car, and stuff didn't fall off. Period. They were sharp and thorough and you can't discount that. I was driving very well during this period; I was sharp and well-conditioned, and my confidence was very good.

It was awesome. To this day I wish it was 1985 and '86 again. Wow! Those were great years in terms of winning races. There was turmoil personally for some of us, but if there ever was a racing heaven, that was it. We were so far ahead of everyone else, my confidence soared. We'd show up at the races and I *expected* to kick their ass.

Financially, that period was a big success, and I made good money. It wasn't about the money; yeah, that's kind of how we kept score, but the money didn't affect my lifestyle or my family. We were still living the same lifestyle as before. We'd bank what we could and beyond that didn't pay much attention to money.

In fact, I'll tell you how dumb and careless I was about money. It was during one of our busy stretches, when we ran a bunch of nights in a row. Hey, we ran something like 130 races each year, and to run 130 races you are humping. We'd run two or three nights a week close to home, and probably two or three days out on the road a little bit, to Indiana, Ohio, Michigan, maybe New York.

Each night we'd settle up right after going to the pay window. Everything was paid in cash at that time, and we'd divide the money and I'd toss my share in my helmet bag, zip it closed and toss it in the trailer.

On this particular stretch we had traveled out to Michigan, and swung out to Chicago to run at Santa Fe Park. We drove through the night back home and got to our shop right about when the sun was cracking over the horizon. Fred Grenoble and Davey Jr. were beat from driving all night, so they went over to the farmhouse to get some sleep. Jeri and I had slept some on the ride home, so we offered to wash the race car and clean out the trailer. We were going to change motors so we could run that night at Williams Grove, so I said I'd go ahead and pull the motor and then Jeri and I would take a nap after noon while

Davey and Fred put the other motor in. Then later that afternoon we'd ride over to the Grove.

I'm washing the car and Jeri is cleaning out the trailer, and she asked if I wanted her to clean out my helmet bag, and dry out my helmet. Sure, I said. A few minutes later she comes walking back with a funny look on her face.

"Have you been splitting the money each night with Weikert?"

"Yeah, each night."

"How long have you been throwing money in your helmet bag?"

"I don't know…a week or two. Or three or four."

She holds out her hand and she's holding $29,200 in cash that was lying in my helmet bag. I'm carrying almost 30 grand in cash, in a helmet bag with all sorts of people coming in and out of the trailer each night. Not exactly a smart way to handle money.

But I didn't think about money. It never occurred to me to count the money and get to a bank, or whatever. I'd toss the money in the bag as an afterthought, and went right on racing.

The thing I remember most about 1985 was how happy we all were. We were clicking on all cylinders, running very well, and things couldn't be better. Obviously, losing Debbie Brown was a huge blow to all of us, but on the race track things could not have gone any better.

I used to kid Davey and them, they'd say after the races, "What was the biggest trouble out there?"

"Keeping the cramps out of my cheeks."

"What do you mean?"

"When you're passing cars that easily, and you're smiling that big, it's hard to keep the cramps out of your cheeks!"

They got a big kick out of that.

But don't get the wrong idea: No matter how many races we won, or how good we did, it didn't affect how we approached the next race. I suppose at the pinnacle of all this I probably got something of a big head, I don't remember. But even if I did, it wasn't much. That's not my nature. I like to win but I don't like to brag. That ain't me.

Plus, remember this: I had been around sprint cars hardcore for about 10 years by this point, and I had seen every part of the cycle. Up, down, up, down, up again, down again. That's the nature of the sport. I had been racing a hundred times a year, for 10 years, so that's maybe 1,000 sprint car races, you know.

My arms never got so long that I could actually reach around and pat myself on the back too awful much. Because I thought to pat myself on the back was absolutely the kiss of death. The moment I got to thinking, "Damn...I'm good!" that's when she all comes unraveled, and you lose 35 races in a row. So I made a conscious effort to never think like that.

No matter what kind of success we had, if somebody asked me I'd say we were just all right. Never anything better than all right. Never.

18

Bumpy

How does that old saying go? What goes up...must come...down, right?

It's hard to follow a fantastic season like we had in 1985, very hard. To race against national caliber competition 130 times and win almost half, that's a once-in-a-lifetime experience.

No matter how good something is, it's not going to last forever. Just like no matter how bad things are going, if you stick it out things get better. Nothing stays the same in life. You're always on the move and things are always in transition: Going up, or going down.

I can't say we were really "down" in 1986, because we weren't. We won 44 races, which is still a great year. We would have won more but we didn't have the luck we had the previous year.

Well, listen to me: We won 44 races and I'm wishing for better luck. Shows you exactly how a racer thinks, doesn't it?

After our strong showing in 1985, Gambler was itching to get us back using their stuff for '86. They finally made a deal with Bob Weikert to give us a car, and I asked for some changes. Their cars felt funny to me...like they were stuck down too tight, and they wanted to tip over. The motor was too high or something. But they made the changes I asked for and the car had a lower center of gravity and felt much better to me.

I don't know, though, if it even mattered at that point. I was so confident, and stoked, I expected to go good every night out. That dramatically affects your team's performance, it really does. It's a mental thing.

However, I'm sure at the time I figured those little details were much more important than they really were. I was still poring over every detail of the car, obsessed with getting it exactly right. Plus, I could be hard-headed on occasion. I was still not keen on using Gambler's stuff, because they had fired me at the end of 1983. Hey, if I'm not good enough to drive their car, why do they want me using their chassis for another car owner? I was just fine using Bob Trostle's chassis.

But Weikert decided to use Gambler cars on occasion, so we did. End of story.

By the middle part of 1986 I had been with the team for two full years. I still didn't feel like I fit in with the Pennsylvania culture and scene, but I didn't spend much time thinking about it. The biggest issue by far was the logistics of living in Sioux Falls and racing each week in Pennsylvania.

Of the 42 months I was with Weikert, my family lived in Pennsylvania maybe 15 months, which spanned May or so of 1986 to August of '87. Jeri and I got a place and moved all of our stuff, to give it a try. But it wasn't but a few weeks that we knew it didn't feel right, so in late 1987 we bought a house back in Sioux Falls and moved back home.

Prior to that, as soon as school was out each year Jeri would bring the girls and we would stay at the farmhouse near Weikert's shop. For about two months this was nice, because I was with my family every day. But when school was back in session Jeri and the girls would go back home, and so would I.

Yeah, *so would I*. That meant each week I made a 22-hour drive from Sioux Falls to Weikert's shop—it's about 1,200 miles—and then on Monday I'd drive back home. I'd spend a couple of days in Sioux Falls and climb into my car for another round. I did this in March through May each year, and again in September and October.

For a while I'd fly back and forth. When I joined Weikert in 1984 you could fly out of Harrisburg, Baltimore, or Washington National (now known as Washington Reagan) for about $125 at the counter. But in less than four years the fare soared to $620 round trip. Don't know why, but it did. That made it too expensive, so the car was my alternative.

Looking back, I probably made that 22-hour drive 20, 25 times each season. Remember, that's round trip; we're talking

22 hours from Sioux Falls to the shop, and another 22 hours going home on Monday.

I would get up Thursday morning in Sioux Falls, and get on the road. It was east on I-90, and somewhere late that night I would pull off and catch a couple of hours sleep. Then I'm back on the road, and typically I'd get to the shop just before noon on Friday. I might get a little nap in the farmhouse before we headed to Williams Grove that night.

On Sunday night after the races—maybe we'd run Susquehanna, or Hagerstown—I'd hang out a little while, talking to fans and stuff, and I'd get on the road around 1 a.m. I'd drive until I got sleepy and pull off, then wake up and roll on. I'd arrive back in Sioux Falls in the early-morning hours on Tuesday.

How did I deal with a 22-hour drive, twice a week? Sunflower seeds, chewing gum, windows down, Diet Coke one after another, music blaring on the radio. It was the Eagles, Credence Clearwater Revival, Linda Ronstadt, stuff like that. We thought it was rock-n-roll but now they call it country.

I'm a little weird but I tried to use the ride to keep myself in shape. When I hit the Pennsylvania border, I would roll up my windows and turn the heater on full blast. It didn't matter if it was 90 degrees outside; I did it anyway. I'd arrive at the shop absolutely soaking wet with sweat from sitting in this sauna for four hours.

I did this to build my stamina. You don't have to be strong to drive a sprint car, but it gets overbearing sometimes. If you can stand things like sitting in a sauna for four hours, even though you're not putting out any physical effort, it sharpens you and makes you mentally tougher.

Plus, I wanted to see if I could take it. It helped pass the boredom of watching those mile markers roll past, one after another, for 22 hours.

I tried to keep in shape physically, regardless of whether I was driving or flying. My off seasons were also very busy, because throughout my career I often spent a lot of time helping whomever I was driving for that next season get ready. I'd spend a couple of weeks maybe in Des Moines at Bob Trostle's, welding up our cars, or maybe Brian Schnee's in Sioux Falls.

Wherever I was, I tried to work out on a regular and frequent basis. If I was at home I'd get up around 6:30 a.m. and go play racquetball with a buddy of mine until he had to go to work around 8:30 or 9 a.m. Then I'd go up to the gym and run laps.

Later that afternoon, say around 5 p.m., I'd come back to the gym, where they had challenge time on the racquetball court. You'd get into the court on a match, and play till you lose, at which time you give up the court. Then you'd challenge somebody on another court. The goal was to keep your court as long as possible. I got to where I was all right at racquetball and I played a lot of those challenge matches.

I'd go back home and spend the evening with my family, and when the news came on television at 10 p.m. I'd get dressed in warm clothing and go for a four-mile run. It didn't matter how cold it was; I ran.

All that physical conditioning made me a better racer. There isn't any doubt in my mind. I kind of enjoyed it, but more importantly it was something I owed to my team. If Bob Weikert—or any other car owner—is buying expensive pieces and parts and hiring good mechanics, the least I can do is hold up my end of the deal and make sure I'm physically ready to race. It wouldn't be fair if I'm falling out of the seat after he has spent all that money.

I'm thinking about our years in Pennsylvania, and the whole idea of feeling like an outsider. I don't want to give you the wrong impression, because the fact is we made many good friends out there during those years, and a lot of those friendships have endured for more than 20 years. I developed a rapport with a lot of fans, and even some media people. I got to know a lot of people.

Weikert's shop was located on a farm near Fairfield, right next to a cattle farm. That's the first time in my life I was actually on a farm. Yet to many Pennsylvania people, I was a "country hick" because I was from South Dakota. I always thought that was curious: Many of these people were living among farms, yet they viewed me as the hick.

It's true the region around Williams Grove was "out in the sticks," but their definition is very different than ours in South Dakota. You go over every hill in Pennsylvania and there's a town with 2,000 people. There are almost as many people in the metro Harrisburg area than in all of South Dakota. It's just loaded with people.

That didn't bother me, and I actually got to where I liked it. Sometimes I'd drive over and visit with Bobby Allen, or go to Steve Smith's apartment and watch "Monday Night Football." I thought that was cool, by the way. One of the very greatest racers, and he invited me to his apartment to watch football. That meant a lot to me.

All in all it was nice to be a part of the scene, and be a part of what was going on there at that time. I have a lot of great memories and, like many things in my life; I wouldn't be interested in trading that time for anything.

During my stint with Weikert, the other car owner in the area who I'd consider to be in Bob's league was Al Hamilton. Al owned a coal mining company and was a very wealthy individual.

Al had Keith Kauffman in his car during this period, and there probably could have been a rivalry built up because what races we didn't win, they were probably right there. But Keith and I were very good friends and weren't interested in being rivals. We were just two drivers who liked and respected each other.

I admired Al as a racer, but personally he rubbed me the wrong way. I never felt like he treated people right. It was all about Al, if you know what I mean. Sometimes wealth goes to a guy's head, and maybe that was the case with Al. Sometimes wealthy people feel like they're just a little more special than everybody else, and you all should recognize that. That stuff doesn't sit well with me. To me we're all the same, rich or poor.

Al once talked about hiring me to drive his car. I just told him, "Al, you don't have enough money to hire me."

He kind of bristled, and said, "Oh yes I do have enough money to hire you."

Well, I got my back up a little bit and looked him right in the eye and said, "No, Al, you don't."

And he didn't. I was just not big on Al Hamilton as a car owner.

Funny thing, I actually liked him as a person. His family was very nice, and his daughter Colleen Clark—who played a big role in taking care of Al's business affairs—was a great lady.

But I was just not interested in driving for Al. He was too self-centered, too focused only on what he wanted, and didn't seem to care much about what the people around him wanted or needed. Sometimes people think they can fix everything with money; just buy what you need to win and be happy. That comes across as wrong to me.

I'm probably not the best judge of character in the world. Who cares what I think? Al was probably a great guy to drive for. But I have to be honest and say something put me off on him very early on and after that I never really gave him a chance. I wrote him off as somebody I wouldn't drive for, and that was the end of it.

Winning 44 races in 1986 with Weikert was not at all a bad season, but all of us—me, Davey Sr. and Jr., Fred Grenoble, Bob Weikert, everybody—felt something of a letdown after winning 53 together the previous season. We didn't win as many big races; we won the Sharon Nationals and our third straight Williams Grove National Open, but finished third at Knoxville behind Steve Kinser and Ron Shuman. Third wasn't bad, especially when you consider we blew an engine earlier in the week and started 18th in the Saturday-night feature.

We started the year out great; we won four straight at Volusia County in Florida in February, then won the opener at Hagerstown. But we weren't quite as sharp as the previous year, plus we weren't as lucky. I remember Fred telling me that we cut down a tire while leading 17 different races in 1986. So the 44 number would have been better if we'd had a little luck.

But what was really happening is that our team was changing. I said it before: Nothing stays the same forever. Every day is one day closer to when something ends, and one day closer to when a new thing begins. You don't really see this at the time but it's there. For everybody.

I can pinpoint the death of Debbie Brown in July 1985 as the beginning of the end for our team. That changed Davey Jr.'s life, as well it should. A man doesn't lose his wife and newborn child without it turning his whole world upside down.

See, Davey had issues. Real issues, emotional issues. As early as 1985 you could see them. I knew something was wrong, but I had no idea how to understand something that complex. Sometimes Davey would say things so completely off the wall, so out of place and weird, that we didn't really know how to take him. Or he'd sit and stare off into the distance, like he was lost in his own little world.

Davey was a very close friend of mine. Of all the people I worked with throughout my entire career, I'm not sure if anybody was any closer than Davey and I.

When I started driving for their team in 1984, Davey Jr. and I immediately clicked as friends. Jeri and I really liked both Davey and Debbie. Debbie was a good-hearted young gal from a very nice family, and she was very kind to us. Kramer Williamson, an area racer, was married to one of Debbie's sisters, and another sister worked the pit gate at Williams Grove. Their dad was a parts salesman, I recall, and he was a very nice guy. The family had a cabin down on the river, and they invited me over a few times when we didn't race on Sunday. I'd take a boat ride and relax and it was a very enjoyable time. Those are nice memories.

Debbie just had the misfortune to contract some kind of blood ailment when she was expecting their first child. She was hospitalized but continued to get worse and they took the baby in a last-ditch effort to save both of them. But Debbie died, and all Davey could do was stare at this tiny, tiny premature baby lying there on a respirator. Soon after the baby died, too.

Davey was holding that tiny baby when it took its last breath. I can't imagine how anybody goes through something like that without it taking them a little bit over center emotionally.

It's got to be completely devastating for a guy in his late 20s or early 30s to lose his wife and child, virtually at the same time. I know it devastated both Jeri and myself. I'm a hard guy and I've seen friends die and I learned how to build a barrier and not let stuff get to me, but when Debbie died I was absolutely an emotional wreck. I could hardly deal with it. On the day she passed I almost couldn't control this outpouring of emotion I experienced. It was so much of a bummer it's hard for me to even describe.

One other big downer from the 1986 season stands out like a thorn in my sock. Late in the year we went out to Phoenix for the Western World Championship at Manzanita. In the pre-race driver's meeting the officials said very explicitly that if a driver jumped the start or restart, they would be penalized a couple of spots on the next yellow flag. In other words, they would assess the penalty during the race if a caution flag allowed them to do so. Fine.

Very early in the race—probably on lap eight or nine of a 40-lap race—I was running second to Bobby Davis Jr. We came to the green flag on a restart, and Bobby's engine stumbled just as we all accelerated. I was already on the gas and so were all the guys behind me, and we had no choice but to run right past him. But I did not jump the restart.

They had two more caution flags after that, so they had an opportunity to move me back if they felt I had jumped. When they didn't, I assumed everything was okay. And the rest of the race was N-C; No Contest. I drove off and left 'em, and won by a half-lap.

I drove around to the front straightaway and climbed out of the car. I had never won the Western World, and I was very excited. But the officials immediately walked over to me and said I was being penalized three spots for jumping Bobby on that early restart.

Man, was I unhappy. I tried to reason with them, but they turned a deaf ear. I'm scored fourth, and that was that.

I was so pissed off I refused to take fourth-place money. Part of my anger was that I didn't trust the Manzanita promoter, Keith Hall. Now, Keith is an okay guy; I liked him personally and we've spoken many times through the years since this incident. In my mind, Keith was one of those promoters who wanted racers to race for nothing. I realize that a promoter has to watch his pennies because nobody else will, but I felt like he was unreasonable at times.

It didn't matter what I thought, however. They made up their mind that I was fourth and that was the end of the discussion.

To add insult to injury, Weikert demanded that I make up the money shortfall between fourth and first, because he reasoned that it was my mistake that cost him.

See, a lot of people believed that Weikert was constantly giving his guys extra money when they won races. Weikert would say in an interview on the PA, "I'm gonna give this guy 100 percent of the money if he wins tonight!" They thought he was making his drivers millionaires. Well, I never got any extra money. And I didn't like him talking like that, anyway. The fact is, he never once gave me 100 percent. That's fine; I'm not asking for a dime more than my standard 50 percent. But I didn't like it when he'd be jawing about giving me extra money, especially when I knew he wasn't serious.

Weikert was a businessman, and he had a firm belief that you kept things on a strictly business basis. Which was fine by me; I felt the same way. So when this happened at Phoenix, and I was penalized, Bob immediately stepped forward and said, "Say, son, you cost me $1,800 with your mistake, and you're going to make it up to me." He made it very clear that if I wanted to keep driving his car, I would come up with $1,800 right away.

This wasn't the only time this happened. At the conclusion of one of our seasons, I received a $7,500 check from the World of Outlaws, my point money for the season. I took the check to the bank and immediately mailed Weikert a check for $3,750, his half of the $7,500.

A couple of days later—and you probably know where this is going—the bank notified me that the WoO check had bounced. I sent it back through but it bounced again.

I immediately called Weikert to explain the situation.

"Bob, we've got a problem. The Outlaws' check bounced, and I already mailed you that check for $3,750, your half. Since their check bounced I need to get my $3,750 back until Ted (Johnson, WoO president) makes good on his check."

After a hesitation of maybe a half-second, Weikert spoke right up.

"Nah, I don't think so, son," he said. "Tell you what…that's our money; now you go get it."

End of conversation.

So now, not only am I not going to get my point money from Ted—and I never did—but I'm $3,750 in the hole because Weikert has my money.

Did I get tired of this? Sure I did. On one hand I can see Weikert's reasoning. In his mind, my mistake cost him money at Phoenix. In his mind, it's my responsibility to chase Ted for our money, because he already got his. But on the other hand he was being unreasonable. If I'm leading by a full lap at a $10,000-to-win race and the engine blows up on the white flag lap, does he owe me $5,000 because it was his car that failed me? He does if you use his reasoning. But I wouldn't even begin to think about asking a guy to pay me under those circumstances. No racer I've ever known would think like that. You're a team and you take your wins and losses together, both the good and the bad.

You might be wondering, "Well…if you got tired of it, why didn't you quit? Don't you have any principles?"

Damn right I'm a principled guy. *Very* principled. But we were winning. There would have been a different line of thinking if we had been struggling. I tried to look at the big picture, and I'd say to myself, "You're gonna quit this deal over $3,750? Or $1,800?" During one of our seasons the car brought in almost a half-million dollars, and my share was $235,000, $245,000, something like that. That's a lot of money, especially in 1985. That would be like $400,000 in today's money. So think about it in present terms: You're in a business deal that's making you $400,000 a year, and you're gonna get mad and walk away because you feel like you got stiffed for $3,750?

Are you?

I'm thinking about that situation with Keith Hall, and it's the first time I've thought about that race in a long time. I'm not sure Keith and I ever patched up our differences specifically. I guess we just agreed to disagree.

Personally, I liked him. But as a racer I viewed him—like I did many promoters—as being on the other side, you know? He was looking out for his interests, and sometimes that conflicted with the racer's best interests. So naturally there was friction there, and there always will be.

My situation with Keith was a lot like a lot of guys I've known through the years: I like him personally, as long as I don't have to race for him. You see, business puts a strain on relationships, and you ain't never gonna get around that fact. It just does. You can't stay friends all the time when money is involved.

Maybe some of these situations came up because my world was changing. When I started racing in 1975, money didn't matter one bit. Just didn't matter. Actually, even for most of the car owners of that time, money wasn't a big deal. They were actually making a little bit of money with their car, so most of the time they were content. But as the sport grew and progressed, things changed.

Not just for me; for everybody. It started costing more, so then it got more serious. Owners began to say—and rightfully so—"Well, we've got to do something different or we can't afford the good parts." It was money.

All along my house payments kept going up, my taxes kept going up, my gas bill kept going up, my insurance premiums kept going up, and it cost more to get up and down the road.

You know the routine. Things were changing. And they kept getting more complicated.

By the end of the 1986 season, Davey Brown Jr.'s life was still in turmoil. Since Debbie's death, he seemed to bounce around emotionally, like he couldn't get his feet on the ground and deal with life.

Sometimes in life guys get the raw end of the deal more than other guys. It isn't fair but it's life. And Davey got the raw end of the deal, through no fault of his own. Maybe he didn't deal with it in the best way possible but maybe he didn't know *how* to deal with it.

It was very painful to watch all this unfolding. He was like a brother to me, but I didn't know how to reach out to him, to help him.

He was a little more bizarre with some things he said, a little more scattered, a little more bumpy. Within a few weeks after Debbie's death, Davey fell in love with one of Bob Weikert's daughters, and they became an item. I guess he was trying to find some sort of place, some sort of happiness in this world.

He went to the doctor for some of his issues and they gave him some medicine and told him to stay away from the race track because the stress wasn't good for him. Even with his new relationship, everything was still a mess. Finally at the end of 1986 Davey left the team.

That was truly the beginning of the end. Things were never the same after that. We had been a cohesive unit, working very well together. But when you take one big piece out of the puzzle, the puzzle is no longer complete.

Of course, at the time we didn't even think about it. We were still balls-to-the-wall wide open, getting ready for 1987.

That season, my third full-season with Weikert, we won 33 feature events. That's still a great year, but again, we didn't look at it like that. In our eyes, 53 had changed to 44, and now 33. Christ, we thought we were terrible.

What's really notable is that our performance at the big races wasn't as good. We won the Jackson Nationals, but that was our biggest win of 1987. We didn't even make the main at Knoxville, finishing ninth in the B-feature. We nearly made it; we went from the back of the B to second before cutting a tire, and ran out of laps trying to get back to a transfer spot.

Our performance wasn't where it once was, there was no mistaking that.

I was slowly coming to the realization that the end was near, at least for me being with Weikert. Davey Jr. was gone; Davey Sr. didn't have nearly the passion and desire as before, and neither did I. We had been so good together, and when it started to come apart it all down it seemed very empty, and hollow.

I had been around enough to recognize that our issues weren't going to cure themselves. We weren't going to get better. I could see it and I'm sure Davey Sr. could, too.

Because we had moved to Pennsylvania in May of the previous year, I had not been back to Sioux Falls in many months. After the Knoxville Nationals, Jeri and I drove our motorhome to Sioux Falls. Jeri had spent some time there the previous month and had bought a house, and that late-August visit was my first time to see the place.

I drove back to Pennsylvania after we won at Jackson, and we soldiered on. The funny thing, we weren't doing badly; we weren't great, and we could still win races. But the magic was gone. Not just for me, but for all of us. You could see it in Davey Sr.'s eyes, and you could probably see it in mine, too. We were kind of going through the motions, just putting in time.

That's no way to race, just putting in time. I knew it, and I also knew the time had come to leave.

I talked to Weikert and told him at the end of the year I was leaving. Bob just laughed and kind of blew me off. You know, said, "Aw, don't bullshit me, you're not going anywhere."

"No, Bob, I'm serious," I told him. "I'm leaving at the end of the year."

He laughed again.

On September 25, we won at Port Royal. That was our 130th and final win together.

Two weeks later we traveled to Syracuse, N.Y. for the Supernationals. I told Weikert this was my last race with him. He still dismissed it as some kind of bullshit talk. I finished second to Dave Blaney, and I stuck my helmet in my bag and went to the airport, and flew home.

A couple of days later they called me. They were getting the car together for a special end-of-year race at Hagerstown on Sunday afternoon, $2,000 to win. Bob said I needed to be there.

"Bob, I already told you...I quit."

"Well, you better be here, by God," he said. "If you ain't here, come hell or high water I'll put Kenny Jacobs in the car."

"I guarantee that's a good deal, because Kenny will do you a good job," I said. "You better go ahead and call him, because I ain't comin'."

I hung up the phone, and that was that.

It was several years before I spoke to Bob Weikert again. Not that we were enemies; not at all. It's just that I wasn't in his world any more, and he wasn't in mine. We didn't have any reason to just sit and chat on the phone.

It was the same for both Davey Brown Sr. and Jr. It was probably seven years before I spoke with Jr. again.

Many years later, in early 1997, I answered my telephone in Sioux Falls. It was a very familiar voice; Fred Grenoble, our old crew member at Weikert's. But it wasn't a social call. Fred was calling to tell me that Davey Jr. had committed suicide.

For a moment it was like a dagger through my heart, because any time you lose a friend it's very painful. But at the same time, I have to admit that I wasn't shocked. With some people you would never see something like this coming, but with Davey, somehow it seemed possible. All the way back to 1985 I could see that Davey had issues, serious issues, and it wasn't so far-fetched that at some point he just couldn't deal with stuff any more.

A couple of years later Bob Weikert died of respiratory problems.

Davey Sr. is still going, but I haven't spoken with him in several years. He isn't a guy to just sit and chat with; he's a man of few words.

I think I said this before, but I'll say it again: I wish it was 1985, all over again. We had something so special, so great, I'd love to go back in time and live it again. Not just winning races, or making money; it was a happiness, a sense that three or four guys were all in perfect rhythm, all joined as one solid team.

Once in a lifetime. That was my experience with the Weikert team.

19

The Big Three

By the early part of the 1980s, there was a phrase I began to hear now and again around the race track. I didn't pay much attention to it at first—really, I never did pay much attention to it—but after a while it kind of stuck and you'd hear it more and more.

The phrase was, "The Big Three."

This was used to describe myself, Steve Kinser, and Sammy Swindell. There were many good racers in the sport then, like always, but for some reason somebody coined that phrase and it stuck.

Like I said, I never paid much attention to it, because I never felt it was accurate. Steve and Sammy accomplished more than I ever did, and I shouldn't have been included in their group. They were alone. The Big Two would have been more accurate. In fact, that's what I used to tell people. I said Steve and Sammy are the Big Two, and I'm the best of the rest. Hey, I'm not whining about it; I'm just stating the facts. Those two guys won more than me, particularly when it comes to championships. I won some big races but I never won the World of Outlaws championship.

I'm proud that people put me in the same league as Steve and Sammy, sure. But those two guys, they were kick-ass race drivers. Above and beyond, in every way.

However, in our defense I can understand why people started the "Big Three" talk. There was a period in those early years—I'm talking 1980, '81, '82, along in there—where the three of us won almost all of the World of Outlaws races, and during the entire 1980s the three of us won all the Knoxville

Nationals. Those two guys won more than me, but we all three ran pretty well.

Of all the guys in my generation, I probably relate more to Steve and Sammy than anyone else. In a sense I felt like we were all in it together, maybe because we all came up about the same time.

I consider both of those guys to be my friends. Sure, there have been hard words at different times but nothing that hurt our friendship over the long haul. Nothing I can remember, anyway.

Those two are as different as two people can be, but I like them both. I'm definitely much closer to Steve, because our personalities are a little more outgoing. Sammy is a much quieter person and is harder to get to know, harder to get close to. But I like him. I've hardly said a hundred words to him over the span of many years but it don't matter; I like him.

Sometimes Sammy made me mad when we raced each other. He was like the "Snidely Whiplash" of the crew in those days, the guy you loved to get mad at. When we were supposed to line up bumper-to-bumper on a restart, he couldn't line up, insisting on getting out of line to try and gain an advantage. If you're on the pole and you're supposed to set the pace and bring the field down for a restart, and Sammy is on the outside pole, you know ahead of time that he's going to jack with you; he's going to want to set the pace.

Mostly little stuff like that. That's the way he learned to race in the very beginning back in West Memphis, and he never changed. That's what he thought it was *supposed* to be like.

That stuff grinds on you. Just grinds and grinds until you're mad at him. Not for any one thing; for every thing.

I once intentionally tipped Sammy over, at Chula Vista, Calif. I was driving for Doug Howells, so this would have been 1980 or so, very near the end of the season. Joanne Howells would give me hell all the time about Sammy: "Why'd you let that little so-and-so run into you like that? Go out there and do something about it!" Usually I'd just go put some cover-ups on my helmet and ignore the whole thing, but I'll admit it used to wear on me a little bit.

I'm leading at Chula Vista—we were running without wings—and I'm really hauling ass, for sure going to win this race. I'm getting into the corner, and in my peripheral vision I

see somebody coming on the inside. I mean, this guy—Sammy—
is clear down in the infield, cutting the corner, making a diamond
out of the turn, and he's coming at full blast. Wide open.

My eyes got wide and I'm saying, "He ain't gonna miss me!"
There was nothing I could do, I'm already wide open and full-
locked on the steering wheel, right up on the cushion. I'm
debating whether to lift and hope he misses me, or stay in the
gas and let nature take its course. He almost missed me, but
clipped my rear bumper and spun me around. I tried to keep
the car going but stalled, so I'm sitting there parked on the race
track, absolutely pissed because he cost me the race.

I restarted at the tail and when the race got going again, I
just idled around the race track, waiting. When Sammy came
up to lap me I tipped him over and he went clear out of the ball
park, it was actually a pretty hard ride. I meant to tip him over
but I didn't mean for him to crash that hard.

I went down to his pit after the race, and I was still pissed.
Now, you've got to understand, for me to have words with
another racer is very unusual. I told Sammy, "Listen, when I
see you again in the spring, I'm going to do that again, until
you stop doing that crap to me."

Of course, nothing changed. He still did all the things to make
me mad and drive me nuts and nothing was different. But at
least I said my piece and felt better.

I think about that argument with Sammy and it makes me
realize how seldom I had to deal with that kind of stuff. I never
once got into a fistfight, or even a pushing match. In hundreds
and hundreds of races, I only had words a couple of times with
people. I might get out of my car and look down toward their
pit and say, "What was that stupid so-and-so doing out there?"
But I stayed in my pit, and I expected them to stay in theirs. On
the few occasions when somebody came to yell at me, I politely
asked them to leave my pit and that was it.

That doesn't mean I had no scrapes at all. When I first started
with Bob Trostle, we were racing in Indiana one night and Bob
Kinser—that's Steve's dad—cracked me one, but that was more
like somebody spanking a kid for misbehaving than anything
else. Me and Bob were cool after that and he's somebody I've
enjoyed as a friend for many years.

Another time Dick Sutcliffe chewed my ass out pretty
thoroughly. Dick was a very large guy, and I recall him grabbing

me by my uniform collar and literally lifting me off the ground. I'm telling you, my feet were dangling a good 12 inches in the air, and Dick was telling me I'd better stop screwing around with whatever it was I did on the track. Whatever it was, it was obvious Dick didn't approve. I remember looking over at Trostle, who was laughing his ass off. Later that night Bob laughed again, and said something like, "Well, I can see that Sutcliffe's ass-chewing did a lot of good, didn't it?" Whatever I did to piss Dick off, I must have kept doing it, because Bob thought it was funny that I was back to my old self so quickly.

Our little run-in at Chula Vista didn't affect how I felt about Sammy Swindell. He's a very quiet, distant person, but I liked him. I liked how he was. He doesn't know this but I like him yet today, and admire him. I'm probably one of his biggest fans but I've never let him know I feel that way. We've hardly had any meaningful conversations, but I admire him. I consider him one of my 10 best friends. That's how much I think of him, and how much I respect him.

Sammy's got all these people watching him at every race, and when was the last time you saw him smoking a cigarette? When did you see him drinking a beer? When have you seen him swearing and cussing at people? You don't see him doing those things. He's always clean and presentable and I admire that.

In fact, he used to infuriate me with something. Nobody— and I mean *no* driver—works harder at the race track than Sammy. He could work like a dog in 98-degree heat and still look neat and clean and dry. That pissed me off to no end. I'd work one pit over from him, get filthy dirty, sweaty, my hair going every which way, and still not get nearly as much done as he did. That drove me nuts, absolutely drove me crazy.

From the very first time we met, I liked Steve Kinser. I was probably friends with most people in the pit area in those early years, but with Steve I always felt a special kind of friendship. My friendship with Sammy, for example, was much more distant. I never went to McDonalds with Sammy and had a hamburger. Never stayed at his house when we were racing near Memphis. But Steve and I did some of those things together, and that probably made us closer as friends.

I probably knew who Steve was before he knew who I was. When I drove for Trostle in 1976 and '77, we often raced in Indiana. That's where Steve got started, around his hometown of Bloomington. It probably wasn't until 1977 that Steve raced more on the road, outside of Indiana. I remember him coming to Knoxville in 1977 to run a red car, I believe the car owner was Jerry Smith.

I knew Steve because his dad, Bob, was King Kong in Indiana, boy, and that's the truth. When you went to Indiana, you knew you were going to have to deal with Bob Kinser, along with Dick Gaines. I vividly remember traveling to Illinois in late 1975 and seeing those guys there, and being a little bit in awe. I had read their names in *Speed Sport* and knew they were guys I could learn from. And I soon realized that Bob had two sons, Steve and Randy. That sticks out in my mind, and I'm sure this was before they had ever heard of me.

I was the type of kid who tried to pay attention to who was really good at the race track. When I'd go to a place for the first time, like Paragon or Haubstadt or Bloomington, I'd study guys like Gaines and Bob Kinser, watch how they acted around their race car, stuff like that. I'd watch mechanics such as Karl Kinser. They were the studs, and I wanted to see what they were all about. I was very green, and was eager to learn.

Bob Kinser was a huge presence in the Midwest during this period. He was big, real big. He was up there with Rick Ferkel and Bubby Jones. He was way beyond me and Sammy, or Bobby Marshall, or any of the other 20-something kids of the day.

When the World of Outlaws was created in 1978, I began seeing a lot more of Steve. Right off the bat we clicked with each other, and we had a lot of fun.

One of the best trips of my entire life came at the end of our 1979 racing season, when I went over to Australia with Steve and Jimmy Sills for two months of racing.

God, what a great time. I've never had more fun than we had on that trip. It was a difficult trip for me in terms of logistics, because I brought Jeri and the girls along, and of course you have to take the kids out of school in order to do this. That's probably why we only made the trip one time.

One thing I remember about the trip is that we struggled with the food. We finally figured out that the McDonalds food was okay, and I'll bet we ate there for 60 straight days, both lunch and dinner. Yes, we got sick of it; but damn, I couldn't take the food those Aussies put down every day. Just couldn't do it.

We raced quite a bit but we also had a lot of downtime. We had a blast, raising all kinds of hell.

One of the things we did constantly on that trip was bet each other on all kinds of stuff. "Kinser, I'll bet you $5 I can outrun you from here to that doorway…" "You're on!" or "Wolfgang, I'll bet I can throw this ball farther than you…" Constantly.

See, Kinser is so ate up with competition he can't help himself. Any kind of challenge, any kind at all, and he can't stand it. He's got to jump all over it because he's got to win. And I figured that out; he was so hot on winning, sometimes you could play with his mind a little bit and drive him nuts. He'd get all flustered and upset; the more I got to him, the more I loved it.

One day our Aussie hosts took us out to the little rental course where you could ride dirt bikes and four-wheelers on this little dirt track. They wouldn't let us get on the dirt bikes because they knew we would probably kill each other and ourselves, but they let us ride these little four-wheeled vehicles where were very much like a Honda Odyssey, complete with a roll cage. We banged on each other and flipped each other over, we must have destroyed their entire inventory. A guy would turn you over and come racing back around to make fun of you, and pull his goggles up and his face was like a raccoon from all the dust, even had dust on his teeth.

During a break in the action that day, I noticed an adjoining farm. There were chickens wandering around, a couple of cows and so on, just on the other side of the fence at the edge of the property. Before long I happened to notice a farmer walking through the pasture, and he disappeared into one of the barns. And I was pretty sure that nobody else saw him.

Hmmmm. Now this is an interesting opportunity.

"Kinser, I'll bet you a hundred bucks you can't catch one of those chickens, wring its neck, and be back over this fence in less than a minute."

"The hell I can't!"

Zoom! He's over the fence, running like a maniac, trying to catch a chicken. Of course the birds are going nuts, squawking, flapping their wings, running, trying to get away. Kinser is down on his hands and knees, yelling, clamoring around, trying to get hold of one. It's a helluva commotion.

Steve finally grabs a bird and lets out a big yell. He jumps to his feet and he's wringing that neck for all it's worth. At almost that exact time, the farmer comes running out of the barn, wondering what in the hell is going on. He sees this big Yank standing there holding a dead chicken, literally caught red-handed. The farmer is absolutely pissed off beyond belief.

You talk about having a shit-eating look on your face, boy, you should have seen Kinser's face. Priceless.

"Hey!" I yelled to the farmer. "That chicken there, it ought to be worth about a hundred bucks!"

I'm not sure what the disposition was that day, but I'm sure it cost Steve a couple of bucks. We laughed for days after that one. I loved it!

See, I'd get Steve like that all the time. He used to get so mad it's a wonder he didn't kill me. His face would get red and his veins would stick out and he'd just stomp off. It was great.

We would all the time flip for pit passes, and whoever lost the coin toss paid for both passes. Well, I had some kind of trick— I don't know if it was a two-headed coin or what, but it was definitely rigged—and I beat Steve like 12 straight times for pit passes.

Finally he got mad and said, "You sumbitch, you're cheatin' me, I quit!"

God, I love that kid. That sure was fun.

One year in Florida we all showed up to start the season, and everybody had gone to these seats with the real high backs, replacing the old seats that stopped about shoulder height.

We always made fun of Steve because when he was ahead of you on the track he could always somehow figure out where you were faster, and he'd move to that line and take it away from you. How he did this I don't know; but we'd accuse him of turning his head around backward so he could block us. He wasn't actually blocking, but rather making you find another line, find another way to beat him. But I'd razz him about blocking and it would piss him off to no end.

He showed up in Florida with one of those high seats in Karl's car, and I walked over to their pit.

"Sonny, you ain't even gonna be able to race this year," I told him.

Immediately he stiffened up and said, "What are you talking about?"

"Hell, look at that seat," I said, pointing. "You can't turn that thick neck of yours clear around to block us any more, because the seat's too high! Karl's gonna have to drill a big hole in the seat so you can see to even race!"

Of course he stomped off with his red face, cussing. I think he stayed mad at me for like two days on that one, which was much longer than usual.

Back to our Australia trip: We were racing at the Sydney Showgrounds, and we often pitched in and worked on each other's car. We got a new engine for Steve's car, and we were getting it bolted in. At the time I was hardly mechanically inclined (I'm not even sure I'm mechanically inclined today), and Steve was probably even less than I was in terms of knowing what we were doing. Now, don't get me wrong; from the beginning, Steve knew what was going on with his race car. He was very keen in that regard. But as far as him getting a set of tools and making it happen himself, that wasn't something he did much of.

We were using these very nice buildings near the track, and soon Steve got his car all together and climbed in to start the engine. The thing fired and kind of shuddered, and then quit. They pushed it back to the garage area and Steve climbed out.

Well, something is wrong. The hood comes off and we're poking and prodding, trying to figure it out. Suddenly Steve looks at his watch, and realizes it's well into the afternoon. Oh, my gosh! It's almost time to go to the bar and drink beer! G'bye! We'll figure out the car later. And away he goes.

I pulled the rocker arm off to have a look. Somehow, every pushrod and rocker arm had come off the valves. Now we're in trouble, because neither one of us knew how to set the valves. Luckily I tracked down a mechanic nearby who helped me get the thing back together.

Was Steve worried about it? Nope! He was already having a good time at the bar.

That trip to Australia…I haven't thought about that stuff in 30 years, and now that I'm on the subject a lot of memories are coming back to me.

Part of the reason we had so much fun is because we were young and a lot more wild and carefree than we are today. Plus, it was three guys who got along really well, and liked to have fun. Myself, Steve, and Jimmy Sills, that's quite a combination.

One evening we're working on the cars in the parking lot of the motel where we're staying, and several of the maids came hurrying down to find me.

"Doug, Doug, come quick," they said, all worried. "Jimmy Sills is having a big tussle with his wife!"

We go upstairs—he's staying on the seventh floor—and there is Jimmy, drunk, mad as hell, pounding on the door of his room. He and his first wife, Karen, have had a little too much to drink and started to fight and she locked him out of the room.

I got him calmed down a little bit, but he's still steamed. Suddenly he says, "Hey, why don't we just throw her out the window! Do you think seven stories is high enough?"

I just looked at him.

"No, Jimmy, for her it's not high enough. All we'd do is get ourselves in big trouble."

"Aw, shoot!" he says.

Now, let me clarify something: I've talked about how Steve and I were good friends, and we were. But there was another angle to all this. During one season—I think it was when I was driving the Howells car—I finished second to Steve something like 19 times in feature race competition.

Did that bother me? Hell yeah it bothered me! I was so sick of that white No. 11 car in front of me, I could puke. I mean, when you're at your best you ought to be able to handle 'em; when I was at my best, I could barely stay ahead of him. He out-drove me and that's all there is to it.

And they lived right, too. One year at the Jayhawk Nationals, Steve won and I ran second. The following day he and Karl brought their car to Bob Trostle's shop in Des Moines, and I was already there, doing some work on Doug Howells' car.

Karl told us that when Steve fired the car for the feature the night before, it never developed any oil pressure but he drove it anyway and won, running all 40 laps with no oil pressure. They needed to pull the oil pan and check the bearings and things before they ran it again. They also wanted to look at the oil pump, which was one of those Barnes in-the-pan sumps, which was a dry-sump system that ran off the magneto.

They pulled the pan down and looked, and the oil pump wasn't even there. It had broken and fallen down into the pan, but was faintly held in place by one of the fittings. It was probably generating a tiny bit of pressure, but 40 laps? That's living right, is what that is.

But no matter how many times Steve beat me, I still liked him personally. Our friendship was beyond what was happening on the race track.

My respect for him goes much deeper than racing. When I think about Steve over the past 20-some years, I know there has hardly been a moment where he didn't know exactly where all his kids were, and exactly what was going on in their lives. He has been a great father, and that isn't easy in his circumstances. Sometimes that meant driving through the night to get home in order to be with one of his kids at a school function, or whatever. But he always went the extra mile to make sure he was involved with his kids. He and his wife Dana have been excellent parents and they've raised three great kids.

Steve is the opposite of what people might think, because they see his gruff exterior and think he's a tough guy. But he isn't. He's got a very soft heart, especially for his kids. He's a very protective mother-hen kind of person, and I think that's great. I totally respect that.

In my office, I don't have much in the way of racing pictures, except one thing. It's a very large photograph of Steve in his Quaker State sprint car. The inscription reads, "To Doug: A good friend and a helluva racer." That means more to me than anything you can imagine. Steve probably doesn't realize this, but it does. It's pretty cool to have the absolute best in the world—forever and ever, Amen—write that on a picture. It means a lot.

Steve and Sammy Swindell have had a great rivalry through all these years, and they've had more than a few scuffles.

Steve is a big, strong guy, and he could probably whip just about anybody out there. But I'll tell you something very few people realize: In all the times Steve has scrapped with Sammy, I'll bet he's never once really hit him. I mean absolutely draw his arm back and unload with full force.

See, Steve doesn't *want* to hit Sammy. He never *has* wanted to. Yeah, he gets pissed off and they might wrestle and scrap, but he doesn't want to hurt Sammy, because he respects him as a person and as a racer. He gets mad at something Sammy does on the race track and in the heat of the moment they get into it, but never have you seen Steve absolutely haul off and bury Sammy. Or anybody else, for that matter.

Lots of people have talked about their rivalry, and believe me, it's real. Those two guys are such fierce competitors they can't stand to lose, and each has stolen a lot of glory from the other. I guarantee they get fired up when they race each other, even to this day. But even though they might not go have a hamburger together, I'll bet each man considers the other to be a good friend. As far as respect, you'd better believe those two guys respect each other as much as any two competitors in any kind of racing.

20

Cast of Characters

Believe it or not, by the end of 1977—even though I had only been racing sprint cars for three seasons—I already knew who the competition was going to be over the next few years. I had already figured out who was going to be really good.

Ronnie Shuman, Sammy Swindell, Bobby Marshall, Danny Smith, and Steve Kinser. There wasn't any doubt in my mind that they were going to be the next generation of winners. No doubt at all. I had seen enough of these guys to know they were going to be good, really good. That group was going to be special.

You know, my assessment wasn't far off. Bobby Marshall quit not too long after that—he drove his family's car through most of his career—because he and his family had jobs and business interests in Texas and couldn't take off and travel like the rest of us. He would have been an exceptionally good racer if he would have had the opportunity to travel extensively and focus on racing.

Danny Smith was ahead of his time in a lot of ways. He was very young when he started, and immediately showed a lot of talent. He was always a nice kid, and I liked him all along. He was calm, and easygoing, and rolled with the flow. I didn't talk to him a lot at the time, but I liked him. Really, everybody liked Danny. You'd have a hard time finding anybody to say bad stuff about him. Not too long ago I learned that his wife had died, and I called him and we had a great conversation. He's just a very good person. I understand he's getting along better now, going on with his life, and I'm glad. I like Danny a ton. I also liked his late father, Mike, and his brother Fred. Nice people.

If you had asked me at that time to rank the top up-and-coming drivers in order, I would have put Ronnie Shuman as number one.

Obviously, Steve turned out to be number one over all of us, but Ronnie had a helluva career, too. He won the Knoxville Nationals, he won a lot of Outlaws races, and then later in his career moved back out West and had many great seasons without the wings in CRA and SCRA. Plus he won the Turkey Night Grand Prix in the midgets about a gazillion times. He was multi-talented and maybe had the best career of all in terms of diversity.

During the early 1980s I got to know Ronnie quite well. I liked being around him. He was professional, and was always ready to race when he got to the track. He was cleaned up and looked sharp, but he didn't put on the boat too much, too fancy. He had an aura about him I thought was great, and I envied him. Even though it was very rare that he would overdrive the car, he got everything out of it that was there.

Ronnie was a smart, savvy guy. Actually, I think his only limitation might have been that he didn't spend the hours working on the car like some of us did. I don't think he enjoyed working on the car that much. At the end of the night he went in one direction and his crew and car went in another. That can hurt you sometimes, because you might not be in tune with what's going on with the car and the crew. Just as I say that, though, I realize again what an enormous success Ronnie had with his career, so obviously whatever criticism you throw his way sure doesn't account for much!

Looking back, Sammy was really plugged into what his car was doing, and I was, too. Steve also was, but not as much, but then again he didn't need to be. He had Karl Kinser, who was God at that time. Together, it was Steve and God; they made a helluva team.

One of the most interesting people I encountered in my career is Bobby Allen. Brad Doty once described Bobby as somebody with a "wicked, warped sense of humor," and that's him exactly. He'd do the damnedest things. Nonchalant as hell, with a dry sense of humor and really wild gags, and he was fun. A very cool guy.

Bob was very smart with the race car, and was ahead of his time. The cars we all build today—four-bar, cross torsion bar cars with light tubular frames—Bobby was building for himself and Lynn Paxton back in the mid-1960s. Today's cars might be a little refined, but they're basically the same car. Bobby's vision was so good, his ideas and philosophy has lasted for more than 40 years, and will probably last another 40. When Bob built those early cars, he probably laid the tubing out and built it on the floor of his shop. Some of the guys today have $5,000 jigs, and Bob probably built his on a cement floor and did it in an afternoon.

He was also one of the early guys to experiment with light stuff. Even though his cars sometimes looked like Junkyard Jones, if you looked at them they were nice pieces. They were simple, with no needless stuff.

Bobby was a little older than me, and all the girls liked him. He was always greasy and kind of ragged, so Scruffy was a good nickname. He would draw the spit out of his mouth and draw it down maybe six inches and then suck it back into his mouth, and then he'd look at a girl and grin. They might look at him like, "Who's this gross sumbitch?" But in another moment they were lovin' him. He was such a cornball, goofy guy, he made you laugh without really trying.

When I came along, Bobby was *the man* in Pennsylvania. Bubby Jones might have been Illinois, and Bob Kinser and Dick Gaines were Indiana, Chuck Amati was Missouri and southern Illinois, Bobby Marshall was Texas, but Bobby Allen and Steve Smith were Pennsylvania. When we raced with wings, particularly when we were out East, Bobby was the guy I knew I needed to beat if I wanted to win.

I mentioned earlier that there was a brief period when Sammy Swindell got on my nerves, and it got me to thinking. For some reason there was a stretch where I was flat annoyed with almost anybody from Memphis. Sammy, his brother Jeff, the whole bunch of 'em. Mostly Sammy, but I was a little annoyed with all of them.

And of course that ain't fair, but that's how it was. There wasn't anything wrong with any of 'em, but for some reason I got crossways with the Memphis bunch and they got on my nerves. I lumped the whole bunch into one bucket: Sammy and Jeff, Mike Ward, Terry Gray, Bobby Davis Jr., plus a few mechanics, Robert Hubbard, Billy Anderson, and Gary "Deuce" Turrill.

Of course this was just for a little while and I got over it.

For example, Jeff Swindell rubbed me the wrong way from the very beginning, and it was a long time before I felt comfortable around him. It wasn't anything bad or wrong, it's just that his personality is very outgoing, kind of rowdy, kind of loud, and that's the direct opposite of me. So I always kept my distance from Jeff. It's funny, I could probably sit down with guys like that today and we'd be good friends. But at the time we were all a lot less mature, and it was pretty competitive, so the combination kind of made you choose your friends and the others you ignored.

Now that we're talking about some of the guys from the earlier years, all kinds of names are coming to mind. For example, Lee Osborne was a good friend of mine, a guy I got to know very well. I often stayed at his house when he was living in Jamestown, Ind., had dinner with him and his wife and family. Our children were about the same age and they played together.

We just loved Lee's wife, she was a very nice lady. I liked Lee a lot, and unfortunately he is one of the guys whom I don't see much any more, but I wish I did. I could stand and listen to him all day long. He could crack me up with his great sense of humor, and make me feel happy and relaxed.

Lee was a helluva fabricator, and was highly underrated as a driver because he owned his own stuff. A lot of people recognized that he was a very gifted person in terms of his mechanical ability, but most people didn't realize how good he was as a driver. He was very talented, much more so than he ever got credit for.

Later on Lee and his wife divorced, and I sure hated to hear that. But life goes on, I guess. I understand Lee has moved back to New York, and married his high school sweetheart! Now that's cool. He's building hot rods and street machines, and is one of the most respected builders in the country in that arena.

Lee is one cool guy.

When I was going pretty good in the early 1980s, that's when I first met Brad Doty. He was truly the nicest, most polite young man you'd ever find. I liked talking with him. I don't remember the first time we met, but I got to know him a little bit and immediately liked him.

He was like so many other guys you get to know only through racing. You don't go to their house, but you might stay at the same motel a lot so you spend some off time visiting. When you get to know someone only in that context, you don't really know them. It takes many years to really know somebody, and the way we lived—one motel to another, competing against each other almost every night—made it very difficult to get to know each other. And I'm not sure I wanted to; to begin with, I was obsessed with the race car, and I also had a family out there with me, and that didn't leave much time for a social life of any kind. So I'd casually get to know guys, if you can call it that, and guys would come and go along the way that you liked but never got the opportunity to build a friendship.

But Brad is such a pleasant person, I'll bet he's friends with just about everybody. He is an easy guy to talk to, and he has a way about him that makes you relax. He's got the type of personality that lends itself to making friends. That didn't mean he was soft on the race track; he'd race you hard, just like everybody else. But away from the track he was a genuine nice person.

I distinctly remember the night he got hurt at Eldora, and I can recall many details from that event. Just a few weeks earlier, Brad and I had switched cars; he got into the yellow Duz-Mor No. 40 for Gary Stanton, and I got into the Kodiak Lightning Chassis No. 18 for Les Kepler. Brad had also driven Gary Runyon's car some, and I suspect his deal was like my relationship with guys like Stanton or Doug Howells, where he could run Runyon's car when he was in between rides.

We went into turn one that night at Eldora, and Jeff Swindell skated across the track. Man, I could see it happening right before my eyes. Cars went every direction and started crashing, flipping, throwing pieces and parts. I couldn't avoid the mess, and wound up crashing very hard. My car really got beat up, and it almost tore that Lightning chassis almost in half.

I got out of the car, and I wasn't feeling so good. I definitely didn't feel whippy. I remember feeling like I had felt a few years earlier at Flemington, when I hit so incredibly hard in the Gambler car. I distinctly remember going back to our trailer, doubled-up in pain. I was hurting, big time. There was a long delay—I'm laying in the trailer dying, at least in my mind—and it became apparent that Brad was badly hurt.

It was obvious my car was hurt much worse than his, but he had much worse injuries. I looked at the two cars, and I immediately said to myself, "What are you whining about, boy? Ain't nothing wrong with you." That took the pain away, but it totally took the wind out of my sails later to learn that Brad was paralyzed.

The next day Jeri and I and our girls went to the hospital in Dayton to check on Brad, and it was a very difficult day. I don't think I was ever at a hospital when a driver got hurt—before or since—but we went down there that day. That's kind of weird, because I don't know why we did. It was one of those times that didn't seem very slick, if you know what I mean. A real bummer.

And we weren't alone. I remember how remarkable it was that so many other drivers and their families were there. Like I said, everybody liked Brad. It broke our hearts to see him get hurt.

Before I even dreamed of driving a race car, there was a name throughout the region that I was already very familiar with: the Weld family from Kansas City.

I admired Greg Weld from day one. He was this hot-shot teen-aged kid, tearing up the region. He retired pretty young from driving, and concentrated on building his business, Weld Wheels.

Greg's brother Kenny was also a great racer, but his personality was very different. Kenny had a brilliant mind, and as is often the case always seemed eccentric to people like me who weren't nearly that smart. We can't think like a brilliant guy, so they often seem strange to us. Kenny wasn't really strange, it's just that he was so much smarter than everybody else he was thinking on a different plain, on a different level. We couldn't relate to that very well. Plus, he was so focused on winning races, he wasn't much fun to be around much of the time.

Later on Kenny got in severe trouble, and actually went to prison—I'm talking Leavenworth—for dealing drugs. Was I shocked he got into trouble? No. Because he was so much out there, nothing would have surprised me.

I had heard rumors, and suspected something weird was going on, because things didn't look right to me. In 1980 Kenny made headlines by building an incredible modified in which Gary Balough trounced the field at the big race in Syracuse, N.Y.

I was there that day, and something wasn't right. Bizarre. If you watched those guys, which I did, they looked bizarre. And I'm not making fun of them, or ridiculing them, but to me they were out there in the twilight zone compared to the average person. Something didn't seem right.

After he went to prison, a lot of people were angry with Kenny. They called him a druggie, a pusher. They were mad, and hard on him. I wasn't mad, but I thought, "How stupid could he be?" A smart, smart guy, going down that path. And hypocritical. He had this imaginary—maybe it was real, I don't know—hatred toward the persona of Jan Opperman, the pot-smoking hippie, compared to the straight-laced Kenny. And Opperman could sometimes out-drive him on the race track, and that bothered Kenny. A person of his stature, being out-driven by this pot-smoking hippie. And then Kenny himself winds up getting involved in drugs. It was stupid.

But Kenny did his time, and cleaned up his act. He got out of prison and invented the 5-axis CNC porting machine that revolutionized how cylinder heads are machined. Hey, his invention didn't surprise me a bit. Kenny could do anything. He could seem eccentric as hell, but he was sharp.

After he got out of prison, Kenny tried to race with the Outlaws. Which was hopeless, because after all he had been through, out of racing for almost 10 years, to try a comeback was a lost cause. Maybe he could have competed at a local level, but not with the Outlaws. And Kenny never ran on the road much, on lots of different race tracks, and that's what the Outlaws are all about.

Then as fast as he came back, he was gone, and he concentrated on his cylinder head business.

It made me very sad when Kenny died of cancer in the late 1990s. I lost both of my parents to cancer, and nobody should have to go through that. Kenny was a guy who had a fascinating life, made his share of mistakes, but in my opinion redeemed himself by not letting it destroy him. He made the best of a bad situation, and that's something I'll always admire.

Bubby Jones, now there was a guy who was *big* when I came along. He was a helluva race driver. I remember Bub being this free spirit kind of guy who didn't have long hair like a hippie, but just long enough to be cool. He was on his own, kind of off by himself, his own man. But when you got the chance to talk to him he was very nice.

And you talk about a talented, race drivin' fool, boy, he was. He might not have gotten the recognition of, say, Dick Gaines or Bobby Allen from along that same time, but there's no doubt in my mind that he was as good as either of 'em. No doubt whatsoever.

About the time I showed up in the mid-1970s, you never knew where you were gonna run across Bubby. He didn't have any connection to one or two series, but he ran wherever the hell he felt like it. That was cool.

Right about the time I got going, and the World of Outlaws were formed, Bubby went in a different direction and started racing more with USAC. Later on he ran Indy, which was neat, and then moved out to California to race sprint cars with CRA.

That's right about the time when the sprint car world divided: wings or not. Bubby went without 'em, and I ran with 'em, so we didn't see each other a lot. But when I went out West and ran Ascot without the wing, boy, Bubby was one of the guys who raced you to the bitter end.

His brand of racing turned out to be different than mine and that's cool. Let me tell you, when you went to Ascot and had to face Bubby and Dean Thompson—Deano!—you had better be ready because those sumbitches were gonna run you hard. Those were the guys you'd see in your sleep, driving you crazy because you could hardly beat 'em.

Lealand McSpadden, now there is one of the sport's all-time great characters.

Our paths first crossed at the 1976 Jayhawk Nationals, at the old Lakeside Speedway in Kansas City. Jeri was sitting in the stands with our girls, because women were not yet allowed in the pits. Sitting right in front of her was a red-haired lady with two young kids. This, we would later figure out, was Lealand's wife Janet and their children.

They started the feature, and Lealand hauled it into turn one and flipped that thing clear out of the ballpark. His car hit a light pole probably 20 feet off the ground, and landed right at the base of the pole. About one second after his car came to a stop, one of those 500-pound transformers fell off the pole right onto his race car. Wham! You just knew this guy was dead.

The red-haired lady jumped to her feet and shoved the two kids at Jeri and yelled, "Watch my kids! That's my husband!" And—zoom!—she's gone.

Lealand wasn't hurt, and Jeri probably had the kids with her in the stands for an hour before the race was finally over. She walked into the pits with four kids—our two and these two red-haired kids—and we had no idea who they were or who they belonged to! Soon we found Lealand and Janet, and gave them back their kids.

That was our first meeting with Lealand and Janet, and they've been our friends for more than 30 years. Sometimes when I happen across Lealand's name in my phone book I'll call him just for the hell of it, because he's so much fun to talk to. One of my all-time favorite people.

He's a guy you never questioned in terms of trying hard enough. God, he could tear up some cars. But make no mistake: He was a helluva race driver. A-number-one, for sure. He'd win or crash, it seemed, and while he won a lot more than he crashed, either way you could count on Lealand to be spectacular.

I flew out to Ascot one year to run the Pacific Coast Nationals, and I ran the first night so I was idle the second. Lealand was there running Gary Stanton's car, and this car was absolutely bullet-ass fast that night. It was a radical car Stanton built for the express purpose of winning Ascot, with the plan of selling it after the weekend.

I'm standing in the first turn bleachers with some friends, watching the feature take the green flag. Lealand is on the front row, and they dropped the green and he smoked that bitch into the first turn like the law was after him. He bent it so far sideways we could see the left-side lettering from the turn one grandstands. The car hooked up and he must have flipped 30 feet in the air, absolutely incredible. Luckily he was unhurt, and after the race I walked to the pits. I saw Stanton standing there wearing a look of shock on his face, and I said, "So, tell me, Stanley, was he fired in mid-air or was he fired in mid-air?"

Stanton never batted an eye.

"He was fired in mid-air," he nodded.

Even if I had been a car owner, and Lealand would have torn my car into little pieces, I'd still love him. There is something disarming about the guy that you cannot *help* but love him.

It's fun to even think about guys like Lealand. I don't want to say "that's when racing was fun," because it's probably fun now for the guys doing it. But if you were lucky enough to meet genuine characters like I did, you never forget those days and they're pretty damned hard to top.

Lealand used to mess with us, and I thought he was kidding around. After a big crash, he'd say to his mechanics, "Say, you can do a plug check now, because I always turn the fuel off when I start to crash. I cleaned the engine out on the way down!"

Then one day somebody showed me a photo. Lealand was literally 180-degrees upside down, sailing through the air, directly in front of the old Ascot sign at the track. And sure enough, you can see his arm reaching up and turning off his fuel! All that time I thought he was kidding, but he was absolutely serious!

Guys like Lealand are never going to be duplicated, not in this time or any other. One of a kind. To know him is to love him.

When I came to Pennsylvania to run Weikert's car, one of the top dogs was Keith Kauffman. He had already won 35 features in Al Hamilton's car in 1984, and when I arrived they won one more feature through the rest of the year. That's because we had a better team; not a better driver, but a better team. The whole package was there.

I stayed with Keith and Kathy Kauffman when I first arrived, because I knew very few people out there. But Keith was a good friend I had gotten to know while traveling around. And let me tell you, Keith Kauffman was and is a badass. A total badass. You might not realize this, because he's very cool and laid back and seems like he's easygoing. But he ain't. Down deep he's a badass. I've seen it.

One night we're racing at Williams Grove, and I hadn't been out there very long. Keith and I are racing very hard for the win, and on the last couple of laps I had to really drive it down in there to pass him. We were running very, very hard and we rubbed just a little bit down in the corner. I won the race, and I'm taking a cool-down lap to get back to the front straightaway and the trophy presentation. As I pass by Beer Hill—that's the big hill in turn three where the hardcore Grove fans sit and drink beer—I could hear the beer cans hitting my car. WHAM! BANG! I'm talking full cans of beer, pounding the top of the wing. The natives were not pleased.

An hour or so later I'm leaving the track, walking out with Keith and Kathy. Keith and I have got our helmet bags on our shoulders, strolling along, headed toward the turn one tunnel. A couple of guys fell in behind us, and began to trash-talk the both of us with a profanity-laced tirade.

"Kauffman, I can't believe what a mother-f***** you are, walking with that little pipsqueak. You're walking with your wife, and you're supposed to be this big man, but you ain't nothing but a pussy. You don't have the balls to even stand up to that little blankety-blank SOB."

They were kind of gaining on us, and were maybe 10 feet behind us. Kauffman paused and kind of turned around, and said very politely, "Hey, listen, guys, my wife is right here, and you don't need to be talking like that in front of her, please. That was just racing, he didn't do anything wrong. Just please leave us alone."

They kept it up. We walked a little farther, and now they're riding me.

"Wolfgang, you ain't nothing but a blankety-blank mother-f******, you little sumbitch. Kauffman ought to whip your ass because you're so f****** ugly…"

Kauffman turned around again.

"Guys, I assure you, he didn't do anything wrong. Just leave us alone. I'm not going to ask you again."

Keith turned back around, but I noticed he moved his helmet bag to his left shoulder.

The two morons kept it up. We walked probably another 30 feet, and out of the corner of my eye I see Kauffman, in one sweeping motion, drop his helmet bag and whirl around, bringing his right fist. This one boy was probably 6-3, maybe 250 pounds. Kauffman caught him under his chin with a right cross, and I'm not kidding when I say that boy's feet lifted four inches off the ground. Lights out. This boy hit the ground, out cold.

It was like a continuous motion, and Kauffman continued to whirl around, picking up his bag, and kept right on walking, hardly missing a step. God, it was impressive.

We walked another 30 or 40 feet, and I noticed Kauffman flex his right hand a couple of times. When you hit a guy hard enough to knock him out, your hand hurts like hell, I don't care who you are. But Kauffman never flinched, he just kind of flexed his hand a time or two and that was it.

Right then I knew Keith Kauffman was a total badass, somebody you really didn't want to mess with.

We got out to the car, and I realized I had forgotten something, so they waited while I walked back through the tunnel and back to my pit for a minute. I cleared the tunnel and saw the EMT folks working on this boy, he's still on the ground and just starting to come around. His buddy is stone sober by now, though. I mean, this kid was probably out for five, six minutes or more. Kauffman laid that boy out, I'm telling you.

Like I said...Keith Kauffman is a badass. File this for your future reference: He isn't somebody you want to mess with.

21

Riding the Peace Train

When I left the Weikert team at the end of 1987, it was more than simply moving from one sprint-car team to the next. In a way, my entire world changed. For three-and-a-half years I had been commuting to Pennsylvania, racing there almost every weekend, and my family and I actually lived there for a little over a year. But leaving Weikert meant I was again living in Sioux Falls and looking for a ride.

Jeri and I decided we were going to live in Sioux Falls from now on, period. No matter who I drove for, we were going to keep our home in South Dakota. We had lived in Des Moines, Lincoln, and then in Pennsylvania, and every time we'd get homesick. We were meant to live in Sioux Falls and that's all there was to it.

To start the 1988 season I hooked up with my buddy Gary Stanton, and planned on running the World of Outlaws schedule. This interested me. I was itching to get out a little bit.

We ran all right, but not great. We won at Kings Speedway on February 24, and our next didn't come until March 16, when we won a $5,000-to-win race at Big H in Houston. We won again in April at Eldora, but we were not setting the world on fire.

I'm not exactly sure of the sequence, but at some point Gary was ready to take the car and go home. See—and I'm sure I've said this before—Gary didn't enjoy living out on the road running a race car. He didn't really dig that. And I knew going in that our deal wouldn't be permanent, so it was no big deal when he wanted to go home.

I like Stanton a lot, and I liked working with him. He is a lot like me; he ain't no genius, and he doesn't give you a lot of bullshit. But let me tell you, Gary could get more done in less time than anybody I've ever known. Some guys will mess around with a car for eight hours, just putzing. Gary would go to the shop and get the same work done in an hour and 10 minutes, then load the car and go have a cup of coffee. And his work was just as good as theirs.

He didn't just dink around to be dinking around. It's like he has this serious streak where he's able to focus on what needs to be done and push everything else out of his mind. I admire that. It's hard to do, because in this business you get all rattled and you don't know if you're coming or going because of all the little details. But Gary knew how to cut through the clutter and focus on what needed done, and do it in minimal time yet still do it right.

Along about this time—I'd say it was April of 1988—a guy out in California began building the Lightning Chassis, which was an identical copy of the Gambler. The idea, I think, was to take a successful idea and make it better. In the end, I don't think they made the car better. I felt like there were some quality issues and they still had a lot of work to do to perfect the idea.

Somehow the guy at Lightning Chassis provided a car to a man from California named Les Kepler. Everything came together at once; Stanton was going home, I needed a ride, and Les had this new car with an open seat`.

Les called me about running the car, and we had a good conversation. When he hired me, I knew going in that I wasn't going to fit and this wasn't going to be a long-term situation. But I didn't have anything else to drive, and I wanted to race. So I said to Les, "I'll tell you what: I'm not driving anything right now, so I'll drive your car. But I'll only drive it on this condition: We take it one race at a time, and the moment that you're done, or the moment I'm done, there are no hard feelings. It's over."

"No problem," Les said. "That's how we'll do it."

We hooked up at Knoxville for the second night of a two-night show—I had ran for Gary Stanton the night before—and didn't run very well. We were doing the "getting to know you" dance, I guess. But things were going okay, and ultimately what I thought would be a one- or two-night deal wound up going almost the entire season.

I have to admit, the more time passed the less I liked the Lightning Chassis. I thought the cars were less than stellar in terms of construction. But Les had fairly good engines, and he and his guys tried very hard to make the car nice for me.

At the time I didn't think much of Les, so I didn't make much of an effort to socialize with him. That sounds bad, but it shouldn't. He hired me to do a job and that was our relationship. I tried as hard as I could every night, and that was my job. I held up my end and I expected him to hold up his. By this point in my career I certainly knew we didn't *have* to be friends.

Les was a flashy guy, and I'm not big on that. And maybe it was a California thing; I had already been through Kenny Woodruff, who was also from California, so there was probably some prejudice on my part. You know what's funny? I like all of those guys today. Once we were no longer working together, we got along great. As friends, they're great guys. But when you race together, man, it strains even the best friendships. And if you weren't already friends to begin with, well, there ain't much to strain.

We used to call Les "Papa Smurf," because he was kind of short and had this white beard like the cartoon character. Boy, Les could piss you off at the drop of a hat. But I must say, the guys working on the car really tried hard for me.

Kelly Pryor was our primary mechanic, and he was a young kid who had raced some, and was kind of mixed up with his life at the time, trying to grow up. He was a nice kid. I admired that he gave me a hundred percent, and really tried hard. He treated me with respect and I admired that about him.

But the situation was kind of hopeless for Kelly. I would tell him what to do with the car, and Les would tell him something different, and both of us would jump his ass if he didn't do as we requested. The poor kid was stuck in the middle so many times, it had to be miserable.

On top of that, the cars just weren't strong enough from a structural standpoint. At the Knoxville Nationals we wound up deep in the "C" and "ran the alphabet," transferring through the "C" to the "B" to the championship feature, where we finished fifth. The car didn't hold up well under the stress, and several things broke loose. I finished the race holding the steering box up with my knees, because it had broken away from the mounts and was floating around loose. Lots of pieces were like that.

Sometimes Les might rant and rave about something, but I didn't pay much attention. He'd bark that I wasn't doing this right, or that right, or lifting too soon in the corners, but I just blew it off. I mean, how *could* you pay attention? This guy who had never driven one of these cars is standing on his trailer, and he's going to tell you when you should lift for the corners? Sure, Les. Sure.

I finally quit in September when we were racing in California, and that was that. No hard feelings between anybody. It was just time to go home.

As the autumn came I was back home in Sioux Falls, uncertain of my plans for 1989. Like everybody else, I had heard rumblings of a new sprint car series called the United Sprint Assn., or USA. Soon the word was passed along that this new group would sanction four races in the fall of 1988, after the World of Outlaws season finished.

The new group was basically formed out of dissatisfaction with Ted Johnson's handling of the Outlaws. Personally, I didn't care one way or the other about either group. I didn't want an allegiance to any sanctioning body. I just wanted to race, wherever the money and opportunity was best.

Harold Annett was involved in the USA in some capacity, and he called me in late 1988 and said they'd like to have me running their races. That's fine, I said, but I don't have a full-time ride right now. Harold had just purchased Gary Stanton's chassis business, renaming it Challenger Racing and relocating to Iowa. Harold owned a big trucking company, TMC, which was also based in Iowa.

Harold explained that Max Rogers, a farmer from Iowa, had purchased one of their new cars and wanted to go racing, but needed a good driver. Bob Olsen, an accountant from Iowa, was also involved in the car. Would I be interested in running the car some for Max? Sure, I said. I mean, I didn't have anything else going, so why not? My first thought was that Max was just a local racer, but I later found out he was actually quite serious, and had arranged to buy his engines from my old friend John Singer.

I finally met Max and sat in the car, and it felt comfortable. We loaded up and headed for Phoenix in October for the Western World, the first official USA-sanctioned race. Singer's engine fit me very well, kind of like one of Davey Brown's engines.

But I promptly rifled the new car clear out of the ballpark on Saturday night at Manzanita. I was chasing Mark Kinser, who eventually won the race, thinking I had a good enough car to win. But in a moment of brain fade, I ran over Mark's tire, and put Max's new car right out in the junkyard, literally and figuratively. I don't know what I was thinking; it was just a dumb mistake on my part.

I figured, "That's the end of that deal!" Crashing big right out of the gate really tests a car owner. You spend all that money and you're just getting started and some fool driver makes a mistake and turns it all into a pile of junk. Some rookie owners throw up their hands and quit, right then. But as we were loading up they told me Max had promised to go home and get a new chassis, and he would be ready to race at Memphis two weeks later.

My dad rode down to Memphis with me, and it was a nice trip. We stopped at the Challenger shop and looked at the new chassis, then took the car to Memphis. The car ran real well and handled nice, and we finished third behind Dave Blaney and Andy Hillenburg.

The final USA round was at Devil's Bowl in Texas, and I passed Steve Kinser on the last lap to win. Not a bad way to finish the year, in fact.

Overall it hadn't been a good year for me, as I had won only a handful of races. I figured 1989 would surely be better than this. Little did I know that the very best year of my career was right around the corner.

While I was driving for Les Kepler, Gary "Deuce" Turrill approached me. Deuce was a good mechanic and he had been around the block a time or two.

"Doug, if I ever got a sponsor and put a deal together, would you drive for me?"

"Sure," I said. "When you get a deal put together, call me. I'm ready."

I figured it would be nice racing with Deuce. He was a good mechanic and a good guy and I had a hunch we would be all right together.

A few weeks later I was out in Phoenix, the night I sailed the car out of the ballpark and banged up my knees on the steering gear. My parents had their motorhome out there, so I was sitting inside applying ice to my knees to keep the swelling down.

Deuce knocked on our door and asked if I could come outside and talk.

"I've got a guy who wants to own the race car, and he wants to talk to you."

"Really?"

"Yeah, he wants to see what it would take for you to drive their car."

I didn't much feel like talking, but I set the ice bags aside, struggled to get out of my chair, and limped outside. I suspect my mood wasn't the best at that moment.

Here is this boy standing there who looks like he's 15 years old. I instantly thought to myself, "Aw, shit." You've got to realize, as a driver you're often approached by people who want to own your car or sponsor you. And they've got maybe three bucks on 'em. They want to give you a $20 bill and put their name in big letters on the side of the car. You become leery of this, and cynical. Everybody's a big spender, ready to set the world on fire. Sure they are.

I looked at this kid, thinking, "He's just a boy! Is he joking?"

Deuce had already made up a proposal detailing what it would cost to race for a year, including the car, the travel, everything. The bottom-line figure was $400,000, but didn't include the driver. That was the only piece missing. How much was I going to cost?

"This is a joke," I'm thinking. "I'm wasting my time. I'm the great Doug Wolfgang, and my time is more valuable than this." I laugh now when I think about it.

The boy's name was Danny Peace, and we began to talk, and I proceeded to tell him what it would cost for me to drive his race car. It would cost him 50 percent of what we brought in with the car, plus 50 percent of whatever sponsorship he brought in using my name. Plus $1,000 cash each week. I was high-balling the kid, figuring I would scare him off.

Danny listened to my proposal, said thanks, and left. I figured that was the end of the discussion. I hated to shoot the kid such an astronomical figure but I figured that was easier than telling him I didn't believe he was credible. A few minutes later Deuce came over and said, "Man, you high-balled him a little bit, didn't you?"

"Yeah, but I don't want to waste my time on this stuff. You know he ain't gonna have that kind of money!"

"Nah, this kid's serious!" Deuce insisted. But I didn't think any more about it and figured we had heard the last of Danny Peace.

Two weeks later we were in Memphis, which is Danny's home town. Right away, I spotted him hanging around our pit. He seemed like a nice enough kid, so I told him, "Danny, you're welcome to stand up on top of our trailer and watch the race if you want." He thanked me, and when I came in after the feature race I noticed he was gone.

A week later we were in Dallas, and I won the Saturday night finale. Jeri and I were in a hurry to get back to Sioux Falls by Monday morning to get the girls back in school. It was cold that night in Dallas, and I hurried through the victory lane interview. I had just finished the interview when Deuce came hurrying over.

"It's a done deal!" he said excitedly. "We're going tomorrow to get the trailer!"

I just looked blankly at him. "*What's* a done deal?"

"The deal with Danny Peace! We're in business…we're going tomorrow to get the trailer, and we want to make sure we can get together with you and get all the details handled."

Suddenly I realized he was serious. I remember some of the details: We would have Brian Schnee build the cars, because he was in Sioux Falls and I could do the cars myself and do them like I wanted.

"So we'll go out to east Texas to pick up this truck and trailer, and we'll meet you at John Singer's on Wednesday," Deuce explained. "We'll give Brian $5,000 to start on the cars, and we'll give you your first week's pay of $1,000. We'll give John Singer $25,000 for engines to get started."

I didn't believe it. Even when my first check cleared, I didn't believe it.

They called me on Tuesday and said, "Are you gonna meet us at Singer's?"

"Yeah, I'll be there." So Brian and I went down there—and Brian was just a kid himself at this point—and sure enough they had the money they promised. We're sure enough in business! They hired Robert Hubbard, another mechanic from Deuce's hometown of Memphis, as a second crew member. The team would be owned by Danny Peace and would be known as DP Motorsports.

I was amazed then, and even though almost 20 years have passed, I'm still amazed to this day. The whole thing was just so unlikely, so incredible.

You might be wondering: Where could a young kid come up with that kind of money? I wondered too, but not too long. Hey, I didn't know if he came from a wealthy family, or whatever. But his checks were good and frankly, that's what matters most. He didn't strike me as a kid who would be involved in drugs or robbing banks; he had nice manners and seemed like a very good person. This might sound silly, but I honestly felt it was none of our business where he got his money.

What I did not know, and wouldn't know until much later, is that Danny's girlfriend was underwriting the team. In the end this would be a very, very big deal.

We had a fabulous year in 1989. In fact, of my entire career, 1989 was my best season. We won 43 races, including several big races: We won the Knoxville Nationals ($33,000), the Syracuse Supernationals ($30,000), the Sharon Nationals ($12,000), the Eldora Sprint Nationals, and the Selinsgrove USA Nationals ($51,000). Our car earned just a tick over $500,000.

We didn't follow either the Outlaws or the USA; we raced wherever we wanted. By the time we were finished we had won 27 WoO races and 15 with USA.

From the opening bell we were red hot, winning 11 of our first 17, and if we didn't win we were either second or third. We raced 75 times in 1989, winning 43, but here's what I think was most amazing: In 75 starts, we finished out of the top-3 only seven times. That means out of 75 races were in the top-3 68 times! For the entire year! That's a testament to the entire team. I was really "on" as a driver, but Deuce and Hubb had our car right every night, and it finished races. Man, it was great.

And we just *killed* 'em on t-shirts. This was a period when racing t-shirts were becoming a big deal. A *very* big deal. We owned our t-shirt concession and sold them ourselves, so it was very lucrative. In prior years—with the exception of my time with Bob Weikert—I hadn't driven the same car long enough to really get a following on t-shirts, or I didn't own the t-shirt rights with that particular car. But in 1989 I finally figured out how important it was to own the t-shirt rights to your name.

By the middle of the season there was plenty of speculation about where Danny's money was coming from. Like I said before, I didn't know and I didn't care. Well, not that I didn't care; it's just that in this business, you see so many weird things going on, people who you think have money really don't, while people you don't think have any money really do. I just figured the kid's parents had money. None of us really knew, though. Later on we realized that his girlfriend evidently had money, but I just let it go. It didn't affect me and it really was none of my business.

The first time I realized there might be something wrong was on August 30, at Silver Springs Speedway in Pennsylvania. We won the USA feature that night, and were pitted outside the race track. After the victory lane interview they pushed the car back to our pit, where a television crew was waiting.

No big deal, right? It was not uncommon in Pennsylvania that a local TV station would come to the races and interview the night's winner. The reporter asked if I would have time to talk on camera. Of course that was all right, so she moved in close with the microphone and began.

"Doug, you're the National champion (I doubt she even knew what this was), but were you aware that this car is being funded through fraudulent transactions involving HUD?"

This was absolutely the first inkling we had that anything was amiss. To show you how ill-informed I was, I didn't even know what HUD was. Didn't have any idea.

I just looked at her and said, "Ma'am, I don't have a clue what you're talking about."

She was professional, and came right back at me. I told her again, "I'm telling you, I don't have a clue what you're talking about. You're talking to the wrong guy, and I'll see you later." And I walked away from the interview.

I thought the whole thing was weird. That's when I noticed the crew was from a Philadelphia station, which was two, maybe three hours away. This puzzled me even more.

That night was the beginning of the entire thing coming out. Deuce was as mystified as I was. For the life of me, I can't remember our conversation at the moment. Surprise, amazement, whatever. But we just put it out of our mind and went on down the road. As far as we knew, the lady from the TV crew didn't know what she was talking about.

We really weren't worried about it. Maybe some of our comfort was the fact that at that point we didn't *need* Danny or anybody else, because we didn't need anyone to give us money to keep going. In fact, we were giving Danny money. He actually got back more than he put up as seed money to get us started. Deuce would get the money at the window, pay me my share, and often he'd have too much cash on him so he would arrange to hook up with Danny and give him more money. He only kept what we needed to run the car, and the car was making far more than we needed to sustain ourselves.

To this day, I don't know or understand all of the details. But in the coming months, the details emerged on what was going on. Danny had met a girl who was around 30 years old, maybe ten years older than him. Somebody within HUD—that's Housing and Urban Development, a huge federal agency that helps low-income people obtain housing—figured out a way to skim money from a certain loan program. They figured a way to get the government to pay more money, and then would intercept the money before it got to the recipient, skimming off the overpayment. The person within HUD apparently recruited a bunch of realtors around the country who happened to be professional young women. They went along because it was free money, and everything was great until someone blew the whistle.

Make no mistake about it; what they were doing was wrong, plain and simple. They were stealing from the government.

Today—and probably at the time—some people might look at Deuce and Hubb and myself and say, "They *had* to know." But we didn't. Believe me, we didn't. I know I certainly didn't know, and I don't believe Deuce knew, either. Look, we were just a couple of dumb guys who knew how to race, and that's about all. High finance? Government programs? That stuff was so far over our heads it was a joke. Way out of our league.

Hell, I don't understand *now* how it worked, and I've had years to study it. I sure as hell didn't understand it then, when the whole thing was brand new to me.

Several of the players involved were convicted of various crimes, and went away to a minimum-security prison for a short time.

I remember being very sympathetic to Danny, and I didn't want to see him get in trouble. In my eyes, he didn't do anything wrong. His girlfriend was giving him money, and he spent it to get the car going. Think about it: If these young women were successful real estate businesspeople, it isn't so farfetched that they would have some money. If your neighbor is a successful realtor, and he offers to sponsor a new ball diamond for the local kids, are you going to demand that he show an accounting of where he earned the money? Of course not. You're going to assume he's on the up-and-up because most of the time he or she is.

And that's where Danny was in all this. He had no idea where she got the money. He was a naïve 20-year-old kid, probably even more clueless than I was.

But the bottom line was the same: DP Motorsports was effectively dissolved at the end of the season. By this time I was good friends with Danny, and I felt bad for him. He was a scared, inexperienced kid, caught up in a lot of things that weren't his fault. In the end he didn't go to jail, nor should he have. But his race team was gone and that was that.

To this day, some 18 years later, we still talk on the phone at least once a year, just to catch up on how each other is doing. He's a nice guy and I enjoy those conversations. He's grown up to be a good person. He moved on to the next chapter of his life, which is exactly the right thing to do in that situation.

Sometimes I look back at 1989 and marvel at what a good run we had. I'm not exactly sure why we had such success, but I've got some ideas.

We weren't doing anything different, really. I kept detailed records in a spiral-bound notebook, with the date, the track, and intricate notes on our setup. We won 43 races that year, and in 39 of them I used the same shock absorbers and torsion bars. We might have replaced them a couple of times, but they were the same number. I just drove the car. John Singer's engines ran very well for us and they felt good.

In fact, those engines were probably the key. We used -11 cylinder heads, which had been the top head that previous season. John had built many engines with the -11 heads, and had them working exactly right. Most of the other teams had sold all their -11 engines and had moved to the more advanced -12 heads, because we all knew the cylinder heads were the key to the entire engine. But in fact most everybody struggled with the new heads in 1989.

We were one of the only ones to stay with the -11 heads, and had an engine that would run easy, nice, and strong everywhere we went, whether it was in California near the ocean, or in Denver at 5,000 feet. Didn't matter if it was hot, the humidity was up or down, whatever. Nothing mattered, the things just ran. That played into our hands perfectly, because the other guys were trying to get through the learning curve of the new -12 heads. The engine builders struggled to figure them out, and the teams struggled to figure out the injectors and the tuning to determine what the new engines liked. Nearly all season they tweaked and fiddled with their new stuff, while we were winning all over the place with old dependable.

Now, you don't stay in front for very long with old dependable. Toward the end of the season, those guys beat me a few times. *Several* times, in fact. They finally were getting their engines figured out, and they were stronger. The following year we couldn't compete with our -11 engines. I was probably strutting a little bit by the end of 1989, telling myself that we were bad sumbitches. But looking back it wasn't so much that we were bad sumbitches, but the fact that the other guys were struggling a little bit.

After the 1989 season the USA series ceased operations, and everyone was back with the Outlaws. I was one of the few guys who didn't go along with either group. I just raced. I didn't care who was sanctioning the event, as long as the purse was where it needed to be. I chased both sides.

It used to chap my ass to see ads in the racing papers saying, "The Outlaws are coming to town!" and see my name listed. Or the same with the USA. How did they know if I was coming to that event? That was misleading advertising, telling fans I was going to be there when they really didn't know. I felt they had no right to use my name like that, unless they made arrangements with me directly. Somebody might spend $20 on a grandstand pass, planning on seeing Doug Wolfgang, and I'm not there that night. So this guy is pissed at me, because I didn't show up. I never planned on showing up at that race, because I was running somewhere else that night. I didn't have a membership with either group.

I had several conversations with different promoters about this, but they didn't agree.

"But you race with the Outlaws!" they would say.

"Sometimes," I'd say. "But sometimes I don't."

But it didn't seem to matter. People continued to use my name, even if I wasn't coming. That annoyed the hell out of me.

After the 1989 season had finished up, Deuce called me on the day DP Motorsports was officially closed.

By this time in my career I figured I had seen just about everything. We had enjoyed a great season with this team, only to be shut down because of some weird connection with some kind of complicated federal government fraud. That was just about par for the course.

Somehow during the winter Ray and Jay Williams from California hired Deuce and Hubbard. They picked up the pieces from the No. 8d car as much as they could, with the idea of keeping the team going. This would be called the Payless Hardware car.

After they hired Deuce and Hubbard, they figured they could get me for nothing. No salary, no percentage of the sponsorship, nothing but a percentage of what the car made. Of course, they were exactly right. I didn't have anything else to drive, so the decision was simple: Drive this car, or sit at home. Hmmm. I think I'll drive this car.

Ray and Jay weren't interested in doing things my way at all. They were fair, and they treated me all right, but they had their way of doing things and my opinion didn't figure in the mix. In a sense I had a bad taste for the deal from the beginning. Again, they were from California, and maybe it was the stereotypes that were flaring up.

In the end they were actually pretty good guys. We stayed together for the entire 1990 season, and did all right.

Notice I didn't say we did great. Well, we *didn't* do great. We were just okay, even on our best days. We won only 14 races for the entire year, and the only big race was the Kings Royal at Eldora in July.

Like I said before, the other teams had made a lot of progress with their -12 engines, and our -11 program was at a disadvantage. At the time we weren't smart enough to see it, or plan for it. The Williams guys insisted on switching to Ron Shaver engines, instead of staying with Singer, and we never really got the program going like we had hoped. We ran the complete World of Outlaws schedule, and finished second in the final points to Steve Kinser.

At the end of the season we parted ways, and I reunited with Max Rogers. My life—not just my career, but my life—was changing at the time, in a way I never foresaw, or even understood. Oh, things worked out all right in the end, but it was a painful and difficult period that's hard for me to talk about.

22

Coming Apart At The Seams

Jeri and I have been together for 34 years now, and we have a great relationship. I wish I could tell you it's been a fairy-tale deal where things have always been wonderful, but that's not true. That's just, well, a fairy tale.

The fact is, in many ways I'm surprised we stayed together. We went through some periods where we fought like dogs, just miserable. We'd yell and scream and act like complete idiots. I thought for sure our older kids would be touched, and maladjusted, because of all of our fighting. But instead they've turned out to be the finest people we could have dared ask for. They are very close to us, and in fact the girls just can't live without their mother. They call her every couple of days and they're all very tight-knit.

And they love me, too, which kind of amazes me. Because I know there were times when I wasn't worth a damn as a father. I was probably a somewhat mean person, yet in spite of that they love me.

I guess it takes maturity to understand your faults and try to correct them, and for many years I wasn't mature enough to do that. Even today there is so much about life I don't understand, why we do things that are good or bad, and how to be a better person.

In my case, I can look back across my life and see patterns, trends that affected me and shaped me as a human being.

To begin with, I was an extremely competitive person. I strived to win every race I ran. That focus and determination might have made me a better racer, but it did not make me a better person. I channeled my desire to win into two things: A very powerful work ethic, and an intense focus on studying every aspect of my performance behind the wheel, looking for ways to improve.

From the time I began racing, I always worked very hard on my race car. That's why I always demanded to be involved in the car; I refused to allow my destiny to be controlled by people other than myself. If I'm involved, I had confidence that details would be taken care of properly. I learned a long time ago you can't always count on other people to do the things they're supposed to do. Even when my crew was top-notch, I still insisted on being involved.

For example, when I drove for Bob Weikert, I had probably the best crew in the country: Davey Brown Sr. and Jr. They did a tremendous job on the race car. However, I only lived a mile or so from the shop, so I'd spend almost every waking hour there, early to late. The Browns both lived some distance away, so they'd head for home at some decent hour but I'd keep working. They might take weekends off in the winter but not me. This was particularly true during the 15 months when we lived in Pennsylvania.

Think about this: On Christmas day, Jeri and I got up with the girls early that morning, quickly opened our presents, and went immediately to the race shop, where I put in a 12-hour day. Many times Jeri and the girls would come with me, just so they could actually see me and talk to me. They would play games and read stories, while I worked.

It's kind of stupid now that I think about it. It's dumb to be so focused on work. But that's the way it was.

My biggest problem, however, was in my head. See, for many years I agonized over every race I didn't win. It's funny; I never considered myself to be special. I was in awe of Steve Kinser and Sammy Swindell, and I was in awe of Pancho Carter. Those were great, great race drivers. Me? I was just okay. Nothing spectacular.

Yet I *expected* to win. How did that work? I was just okay, and Steve and Sammy were gods, yet I expected to beat them every night. How did my brain process that? How did I talk myself into *expecting* to win?

When I didn't win, I was miserable. God, I'm the most insecure guy in the world, and I could win 20 in a row but when I lost number 21 I was in agony, worried that my career was over, I was washed up, I've lost it, on and on. I drove Jeri crazy with all that. I'd replay the race over and over in my head, convincing myself that the mistake I made on the parade lap cost me the race. Cost me the race! I might lose a race in Pennsylvania, and the next night I'm racing in Kansas. As I replayed the race 72 million times in my head, I might drive through the night to Kansas, still rolling the past race through my mind, focusing on the mistake that I perceived cost me the race. It was all my fault. Even though I could never change the outcome, I'd endlessly replay it in my mind, beating myself up, tearing myself down, telling Jeri what a miserable failure I was as a race driver. Night after night, over and over again.

I don't know how she stood it. I don't know why she didn't just leave me.

In the midst of the growing anxiety and stress and strain of our life, let me tell you about something that almost led me to leave sprint cars, and change my whole life and career.

It was 1987, and I was in my final year of driving for Bob Weikert. Jeri and I were living in Pennsylvania, and my life wasn't very happy at that moment. Davey Brown Jr. had left the Weikert team a year or so earlier, so we were a shell of our former selves. Our team was clearly on the downside and it was very frustrating. Jeri and I were homesick and did not like living in Pennsylvania. To put it bluntly, life wasn't a helluva lot of fun right then.

Early in the year—February or so—the phone rang in Weikert's shop. It was Richard Childress, the well-known NASCAR car owner. He had seen my name in the racing papers for the past couple of years, and was aware that I had won a lot of races. Out of the blue, he was calling to ask if I had any interest in driving a stock car. This was a time when Winston Cup—long before it was called Nextel Cup—was changing, and growing. Richard was very much a visionary and he could see the future of multi-car teams. At the time he didn't have a Busch car, or a second Cup car. He had only the famous No. 3, with Dale Earnhardt driving.

Richard asked if I had thought about trying stock cars. I was very honest and told him no, I hadn't. I tried to explain that I was probably 21 years old before I knew who Richard Petty was. That's possible when you grow up in South Dakota, you know.

The next day Richard called back and asked if I could get to Daytona the following day for a test. He said no matter what happens, it wouldn't hurt to take a few laps and see how it felt. If it worked out, maybe he could get a sponsor and run me as a second car to Earnhardt. If it didn't, I could always tell my grandchildren I once drove a Winston Cup car. I said sure, I could probably do that. The whole idea was intriguing, but I wasn't obsessed with the deal. The only thing I promised Richard was that I would do the best I could. He said that was cool and I bought my plane ticket out of Washington, D.C. for the next day.

The next day was gloomy and crappy in Daytona, but by noon they were ready for a few practice laps. The car was owned by Bobby Wawak, who had a business relationship with Richard, who was also there with Dale testing the No. 3 Goodwrench car. Before we got started, Dale took me around the track in a street car. He was eating a steak sandwich with one hand, holding the wheel with the other while driving me around the big tri-oval, telling me how to drive the race track. No seat belts, nothing, and he's running 125 mph in this street car, wide open. Like it was no big deal. It was great!

Of course I'm pretty impressed. At the time Dale wasn't quite God yet, but I already liked him. I had picked him out as somebody to watch. One of my heroes.

I made a few laps, trying to get used to the car. Finally I spun into the infield, and pretty soon the practice day was over.

Richard arranged another practice session at Charlotte, and not long after asked me to come to North Wilkesboro for the April race. He had arranged for me to drive an Oldsmobile for a local guy, Roger Hamby, in the Hesco Exhaust Systems car. This was early April, and our pre-qualifying practice session was snowed out. I had no laps in the car, and had never seen the track before, so it was a hopeless deal. I missed the show, and of course had no provisionals. They put Slick Johnson in the car— I think he was killed a couple of years later at Daytona—and he started 31st and finished 19th. It wasn't a bad car, but I didn't have the experience to put it in the show.

You know what's interesting? Slick Johnson won $4,045 that day. During that period of my career, it was a very rare week when my car didn't make $4,045. It wasn't hard to see that, frankly, at this stage for me to come to Cup and run 19th every week meant a very significant pay cut.

That reality had already occurred to me, a couple of years earlier. See, Cup racing wasn't anything like it is today. The guys racing Nextel Cup today are millionaires, almost automatically. But that wasn't the case in 1987. I distinctly remember a couple of years earlier when I won the Kings Royal at Eldora, and made $51,500. The next day on the way home I listened on the radio as Cale Yarborough won the Talladega 500, and he made $48,655. I looked over at Jeri and said, "Gee, that's not too bad…it took Cale three hours to make $48,000, and I made $51,000 in about 17 minutes!"

Don't get me wrong, I admired those guys. But when it came down to decision time, I was walking in tall cotton in sprint cars. And if I went South, I probably wasn't going to get into Junior Johnson's car. Nor would I have held up my end of it if I would have. That's just the way it was. I would be starting at the bottom.

But if I wanted to pursue it further, the opportunity was there. Richard was very supportive and if I had pestered him and tried very hard, I probably could have gotten a couple of chances to make a race somewhere.

Jeri and I didn't stay for the race that day at North Wilkesboro. It was cold and nasty, I was disappointed, and we were griping and fussing with each other. Our tempers were frayed and we were stressed out to the max. We got into our motorhome, and drove the small highway from the track toward Interstate 77. My mind was swirling with everything. What do I do? Do I turn right on Interstate 77, drive to Charlotte, and pursue this thing? Or do I turn left, heading north back to Pennsylvania and sprint cars?

Jeri and I were talking, arguing and stressed out, and when I saw the approaching signs of the Interstate I reached my hand for the signal lever and without any hesitation pulled it down. We were going north.

That's just how it went down. When we got to Pennsylvania, within a few hours Jeri and the girls were on an airplane, headed for Sioux Falls. She immediately bought a house there, and—BOOM!—that was it. They came back and finished the school year in Pennsylvania, and the house was finished in August after the Knoxville Nationals and we moved. Just like that.

That was the end of my Winston Cup aspirations. I won several major sprint-car races after that, and never looked back. But part of the reason for my decision was the growing stress of more than a decade of travel and moving, and a constant sense of displacement, and the fact that I was in this big emotional upheaval all the time. Jeri and I both acknowledge that our personal stress and strain was part of the reason for how it worked out, and we're not proud of it. But that's life.

By 1989 I began to realize that something was very, very wrong in our relationship. Jeri recognized it too, but neither of us knew how to deal with it, or even understood what was happening to us. That year—1989—was the most difficult period in our marriage, even though 1989 was the biggest, most successful year of my career. The best year I ever had, on the race track. And the worse moments I ever had, away from the race track.

I would have bet money Jeri and I were going to split up. In fact, on the day I won the 1989 Knoxville Nationals—that very day—we were staying at Knoxville, and our kids were staying with some friends at a nearby campground. Jeri and I were in a huge fight, and I was so angry I demanded she get into the car because I was going to take her back to Sioux Falls. We were so completely sick of each other, screaming and fighting, I couldn't take it any more. I figured I could make it back to Sioux Falls, drop her off, and haul ass back to Knoxville in time to make the A-main. We were literally halfway to Omaha before Jeri finally got me calmed down, and we both agreed to turn around and go back to Knoxville. At that moment I was positive our marriage wasn't going to make it.

Jeri and I are both very private people, but I'm sure our friends knew something was wrong. We didn't care, because we were antagonizing each other so badly. I didn't care if anybody knew or not. Nor did I care what they might have thought.

You're probably wondering: How did I have the greatest season of my career in the midst of all the strife and strain and fighting? I really can't answer that. I guess I had the ability to put it out of my mind when it came race time. I'd pull that visor down and forget all the other stuff. Racing was my escape, my oasis.

I remember Deuce Turrill saying, "Son, you're amazing."

"What do you mean?"

"I have never seen anybody that can get mad and scream at his wife, have 50,000 people crawl all over him, six promoters on the telephone wanting him to do this or that, 14 manufacturers wanting you to try their part, without one moment to yourself, yet you get into that car and run up front like nothing was going on. How do you do that?"

I didn't know then, and I don't know now. It's true, though; I had the ability to shut everything out once I got into the race car. Nothing else mattered. Nothing. The only natural thing at that point of my life was sitting in the race car. Everything else was stressed, strained, and work; but sitting in the car I was completely at peace with the world. Even at the time, I recognized this. I would crawl into the car, cinch up my belts, wave for the push truck to go, and then breathe an enormous sigh of relief. "I'm safe now." My escape from reality. Now we can rock.

Jeri and I both knew what the problem was: racing. But what are you going to do? What do you do when you realize your career, the way you earn your living, the thing that has totally defined you for all of your adult life, wasn't good for your spirit? What are you going to do, really?

Think about our lives in the late 1980s. We had some incredible travel hours to Pennsylvania from 1984 to 1987, and actually moved our family out there for 15 months. That wasn't happy, so we moved back to South Dakota and now we have the long drives, and I'm away from my family again. Then I'm back on the World of Outlaws circuit, living like a vagabond and away from my family for weeks at a time. How on God's earth can a family be happy in that situation? Where is the happiness, the peace? You go home and make your family happy, and your career falls off the map; or you follow the racing and you're separated from your wife and children for weeks at a time, or you choose to drive 22 hours every Monday and every Thursday. God, it's impossible.

That was our dilemma.

See, by this time Jeri and I liked spending money, and I liked winning. We were very much into those things. The money I wasn't especially interested in, even though everything we did seemed to center around money. I didn't want to just win 35 or 40 or 45 races; I wanted to win the *biggest* races, meaning the ones that paid the most money. So if you're not counting the money, why do you want to win the biggest races? It's a double-edged sword. I didn't care about the money, yet I wanted to win the biggest races.

And Jeri was chewing my ass out because I wasn't doing what I should be doing in terms of my family life, but on the other hand she liked to have a nice home, a nice motorhome, new clothes, and the freedom to do what she wanted when she wanted. I'm certainly not cutting her down; we've talked through all this and we both now realize what we were doing to each other.

We weren't screwed up all the time, of course, but that night at Knoxville in 1989 was probably the lowest point. The best year I ever had, and the worst. And I cannot tell you how, or why, we got there, and I cannot tell you how we got out.

If that big fight at Knoxville was the lowest point of our personal difficulties, that means the period after that started to get better. And it did get better, gradually. Through 1990 and into the 1991 season, we began to talk about things and figure out what we needed to do to get better.

You know what's strange? I'm not even sure how it got resolved. Isn't that the funniest thing? We were on the brink of it all going down the tubes, but somehow we got through it. I don't know that I consciously did anything different, or if she did. But we both recognized we were in trouble, and we had to step back and think about how to treat each other a little better to make it work again.

In late 1990 I reunited with Max Rogers, the Iowa farmer. Max still wanted to race, and my deal with Ray and Jay Williams had gone away, so Max and I decided to go racing.

But this time it was different.

This time I wanted to run the big races, but I didn't want to run all the time. I wanted to be more selective. And I didn't really care where we raced; I just wanted to race, and cut back my schedule a little. I was nowhere near ready to retire; that's not what it was about. Jeri and I were starting to slowly get things back together between us. Our daughters were getting a little older, and we had a new baby girl. Allie was born in

February 1990, and Jeri and I talked about trying for a boy, so we weren't finished yet.

I was actually becoming a different person by this point. Don't get the idea that I was a great guy; I don't think that's accurate. I wasn't a great guy. But I wasn't in the league I was before, where I made people around me miserable. I had improved in that regard, I think that's a safe statement.

Mellowed? Maybe that's a good word. Just when Jeri and I thought we were done as a married couple, we discovered each other. We weren't done, after all. In fact, when we looked at in honestly, we were all right. Some of the stuff I was doing wrong I wasn't doing on purpose, nor was she.

No longer did I want to go to the races seven nights a week. I still wanted to be pretty good when I went, but if I missed a Tuesday night race somewhere, no problem. That didn't mean I was suddenly gonna run in the back of the pack, either.

I'll tell you a little secret: I was just starting to get real good. In the past I had holes in my repertoire, so to speak. But now I was starting to get some balance in my life, and that was really, really all right.

One of our issues was that Jeri wanted me to pay attention to details a little more. There are many things going on around a race track, and even if you aren't part of it, you're part of it. And I was part of it; I was there. I didn't chase women, and I wasn't a drinker. I was into fitness, and being ready to race 24/7. I was trying to win all the races, but I was also noticing how miserable that made everyone around me. So I started making an effort and I could see how things between Jeri and me were starting to come back the other way, in a good direction. I liked that. It felt good. I never liked fighting, and we didn't start our relationship by fighting. In our early years, rarely did we have any turmoil. I never liked it; even when I was screaming my loudest and completely pissed off, I didn't like fighting with Jeri. I know she didn't like it, either. We aren't that type of people.

But having some balance in my life actually made me a more effective race driver. Even though I wasn't as blood-and-guts as before, my performance was not worse, but better. It amazed me. My mind was right and I was sharper and physically stronger because I was relaxed.

There is often a perception that a lot of bad behind-the-scenes stuff goes on with racers, things like drinking, partying, chasing women, carousing. But from my perspective, there wasn't much of that going on around us. I'm not saying some things didn't go on, because I'm sure they did. But it was by far the minority.

Most of the guys I raced against were so wrapped up in trying to win, trying to get the car better, they didn't have a lot of time or energy to do other stuff. These guys are athletes, and they weren't into putting stuff into their bodies. Plus, guys my age, when we started we hadn't heard the word "cocaine" yet. Didn't know what it was about, and wasn't interested. I didn't even smoke cigarettes. About the worse I ever did was get drunk and raise hell, and I had quit that stuff *many* years earlier.

There might have been rumors surrounding the racers of the World of Outlaws in the mid-1980s of cocaine use and so forth, but I honestly don't know if it was true or not. See, I kind of kept to myself, and my family always—or almost always—traveled with me. If guys were doing that stuff, it was certainly outside my circle.

The perception is that a racer is vulnerable to things like drugs or women. You're on the road, you're lonely, you're generally somewhat self-centered, and sometimes it leads you to do things that aren't right. But I was fortunate to grow up with very solid grounding, and a strong sense of right and wrong. It's wrong to chase women if you're married. It's wrong to get drunk and obnoxious. It's wrong to take drugs. So it was not a difficult thing for me to walk the straight-and-narrow, because that's how I grew up. It was the same with Jeri; our values were strong and they defined what kind of people we are.

Plus, I think I was less vulnerable because I wanted my family with me at every possible opportunity. It was probably a hardship sometimes because we had to hurry back home on Monday morning to get the girls to school, but it was worth it. We were a tight-knit family, even through our stressful times, and we're a tight-knit family to this day. I'm glad.

23

Knoxville

When I think about the Knoxville Nationals and how that great event has fit into my life, one thing really stands out in my mind.

A console television.

Not one of those little portable jobs you set on a TV tray, but a big floor model with a sharp color picture and big round speakers on each end, wrapped up in a wood cabinet.

In 1977 as my sprint-car career was just starting to go all right, Jeri and I were living with our two girls in Des Moines in a single-wide mobile home provided by Bob Trostle's partner, Dave Van Patten. We weren't starving but we sure didn't have much in the way of material things. The one thing we both really wanted was a console television.

The more I thought about it, the more I wanted that big TV. We were watching TV on a little black-and-white portable, and man, I could just imagine how good that console TV would look in our living room. But I had priced those things, and no way were they within our budget. The only way I'd get one was to come up with the money up front, because borrowing from our folks for something as frivolous as a TV wouldn't seem right. And bank financing was out of the question; I was a lowly know-nothing sprint-car driver, so no way was I gonna get credit to buy a TV.

I knew the Knoxville Nationals paid more money than any race all year, and I got to thinking: If I could win that race, I could buy us a console television. God! Wouldn't that be great, to bring that big TV into our living room, where we could sit on our couch and look at the great picture?

Man, I wanted it more than anything I can describe to you. It was like this giant gold ring that seemed so far away it was impossible.

That's what the Knoxville Nationals meant to me, early on. It was like a ticket, and if you could get it punched all kinds of great things would happen. You'd be number one in sprint-car racing. You might get to the Indy 500. And for sure you could buy the best damn console television in the store.

I'm not really sentimental about Knoxville Raceway, but the Knoxville Nationals I'm sentimental about, still to this day. Even this past summer, when we weren't there and I tuned in on Saturday night on the Speed Channel, my palms were wet with nervousness. They never did that even when I raced, but to watch it on television got me completely fired up.

My first Nationals was with Bob "Buns" Richardson in 1975, and we did all right. I ran second in the B-main on Saturday night, then drove from 24th to work my way up to fourth when the engine blew up. By 1976 I was teamed with Bob Trostle, and we were going good on a weekly basis at Knoxville and won the season points championship. But we ran sixth in the B-main at the Nationals.

One year later I won the Nationals with Trostle, and I'm embarrassed to tell you something: I don't remember one solitary thing about that race. I've got photographs of myself and Bubby Jones and Lealand McSpadden in the trophy presentation, but I can't remember any of it. That makes me very sad because winning it with Bob was one of the most special moments of my career, and I wish I could remember and savor every detail. I feel bad, because it's downright disrespectful to both Bob and Knoxville that I can't remember something so meaningful.

But I'll tell you what I *do* remember: We raced on the day following the Nationals, but we were home Monday. First thing Monday morning, as soon as the K-mart opened up, Jeri and I hurried down there and bought that console TV. We paid $525 and I couldn't have been prouder if the governor of Iowa came to our trailer and sat and watched TV with us.

My recollections from 1978 are much more detailed. I was driving the Speedway Motors car for Bill Smith, and one week before the Nationals I crashed hard at the Eldora Nationals. We hurried back to Lincoln and took the car apart and began making repairs, watching the clock because we were scheduled to race in the Wednesday-night preliminary at Knoxville.

We had a 430-cubic-inch engine that we had run a few times that season, and it was strong but had given us some trouble. It was fast when it ran, though, so we figured it would work for the Nationals. We had the engine freshened up, replacing the parts we thought had caused the trouble.

Most of our stuff was worn out by then, so we were scrambling. Smith gave us good stuff but by this time I had blown it up, burned it up, broke it, tipped it over, and generally made a mess of it. If it wasn't worn out it seemed like I broke it.

It was fairly early on Wednesday morning and I was getting everything buttoned up. To get to Knoxville you had to leave Lincoln by 2:30 or 3 o'clock in the afternoon on the day you raced. You have to realize the Nationals were not nearly as big a deal as they are today. It was a big deal in 1978, yes, but not like it is in 2007. Today you've got to be in line at the pit gate by early afternoon. Hell, back then if you got there as late as 6:30 you were still all right.

The guys who helped us then were home getting ready, and I was finishing some last-minute stuff. We figured it would be a good idea to fire that new engine up before we left, so I crawled in and Jeri pushed me in the alley behind the shop to fire the car. Then she was going to hurry home and gather our clothes together and run a couple of errands.

I drove the car around to the shop door, and left the engine running to warm up. The idea was to adjust the timing once the engine got warm. I climbed out of the car and walked into the shop, and heard the phone ringing. I answered the phone, and while I was talking I heard something go, "clunk-clunk, thud!" out in the driveway. I finished the call real quick and ran outside, and that damned engine had blown up right there in the alley.

I was all flustered and immediately got my pal Smith on the phone.

"Hey, sonny, you know that great motor we were going to win Knoxville with? It just blew up."

Smith must have had his own problems that day, because he just said, "So go tell somebody who gives a shit!" You know, it was one of those don't-give-me-your-problems discussions.

"Well, what are we going to do?" I asked him.

"I'm not doing anything," he says. "*You* had better do something!"

I called Frank Brenforder, a local fellow who had helped a ton of racers down through the years. I asked for his suggestions, and he told me to call Larry Danhauer, who built racing engines on the side outside of his day job. These weren't full-blown exotic high-end units like Earl Gaerte built, but Larry did a good job and his stuff stayed together nice. At the time, many sprint cars used a small-block Chevy engine with a stroke of three-and-nine-sixteenths, which figured out to be 366 cubic inches. That was a nice combination that ran good but it wasn't a killer deal by any means.

Larry went above and beyond to help us, and worked with me until three in the morning Thursday, putting all the pieces on his short block. Oil pan, front cover, heads, injectors, oil pumps and drives, water pump, and so forth. We had to make sure everything fit, and the pistons weren't hitting the valves and things like that. We fired it up that next morning and it looked like it might run all right.

We hustled to Knoxville that afternoon and arrived around six p.m. The officials immediately told me I couldn't race, because I had missed my allotted spot the night before. I was the defending champion, and race director Ralph Capitani came to my defense and straightened everything out.

I set fast time and finished second in the feature that night, giving me a good starting spot for Saturday night's championship feature. I beat Steve Kinser into the first corner, and was really going good until a brake line was torn off the right rear of the car and I lost all my brakes. This was a big deal for me, because I always used a lot of brake to drive the car. I'd hold the throttle wide open through the corners and use the brakes to set and turn the car. Without brakes, I was off-balance and it wasn't at all comfortable.

Plus, you've got Steve Kinser all over you, and that ain't fun. Very late in the race we came up on lapped traffic, and I went into turn one just as I caught a slower car. I squeezed past him on the outside, and I was hammering my car for all it was worth to stay off the fence. If it would have hiccupped I would have flipped clear out to the highway. But Larry's engine did all right and I beat Steve to the checkered flag.

It's funny, I remember that race, and the victory celebration, like it was yesterday. It wasn't any more important than the year previous, but for some reason the details of 1978 are vivid in my mind. Weird.

The difference in the two years is amazing. In 1977 you couldn't have told me I wasn't going to win the Nationals. We were going on such a high, winning so many races, I felt like a sure thing. But in 1978 on the drive down I didn't figure I had a chance, because we were scrambling and disorganized because of the last-minute engine drama.

Maybe that's why I remember 1978, because it was such a struggle and it had such a happy ending.

Either way, it's nice to win the Nationals. Very nice.

I came back to win the Nationals again in 1984, and in many ways that was probably my favorite victory. All were special, but that race meant a lot because of my situation at the time. My career had been stalled a bit, and I was 32 and actually questioning if I might be over the hill. But winning Knoxville helped me get past that idea, and boosted my confidence tremendously.

Plus, it was like a big plan came together just right. I joined Bob Weikert's team because I thought the car was capable of winning a big race or two, and within a month we won the Knoxville Nationals. We came back and won the Nationals again in 1985, so that period was really satisfying.

The sport was really changing during this period. In the 1970s there were three truly big races: the Knoxville Nationals, the Western World at Manzanita, and the Pacific Coast Nationals. But by the 1980s there were many other races bigger than Manzy and the Pacific Coast race in terms of purse. (Personally, I ranked the Pacific Coast event as one of the biggest in the country no matter what, because it was so hard to go in there and beat those guys.) The Kings Royal at Eldora, the Syracuse Supernationals, the Eldora Sprint Nationals, the Williams Grove National Open, those events really came into their own in the 1980s.

I once considered $5,000-to-win to be a bona fide big race. But somewhere along the line I jumped the number to $10,000. Then again I changed it to $20,000. I remember riding in the truck after a particularly satisfying win and turning to Davey Brown, one of my mechanics at Weikert, grinning real big and saying, "Now, by God, that's a *bona fide* feature win, ain't it?" Maybe we won $10,000, and we were bragging.

When Earl Baltes announced the Kings Royal at Eldora, I remember it distinctly. $50,000 to win! Now we're talking some real money. I believe that influenced other promoters to raise the bar a little bit to keep up. I think Earl and Knoxville went back and forth for a little bit, he created a $100,000-to-win race, the Historical Big One, for a few years, and that prompted Knoxville to keep moving its purse up as well.

As the money increased, I don't think most of us thought much about it. It didn't change anybody's lifestyle, I suppose, although I bought a bigger motorhome, and maybe got a little nicer home back in Sioux Falls. Then through the years we moved a couple of times and got a nicer house. But it was never a rapid ascent up the social ladder, believe me.

I got as big a kick out of winning a race and feeling like King Kong, even if I didn't get paid much. That's why it wasn't only about the money; I got a huge satisfaction any time I won against the top-flight guys.

People sometimes ask me if winning the nationals ever got to be old hat. I can answer in two words: Hell, no! My fourth in 1985 was just as exciting as my first in 1977.

By that time I had realized my goals had changed. Any chance I had at getting to Indianapolis had passed me by, no matter what, without even having a shot at it. I figured since I wasn't gonna make it to Indy, I might as well race the biggest races I could in sprint-car racing. So for me, the Knoxville Nationals was my Indy 500, and by God in 1985 I had won it four times. That's a very satisfying feeling, believe me.

I wasn't all that disappointed that my Indy dreams had faded. The good news was that sprint cars weren't paying $400-to-win any more. This is not your average job. I wasn't making $10 million a year, but at the time my friends were making $15,000-20,000-a-year, and I was making more than $100,000. Maybe $200,000, and a couple of years, more than $300,000. I'm no dummy; I could see that this sprint-car deal wasn't all that bad. And we hadn't even got to the point of selling T-shirts yet.

In 1989 we came back and won Knoxville again. To be honest, going into that race you couldn't have convinced me I wasn't gonna win. Sure, God could strike a blow on me by flattening a tire or something, but unless something weird happened, I knew I would win. We were having such a great year, and my car was so strong, I figured I'd lead every lap and win. I wasn't being overconfident, but I knew we would be all right. I would have been really disappointed if we hadn't won, because it would have taken an act of God to beat us. That's how strong we were.

Here I am bragging about winning Knoxville! I'll tell you a secret: You know the most important factor in going good there? Luck. It's really as simple as that.

You can think all you want to be about being a super-stud and handling the deal, but if you don't have perfect luck you ain't gonna get it done. You can tell yourself that you can do it no matter what, even if you're running on seven cylinders. But if you're running on seven cylinders you ain't gonna beat Steve Kinser and Sammy Swindell, I don't care who you are. So get over it, and be honest: Being lucky at Knoxville is more important than being good.

Things have to go perfectly in order to win it. Nothing can go wrong for two or three days, nothing. If you have a slow leak in a tire you're in trouble, something as simple as that. Sometimes if you draw 100 on the draw coming through the gate on Wednesday night, the whole weekend is junk because the track will go away and become so slow you can't get a good qualifying time, even if you are a superstar. If you start in the front of the heat, maybe you're 29th on the qualifying results and even if you recover, because of the track conditions going away so quickly you're still going to start 17th or 18th in the main event on Saturday night. You don't have any control over that.

It was in the 1980s when they moved to the new, much more difficult format at the Nationals. As a racer, I didn't want the change. Naturally, I wanted to get fast time and start in the front. I didn't want to start 10th in the heat race.

But the funny thing is—and I still think it's this way— sometimes if you're exactly right you can start 10th and drive right through 'em. Because you and your car are just…*right*. The next year, maybe you start 10th in the heat and barely get to sixth in the heat.

I firmly believe that if you haven't run into a problem, if you haven't experienced several different scenarios, you're not ready to win that race. You've got to experience the good stuff, and also experience the bad stuff, too. If you experience the bad stuff and you know what you did to overcome it, the next time you're all right because when it happens you will be more in control of what's going on. But without that experience, you're not going to be able to overcome it at the Nationals, with all the competition, all the cars, and a difficult format.

You might think you can just luck into it at the Knoxville Nationals. Well, God works in mysterious ways: He ain't gonna let that happen. That's just the way it is. If you aren't prepared, you don't have a chance.

Before you learn how to *win* the Nationals, first you have to learn how to *lose* the Nationals. For example, Donny Schatz won in 2006 after finishing second several times. He has started on the pole and had all kinds of things happen that prevented him from winning, even weird things like flattening a tire and hitting the fence on the first lap. So Donny has been there, and has experienced the bad things. But through that he and his team figured out what it takes to win, because they've seen things go wrong and learned from each experience. This past year when Donny finally had some decent luck, he was ready.

The qualifying process at the Nationals is as grueling as the race itself. You time trial on your preliminary night, then run your heat race and hope you qualify for that night's feature event. You get points for each time you're on the track, and after the preliminary nights the lineup is set for Saturday night. You always hope you're locked into the championship race, and if not you have to race your way in through a series of qualifying features with a letter designation. If you're in one of the top spots in the E-main, for example, you transfer to the tail of the D-main. If you can race your way into another transfer spot, you move to the C-main, and so on.

This process is known as running the alphabet. It's a great chance to be a hero if you can do it, but no racer would ever wish that upon themselves. It's very tough and has only been done successfully a few times.

I found myself in this predicament two times, in 1988 and '90. In 1988 I went through the C to the B and into the championship feature, where I finished fifth. In 1990 I again finished fifth in the final, but had to come all the way from the D-main to do it.

You know what's funny? I won the Nationals five times, but when people approach me to talk about Knoxville, 95 percent of the time they want to talk about me running the alphabet. They don't bring it up that I won five times! No, their eyes get wide and they get all excited and they talk about me passing those cars to transfer from each qualifying feature. Why is that?

Well, it's because that is a memorable thing, and you're doing it the hard way. The best way is to qualify for the front row and lead all the laps to win. But the hard way is when you're coming from deep in the alphabet and you've got to pass 40, 50, 60 cars to make it. As a driver it's memorable, too. I still vividly remember those nights in 1988 and '90.

However, the two nights were so similar, I have a hard time distinguishing which was which. For example, I don't know if it was 1988 in the Kodiak car or '90 in the Williams car, but I distinctly recall that by the tail end of the B-main the crowd was standing up and making more noise than the engine in my car. I could hear them, even though my engine was screaming, my helmet was on, and my earplugs were in place! Amazing! If I close my eyes I can hear that sound yet today.

I can also distinctly remember one other lap during my Nationals career, like it happened just yesterday. It was 1984, in the Weikert car. Sammy Swindell was leading in the Raymond Beadle No. 1—the Old Milwaukee car, I think—and it was maybe nine, 10 laps into the race. I caught Sammy coming off turn two, and passed him down the backstretch. When I came off turn four, the crowd was so loud, I thought Sammy had taken it out of the ballpark behind me. You know how they jump up and scream when something weird happens? I thought Sammy got excited and took it out of the place. But they were yelling because I took the lead. That was a noise I'll never forget. To this day, at this moment, I get goose bumps when I remember that sound. The crowd was with me, it was like they were riding in the seat right alongside me.

In some ways this was amazing to me. Remember, I had been a Knoxville regular only a couple of years—1975 through '77— and I wasn't from Knoxville originally. I wasn't a born and bred Hawkeye. I lived in Des Moines when I drove for Bob Trostle, and worked for him, but I was never considered a local guy. So for the crowd to get behind me like that, it really lit me up. I wasn't one of them, yet they embraced me. That's the time when I began to realize I was gaining on something. Maybe I could become a fan favorite there at Knoxville. That moment, and that night, really affected me.

Steve Kinser was a hometown hero at Bloomington and the Indiana tracks, and Sammy was big in Memphis, Devil's Bowl, and different places. But the Outlaws didn't go to South Dakota yet, and I didn't know if I had a hometown following anywhere.

That night I began to feel that Knoxville was something of my hometown, and that felt good.

I could never quite figure out why people chose to cheer for me and become a fan. I always saw myself as just another guy, nothing special. And as I look back today I realize that's partly what attracted people to follow me. I was just a normal guy. I tried to look at myself as the fan's equal, not as anything better. I always believed in treating people the way I'd want to be treated.

For example, one day we had a big line of people waiting to buy a T-shirt, and it was very hot. The sun was beating down. A young mother was standing in the line, in the hot sun, holding a crying baby. Soon it was obvious that the baby needed a diaper change. Jeri or my girls approached the young gal and asked if she'd like to bring the baby in our motor home to change the diaper. This was very typical for us. Maybe a small kid needed to use the restroom, so we'd invite them in to use ours. If we had sandwiches, we'd probably offer them one, or some potato chips. That's just how we were made. That's what you do for others.

Today, if I'm working in my shop and a fellow comes by and we begin to chat, I'll probably offer him a chair and a cold drink. That's what you'd do at your house, right? That's just what normal people do. And I'm just another guy, although you might wonder about the "normal" description because naturally I'm a little weird!

I think that's one of the key elements in why people chose to follow me and my career. For many years I've been humbled that people were so kind with their attention and their compliments. They were very good to me. I always felt a strong sense of loyalty to those people.

It was also a combination of many things. For example, Steve Kinser was viewed as somewhat invincible, and Sammy was like Superman but very quiet. Sammy, in particular, is a very quiet person. And Steve ain't at all quiet, but he had this big, bull look to him that said, "Stay away from me, boy!" People might have viewed him as difficult to approach because he was just so tough-looking. Especially younger fans, or ladies. Not that he wasn't good looking; the girls always thought Steve was great looking, especially when we were younger. But he appeared bigger than life, and they were afraid to approach him sometimes. But me, well, people looked at me as just good ol' Doug. I wasn't Huckleberry Finn, but I probably could have been.

The Knoxville Nationals was where the sport began to change, and become more of a business. That's what we eventually realized we were in: a business. It wasn't like that in the 1970s, but by the tail end of the '80s it was obvious the sport was changing. Some things were good; like selling T-shirts, because that became a very lucrative business for the top racers. But other things were bad, because they made life much more complicated.

My family and I recognized that part of our business—and we looked at this somewhat differently than many of the other guys, I think—was not just selling T-shirts, but selling Doug Wolfgang. If you could sell Doug Wolfgang, that sold the T-shirts. We made it a point to interact with the fans, and all of us were approachable. In fact, our oldest daughter, Niki, could sign my name as well as I could, and soon people began to insist that she sign my signature on their shirt! They'd ask me if she was there to sign my name; I think they got a kick out of that. She could do it perfectly.

My wife and kids were a big asset to my career. I won races, yes, but they sold the name. They organized the T-shirts, arranged for me to do signings, things like that. We were a team: I won the races, and they ran the concession program. That was our business.

It wasn't that way in 1978, although we sold a few T-shirts then. But nobody thought about it like it was business. It was kind of fun to have a box of shirts, but you'd usually give away half of 'em. But at some point, maybe the early 1980s, the fans caught on and suddenly racing shirts were hot. We never had many shirts with Doug and Joanne Howells, and I'm not even sure we had them in the Gambler car, although we might have. We definitely didn't even have 'em with Weikert's car. In the beginning Weikert asked if he could use my name and make shirts with the car on 'em, and I said sure. Then I saw that the more races we won, the more shirts they sold. They almost ran the car off of T-shirt sales; all the diesel fuel, traveling costs, stuff like that, it was substantial. Still, they only dabbled in it. It wasn't anything spectacular. But as I noticed they were selling a lot of shirts, we decided to pay attention to that side of the business a little more.

But that opened up some conflicts between car owners and drivers over who had the rights to T-shirts. It was a conflict with me, for sure, and I know most of the other guys had similar issues. When you talked to somebody about running their car, often that's the first thing they insisted on: They wanted the T-shirt concession, because that deal was very profitable.

I always felt I should protect the rights to my name. I spent my entire career building my name, and if anyone was going to profit from it, it should be me. Yes, I realize you have to have a car to make your name, but people aren't buying the T-shirt because it's got the car number; they want the name of their favorite driver.

In the very early days, even before he formed the World of Outlaws, Ted Johnson was signing up guys to a T-shirt deal. He offered something like 50 cents a shirt, I think. Shirts sold for $5 each at that time. But I felt it wasn't worth giving up the rights to your name for just 50 cents. We'd only sell a half-dozen shirts anyway, so it wasn't big money. But the principle was strong with me. The same was true for the die-cast cars that came along later.

It's a fine line to protect your name and still do things that promote the sport. However, in my mind I was promoting the sport in the proper way. I wasn't a bum, I was good with fans, I treated people with respect; not just the fans, but the promoters. So I felt like I held up my end of the bargain, but in my opinion signing away the rights to my name was asking too much.

So much has changed in the sport, mostly related to business issues like this. In earlier years things were simpler, and we didn't have to deal with this stuff. But I guess it's an inevitable part of the sport growing. Look at NASCAR: I enjoy watching that program on Speed TV, "Back in the Day." You see old footage of places like Darlington, and there is a corrugated tin fence around the place all bent up from people running into it, and those small grandstands just packed with people. I love that! None of that is left in NASCAR, not today. It's all big, it's all modern, and it's all business.

Knoxville has changed, too, and that's just the way it is. For example, we always sold T-shirts right out of our trailer in the infield, or maybe we'd set up a table near our car after the races. In the later 1990s they opened a trade show in one of the barns where drivers set up T-shirt tables. However, a few years ago Knoxville announced that you had to give a percentage of the t-shirt money to the track.

A lot of people were aggravated by that rule. I don't know what's right, but it's obvious the track has the right to say, "Don't use my race track to sell your shirts without giving me a percentage." I understand that completely. Then again, look what happened: Everybody moved their T-shirt sales into trailers across the street, because it's cheaper to pay rent on a spot there than to pay a percentage to the track.

It goes back to that natural conflict between the racer and the promoter. Both are trying to survive, and it's tough out there. I never raced simply for the money, but you have to have money to live. Plus, nobody likes to be taken advantage of. I think people are especially sensitive to that.

When you're in the public eye people approach you with all kinds of ideas, products they want to market using your name, and so on. I don't know anything about stuff like that. So maybe you say yes to this little thing, or that little thing, and pretty soon you get uneasy and you say, "Hey, wait a minute…what's happening here?" You feel like you're losing control, and naturally you fear you're being taken advantage of. It's just a natural outgrowth of the business side of sprint-car racing. It's not about being greedy, it's about trying to protect your interests.

I never considered hiring an agent, because I had some people along the way who helped me. Bill Smith would give me good advice, and he's a much better businessman than I am. And he had one of his high-school friends who is an attorney help me two or three different times. They gave me proper advice and care. And there were other people as well who helped me. I went through a period, like all kids, where I didn't think my parents were very smart, but I learned that they weren't dumb. I'd ask their advice sometimes and what they told me I really didn't want to hear, but as time went on I realized they were able to see things through eyes much wiser than mine. So I eventually learned to listen to people I trust.

I was lucky in my career to see purses grow to levels we couldn't have predicted. That was great, because it allowed guys like me to make a living driving sprint cars. But the down side is that it forced all of us to deal with business issues that sometimes we didn't like.

You know, even after all this talk about business and money, that's not what the Knoxville Nationals are about. Not at all. If they lined you up in front of those 30,000 screaming people, and you're racing against the best in the business, it wouldn't matter if first place paid $100. You're going to race as hard as you can, every lap, because more than anything you want to be able to say you won the Knoxville Nationals.

It was like that when I came along in 1975, and it's like that today. There ain't anything like the Knoxville Nationals!

I have one more really sweet memory from Knoxville. When I won the Nationals for the fifth and final time in 1989, I made my way to the victory podium to begin the trophy presentation. I was all pumped up and excited, completely jazzed.

The photographers were blazing away and the whole scene was chaos, and very exciting. I realized someone was handing me this big trophy, and instinctively I took it from their hands. I looked over and suddenly realized the Nationals Queen was Amy Richert, daughter of the great IMCA sprint car racer, Jerry Richert.

All of a sudden, standing there on that podium, I could picture Jerry on the race track, years earlier. I was a small kid watching from the stands, completely mesmerized by this man. Everybody else was putting around the bottom, but Jerry Richert was up on the fence, turning that engine 30,000 rpm from the way it sounded. He was sideways and spectacular, and even though he'd only win the race by three feet it looked like he was going 3,000 miles an hour. He had a style I really liked and as a young boy he affected me. He was one of the great stars that made me want to be a race driver.

Later on Jerry got to be a friend of mine, but I was still in awe of him.

When I looked down and saw it was Amy presenting me with the trophy, I almost broke down and cried. That meant more to me than winning the race itself.

It isn't very often that a man has a chance to touch his heroes. At that moment of winning the Knoxville Nationals, I felt like I could touch Jerry Richert. That was a really special moment, at a really special race.

24

Lakeside Speedway, April 1992

Sunlight was peeking through the windows. I was lying on my back, and my eyelids slowly fluttered open. My eyes glanced around the room, and a clock on a nearby wall showed 6:30. Morning or evening? I didn't know, but something about the fresh sunlight told me it was morning.

As I lay there, I began to sort out my surroundings. There wasn't so much a fog in my mind, but rather a big emptiness, like a mystery. Where was I? What's happened?

I realized something was wrong with my body. My eyes worked okay, and I could hear, and smell, but nothing else seemed right. My head seemed kind of bound up, and my legs felt weird.

Soon the door opened and a lady walked in wearing a nurse's uniform. I realized I was in a hospital of some kind, but where?

The nurse was very kind. She began to quietly explain things to me. Today was May 11, 1992, and I had been in a bad accident. The accident took place several weeks ago, on April 3. I had been unconscious, she explained, for about five weeks. I was in Kansas University Medical Center, in Kansas City, Kan. She didn't tell me much more, but encouraged me to rest.

Slowly, as the day progressed, I began to understand my situation. My neck was broken, as was my sternum. I suffered a serious head injury, and that's the reason I had been unconscious. Most of all, I had been terribly burned.

It wasn't a total shock that I was here. Somehow it had registered with my subconscious what had happened, so when

I woke up I didn't have any problem accepting that I had been in a crash.

However, the past five weeks were a complete blank in my mind. I had no recollection then, nor do I today, 15 years later. But May 11 began my awakening, when I started to slowly put my life back together. It was going to be a long, long haul.

That first day made me understand what pain is all about. I was a tough guy, or *thought* I was a tough guy. I had suffered broken bones and stuff like that at various times in my career, but always raced right through those injuries. But this deal, this was something totally different.

Burns are a terribly destructive injury, and very difficult to treat. All the damaged tissue has to be removed, in order to clean out all possible impurities. Even though your skin is destroyed, your nerve endings are still there, and they register pain to the touch.

Each day around noon I underwent a process called debridement, where they scrub the burned area to remove the damaged tissue. This is excruciatingly painful. You think you're going to die, and sometimes you wish you were dead. They can't give you pain medication because the amount needed would either kill you or quickly addict you. So you've got to just tough it out and get through it.

As soon as they're finished you feel great, because the process helps remove bacteria from your bloodstream. However, with each passing hour more bacteria forms in your bloodstream, and you begin to get sick and feel very bad, like a severe flu. Your entire body aches.

That was suddenly my new routine. Feel bad until it was time for debridement; then suffer the excruciating process; feel relatively good for a few hours; begin to get sick and feel bad as the bacteria accumulated in my bloodstream. Go to sleep that night and know tomorrow is going to be just like today.

One of the worst moments of my life came soon after I woke up. Somehow I was propped up a little bit in bed, and I lifted the sheet. I could see that my legs and lower body had been horribly burned. Not just a little bit; some spots on my legs were so charred the bones were exposed.

Right at that exact moment, it was crystal clear to me: I was never gonna be Doug Wolfgang again. Yes, that was still my name, but the Doug Wolfgang who was a successful race driver, that guy was DOA. Dead. Gone. I knew as sure as life that I would never again be able to perform at that level.

That made me very sad. I *liked* being Doug Wolfgang. I wanted to be him forever. But now I knew I could never be him again, not ever. It made me want to cry.

Jeri was there with me, and she talked to me that first day. I remembered something right away: She was pregnant! We were going to have a baby, hoping after three daughters to have a boy.

That first day was a bit of a blur, because my mind was trying to absorb so much. I was conscious through my first debridement, which was memorable but not in a good way. The nurses talked to me throughout the day, and among everybody I started filling in the blanks a little bit on my situation.

It's a helluva thing to be asleep for five weeks. A lot happens in that time, let me tell you.

Late that first night, a nurse came into my room and woke me up. It had been 12 hours since my debridement, and the bacteria level in my bloodstream was high, and I felt very weak and sick.

"Doug, you have a phone call," the nurse told me.

I was annoyed that she woke me.

"I don't care who it is, I'm not feelin' good so I'm not talkin'."

"No," she said, "you have a phone call and you will answer this call."

"No, honey, *you* don't understand. I'm not feelin' real slick, and I'm not into talkin' on the phone right now. I don't care who it is."

She looked right at me and glared.

"Doug, you *will* answer this phone right now."

I guess she kind of got my attention.

"Well, okay then."

I answered the phone, and it was Jeri.

"You're the proud owner of a baby boy," she said.

I was so happy I wanted to yell, but so sick I couldn't do it. If you've ever had a child, you understand the euphoria of the moment of birth. But I was so sick, and weak, I couldn't even enjoy it.

It's a helluva thing when you're so goddam sick you can't celebrate the birth of your only son, and all you can do is nod your head and cry and feel like you're going to die.

By all rights, I *should* have died.

When they got me to the hospital the day of the accident, the doctors were very honest with Jeri. They told her I had a 10 percent chance of survival and a zero percent chance I would ever walk again. That's pretty rugged news for a lady who is almost eight months pregnant with three kids at home.

Several things could have killed me. The head injury, for one. I could have breathed fire and died on the spot. And the real menace was infection, which is a big-time threat for any burn patient.

I don't know why, or how, I lived. I guess the main factor was my strong will to see my wife and kids again. In fact, I later learned that when they loaded me into the ambulance after my crash, I suddenly woke up for a few seconds—I had been unconscious since the moment of impact—and very lucidly asked, "Is my wife here?" Then, as quickly as I had awakened, I was out again, and didn't wake up again for five weeks.

That's kind of a mysterious thing to me. Sometimes I wonder if I somehow knew I was going to die, and I wanted to say goodbye to Jeri. I really love her, you know.

The day after Robby's birth they wheeled him down the hall in a little cart, and placed the cart along the corridor near a window. They loaded me into a wheelchair and rolled me to the window, and I could actually see the little guy for the first time. He couldn't come into my ward because it was environmentally controlled to help prevent infections. Not for him, but me.

I don't remember much from the next few days. Things were kind of coming and going, and it was probably a week later that I have a clear memory of anything. They wheeled me down to a small conference room, where several of the nurses had brightened up with birthday decorations. They brought Robby in and I was allowed to hold him for the first time.

It was an unforgettable moment, partly because it was something of a breakthrough for me. But also because of the incredible kindness of the nurses to go out of their way to not just make it happen, but to make it special. They decorated the room like it was a birthday party, and if I live to be 100 years old I'll never forget that simple act of kindness and generosity.

For the next few weeks I was very much up and down. I was making tiny progress, but I was whipped. Totally weak. But I finally had another breakthrough when I could pull myself up and actually hobble one or two steps under my own power.

It sounds simple, just putting one foot in front of the other and walking. But it took absolutely every ounce of my energy and strength to make two steps. It's hard to describe how difficult it was, because my legs were pretty much destroyed. Nothing worked right, and I was completely starting over.

We were surprised in late May when they told us I was being released. We didn't think I was ready, but okay, whatever, I'll go home. When the day came they wheeled me out to our motorhome—Jeri had been staying out there the entire time, even with the new baby—and helped me up into the bed. I lay there for the six-hour ride back to Sioux Falls, and Robby lay on my belly, sleeping.

I was home only for a couple of days before I was back in the hospital in Sioux Falls. Several burn areas weren't healing properly, and I was in bad shape. I still had trouble with infections and weakness, and every day I was completely whipped. It seemed like it took all my strength just to breathe and have an occasional meal.

I was hospitalized for another month. That's when I began to grasp a phrase that would become part of my daily language: reconstructive surgery.

At first you think only good things when you hear you're going to have reconstructive surgery. You're damaged, and they can fix it, right? Great! But I got to where I dreaded the very thought of more surgery. I had two or three major surgeries while hospitalized in Kansas City, and back in Sioux Falls I began to prepare for more.

At the time I had no inkling that the reconstructive surgery thing would stretch on nearly as long as it did. To date, there have been so many surgeries I can't count them all. Fifteen? Sixteen? Seventeen? It's still not over; as recently as last year (2006) I required surgery on my leg to remove some debris from the fire that was causing me to get sick.

By far and away the biggest challenges were my knees and my Achilles tendons. My Achilles tendons were burned so badly they were severed from my calf muscles, and it took a long time to get that area fully cleaned through debridement. They then went up into the back of my calf and transplanted something to take up the distance of the tendon that was destroyed. It was a very delicate process and that alone took several visits to the operating table.

Many times a burn victim suffers the worse damage to their skin, because you're normally only burned for a few moments and then the fire is out. Of course it takes only a few moments to suffer severe burns. If you're in a fire for more than a minute or two, generally you're dead. But my situation was unusual in that my burns were confined to the lower part of my body, but I was in the fire so long the damage was far deeper than normal. Like I said, the bone was exposed on several spots on my legs because all the tissue had literally burned away. Yet I lived because my upper body was not enveloped in fire, and was not burned. Plus, I was incredibly lucky that I didn't breathe any fire.

It seemed like my recovery was moving so slowly, it wasn't moving at all. I was getting better, but it sure didn't feel like it. In a way it felt hopeless, because I was beginning to understand how badly I was hurt and how long this whole process was going to take.

For example, they couldn't really begin the reconstruction of anything until they had completely cleaned out all the dead tissue. That was fairly simple on the areas of outer tissue, but because my burns were so deep, the cleaning out process was a lot more involved. It took a long time, and a lot of scrubbing and grinding, to get the exposed bones cleaned, as well the muscular tissue and tendons, things like that. They couldn't do it all at one time, and had to move slowly until each area reached a point where it could withstand surgery.

We really had two major challenges. Repair the mechanical things that were damaged, such as my knees, ankles, feet, and Achilles tendons; and begin to repair and replace all the skin that was destroyed throughout the area.

The reconstructive surgeries were aimed at the mechanical things; reconnecting muscles and tendons, for example. The skin repair would require grafting, which means taking healthy skin from other areas of your body and placing it over the burned area, hoping the new skin will "grow" and begin to function properly.

The grafting deal was almost as tough as the burns themselves. It was very difficult, and very painful. I was sick all over again from the pain, the stress, everything. Plus, you're back to fighting the infection worry, all over again, only this time it's worse. You're worried about infection not just on the burned area, but where they took the healthy skin, too.

All in all I was one miserable sumbitch. And there wasn't anything anybody could do, because it was just going to take time. A *lot* of time.

When you're laid up, you have a lot of time to think. I bounced around from feeling good and optimistic one day to feeling sorry for myself the next. Good days and bad days, for sure.

I thought about this for many hours, and came to the conclusion that I clearly knew the most disappointing thing in my life. You know, everybody has things in their life they regret, but usually it's a toss-up on which single event is the most disappointing. Not in my case. I knew exactly the decision in my life that I was most disappointed with.

It was this: The day I crashed at Lakeside Speedway in Kansas City, I shouldn't have even been there. It was a World of Outlaws race, on pavement, the first time we would be on pavement in forever. In fact, I had only driven on pavement three or four times in my entire career. I had no business running on pavement; I'm a dirt racer, and pavement didn't interest me, unless it was maybe a Winston Cup car or a chance to drive at Indianapolis.

I was driving for Max Rogers, and we had planned on racing in Bloomington, Ind., that Friday night, and Eldora the following night. That made sense, right? We had a dirt car, and we should race on dirt. Common sense. But the promoter at Lakeside called me and said they were a little short on advance tickets, and he figured if he could get me to race at Lakeside, it would help put people in the grandstands.

I told him, "I'm sure we could, but we aren't coming for nothing…" Actually I referred him to Max, because I didn't know what he wanted to do.

Max called me later that day and said, "This guy will give us $2,000, and two free motel rooms if we'll come down there and race."

"I can get us some tires from Hoosier," I told Max. "What would you like to do?"

"We'd just as well go down there," Max said. "That's a lot of money."

So he and I agreed. It wasn't like I had my heart set on racing on the pavement; I didn't. It was only about the money, and I hate that.

To this day, that's my greatest disappointment: It was money that brought me to Kansas City. The very thought makes me sick to my stomach.

Well, let me backtrack, now that I think about this. Maybe that *isn't* my greatest disappointment. Maybe my biggest disappointment is that at the moment I got burned at Kansas City, I was just starting to get good.

Yeah, I know what you're thinking: I had already won more than 400 sprint-car races. I had won the Knoxville Nationals five times, plus plenty of other big races. But I'm sincere when I say that on April 3, 1992, I was just starting to get good.

Here's what I mean: After almost 20 years of beating my head against the wall and doing it the hard way, I had finally begun to understand how to get my mind right to really be successful. I had made an important, wonderful discovery, but it came too late to really capitalize on it.

I had discovered that if I eased up just a little bit, and changed my attitude, I was a much better racer. I had my mind right and now those other boys were *really* in trouble. I had finally perfected the physical skills in the cockpit, but now could match it up with the right mental attitude, and I felt like a new man. Felt like a million bucks, every time I got into the race car.

See, racers tend to be blood-n-guts, because we don't want to show any sign of weakness that might indicate we aren't totally focused. But I had discovered that if "being focused" means you're making yourself sick with hardcore desire, you aren't very smart.

For example, there was a time that if I wasn't racing every possible night of every week of the year, I was miserable. Miserable! I was so consumed with it I wanted more, more, more. But after almost losing my marriage because of being ate up with competitiveness, and making everybody around me miserable, I figured out I didn't have to go at it quite so hard, and yet I could still enjoy racing.

What a discovery! And when I partnered with Max Rogers in 1991, we both decided we'd kind of ease up on some of the road trips in order to give other segments of our lives some breathing room. It was the beginning of a transition for me, and a great period of my life where I was awakened to so many more things around me. Max told me he couldn't go to Syracuse in October 1991 because he had to harvest. Okay…harvest! And I explained that I'd have to miss a particular weekend to attend my daughter's graduation. Max said, "Okay, go to the graduation. That's cool!"

Yet here's what I found: When I took a couple of days off and did family stuff, when I got back into the car I was not only happier, but *a better race driver!* I was actually more effective and efficient because my mind was right.

You could have preached this message to me endlessly in my younger years, but it would never have registered. God couldn't have convinced me, even if he came down here in the flesh and personally explained it to me. But when I discovered it in the early 1990s there wasn't any doubt that it was true.

(It shouldn't have taken me my whole career to figure this out. Some years earlier, as I fell in love with fitness and exercise, I discovered that if I slowed down just a bit on my fitness regimen, I actually made more progress. I should have been smart enough to apply the same concept to racing, but I guess I wasn't that smart.)

You see, too much can be…*too much*! When I eased up and got back to a more realistic level, I got better.

I know without a doubt that the day I got burned I was as good as I ever was. No doubt about it. Maybe *better* than ever.

It was a bittersweet moment when this all became clear to me, lying there burned to a crisp.

I lay on that bed, and laughed out loud. Wolfie, you big dummy. Just when you had it figured out, you get burned up. Ain't that a pity?

25

Long Road Back

Recovery is a big word. It means to get back to normal, to where you were before. That implies that you get *all* of it back.

When I think about my life after the Lakeside accident, recovery is not really the right word. Because I knew at the time, and history has proven my intuition right, that I would never recover. Not fully. The injuries were too severe, the damage to my body too much.

Thinking back to that first day in the hospital, things looked pretty grim. Because my burns were so severe, over such a large area of my lower body, the doctors were pretty confident I wasn't going to live. The infection risk, the loss of skin tissue, and so forth, it was unlikely my body could withstand this.

Even if I lived, they were positive I wouldn't walk again. My lower legs—particularly my knees and below—were damaged severely, and I'm talking whole muscles and tendons destroyed.

I don't know if it's because I'm stubborn, or stupid, whatever, but something inside drove me to want to survive. When I sort it all out today, I think it was simple: I had a loving family—a great wife and four children, including a brand new baby boy— and that was my incentive. I wanted to live to see my younger kids grow up. I wanted to spend my twilight years with Jeri.

Racing? Forget it. When I lifted my bed sheet two days after waking up and saw my lower body, I instantly knew my career was over. Instantly! Not to gross you out, but you can't imagine how ugly the sight was. It was so repugnant even I didn't want to look at it.

I was still hospitalized when Danny Lasoski, a racer from Missouri, came up to see me. Danny was an eager racer and frankly I think he was hoping to drive Max Rogers's car, but sort of wanted to know if I was officially done. I laughed when Danny asked me if I was going to race any more. I lifted up the sheet and told him to look at my legs.

"You look at those legs and tell me if I'm gonna race again," I told him. "I'm telling you, I'm finished."

On the day of my accident, I was 39 years old and weighed 165 pounds. I was very serious about my fitness regimen and my body fat had recently been measured at 7.5 percent, which is very low. I was in top physical condition and there isn't any doubt that helped tremendously in my getting through the summer of 1992.

When I was hospitalized in Kansas City and again at Sioux Falls, my primary goal was simply to survive. That's what carried me through the debridement sessions, which continued to be terribly painful, and motivated me through the many visits to surgery.

When I was released from the Sioux Falls hospital in July, it was fairly obvious I was going to live. That hurdle was behind me. So I turned my attention to learning to walk again.

First I had to use a walker, and then a cane, but before long I could actually make some steps without assistance. That was really a breakthrough, and kind of inspired me.

I wanted to get back to the gym. I knew I couldn't do much, but I was getting back into some kind of a routine would help me get better. Running was out of the question, but at least I could use the stationary machines for strength and cardio training.

Late in the summer—this might have been in the fall, I honestly don't remember exactly—I was strong enough to try it. I started lifting weights on a Nautilus program, and my walking had improved to where I could actually use a Stairmaster.

I continued to work on using my feet, even though nothing worked right. I finally got to where things had healed enough that I could run, but it wasn't pretty. It was awkward, almost like a fawn learning to walk on those new spindly legs, because nothing worked like it used to. I had ran hundreds of miles over the past few years but now I was starting over, because my legs had been, shall we say, "reconfigured."

But the running was a real breakthrough, and it seemed that my strength and stamina began to come back more quickly. Not world class, but I could see progress, and I started to gain some weight back. I had been down to 130 pounds at my sickest, but soon the number was coming back up. My appetite came back, and I began to eat more heartily.

Boy, this was great. For the first time in probably six months, I felt encouraged about something. My feet and legs were still a horrible mess; not only did they not work right, but they were hideous to look at. But when I began to get stronger, it gave me an emotional lift you cannot believe.

I felt like maybe, just maybe, I could be normal human being again. I would take a walk with Jeri, and we could go to the gym together. I could run and play with my kids. I could do things a normal person does.

But what about racing?

Max Rogers and I had talked, and he told me that if I still wanted to race he would put a car together. He wasn't rushing me, but the opportunity was there.

Very late in 1992 I began to wonder if maybe I could actually race again. Max and I talked, and we decided that we'd try to start the 1993 season with the World of Outlaws in Texas, which would be in mid-March. When I made that decision, I really started to gas it up in terms of conditioning. I began two-a-day workouts, six days a week. I was really getting after it. Now that I had a specific goal, a target, I was really humping.

Even though in my mind I knew I was never going to be the same racer as before, I think something was telling me, "You're the great Doug Wolfgang! You can do anything! It will be just like it was!" I might not be killer-fast, but I figured I'd be pretty good.

But when I arrived in Houston, I was a duck out of water. Not only did I not have the physical stamina, but my head was ringing and everything was weird. Remember, in addition to the burns I had also suffered a broken neck and a serious bruise on the brain. My head was ringing and I couldn't judge distances, and felt completely disoriented.

It was all I could do to run 15 consecutive laps, even when all by myself on the track. But I did a couple of stints, and made some pretty fast laps. You don't forget everything right away, I guess.

I remember a lot of people being glad to see me. Things were kind of a whirlwind, and I was trying to focus on racing, so I don't remember a lot of specifics. Bobby Davis Jr. was there, and I remember walking up the pit window at the same time as he and his wife, and how they were genuinely happy to see me. Steve Kinser was pitted next to us and he knew I was disheartened when I didn't make the main event. That hadn't happened very many times in my career, to miss the main event when there was nothing wrong with my race car. But Steve didn't act weird, and he didn't feel sorry for me, but he didn't act like I was a dud, either. He was just kind of there quietly, like a friend, wishing there was something he could say or do to make it better.

The next day we drove up to Dallas, and we were going to work on the car for the Friday and Saturday races at the Devil's Bowl. I knew something was wrong, and Max approached me quietly and said, "Let's talk."

He asked what I thought about everything. I think he could see what I was thinking.

"I'm not ready, Max."

"Well, I didn't think you were. You'd better make a decision on what you want to do from here."

"I think I'm not ready…I think it's gonna be a few more months yet."

"I thought you'd probably see it that way," he said. "I've been thinking that way myself."

Max wasn't upset, he was just being honest, and so was I.

So we went home. The experiment had not worked out anything like I had hoped.

I guess I probably knew going in that I wasn't ready, but I didn't want to admit it, not even to myself. I was ready to be Doug Wolfgang again, the *real* Doug Wolfgang. I didn't want to be the guy I had turned into: injured, weak, helpless, alone. So my goal was to somehow to work hard at the gym and use it like a job—bust your ass, twice a day, six days a week—to reach back to find something that I had lost.

When I proved I wasn't ready to race, it was kind of a relief in some ways. I had tried my hardest, and I couldn't yet get going. So when I went home, I kind of cruised for a while. I kept working out, but not at nearly the same level of intensity. And a funny thing came to me within a month: I was getting stronger, and doing less. It was becoming more fun. It wasn't a "have to" any more. You know, pushing yourself to do every rep, every set, every day. I let up a little bit and it turned out that the less intense my approach, I actually gained more. I might miss a workout here or there, and some days instead of an intense workout I'd bring a magazine and sit in the sauna and talk with a few friends. When I didn't feel like it, I didn't force myself.

I didn't realize it at the time, but I know it now: It was all about time. I hadn't healed enough yet to begin making gains with my body. It probably helped to work out at that intense pace, but the fact is, my body wasn't yet healed enough to gain at a normal pace. I was maxed out. But after a few more months, my body was more healed, and I was stronger, and the more relaxed approach was exactly what I needed at that time.

Max and I stayed in touch, and I kept telling him I wasn't ready. Finally about June or so, he said, "What are you thinking?"

"I don't know, Max. I just don't know."

"You know, I'm thinking that I'm probably gonna sell my stuff," he said.

"I guess I would do that," I told him. "I mean...I don't think I'm gonna come back tomorrow and be the best I can be."

"That's fine," Max said. "I want to race, but I'm not ready to put somebody else in the car that I'm not comfortable with, someone who didn't have the knowledge and didn't have what you had going for you. So I think I'm gonna sell my stuff."

I don't blame Max one bit for selling his stuff and moving on. He went above and beyond for me, in terms of working with me and being patient. He was a good friend and I appreciate him very much.

In the meantime I had begun to visit my brother-in-law, Brian Schnee, to help him out with some welding. Brian was and is a very successful car builder located in Sioux Falls. I wanted to help Brian out maybe a couple of hours a day. Not so much like a job, but to have something to do. At first it had to be set up for me to be pretty easy, because I wasn't flexible enough to stand in one place with a welding helmet on, bending in all the different positions you need in order to weld a chassis.

I had done a lot of welding before my accident and had always used my left hand as my filler feed hand. But the accident had badly burned my left hand, and in fact I lost portions of a couple of fingers. I had to learn a new way of welding to accommodate the loss of those digits. This took some time, but I slowly figured it out, two or three hours a day. I also discovered I was building stamina, and pretty soon I wasn't exhausted after just a couple of hours of work.

Then came a surprise, the kind of bonus that drops from the sky and catches you completely off guard.

Ron Tisdall lived near Brian's shop, and he raced a 360 sprint car on the local circuit. Ron was preparing two cars for the Jackson Nationals on July 31, and one car still needed to be finished. From out of the blue Ron asked if I'd be interested in driving one of his cars.

"If you'd like to drive it, come over and help me put this thing together," he said.

I was kind of taken aback, because I hadn't been in a sprint car for several months and frankly hadn't even been thinking of the possibility of driving again.

The idea intrigued me, so I went over to give him a hand. Robby came with me, he was just a little guy beginning to crawl around. I helped Ron bolt the car together, and then I contacted Hoosier Tire to see if they'd help us with some tires.

I'll be darned if I didn't win the Jackson Nationals!

I didn't feel that great, and I had a lot of rust, but somehow I cruised along and won. Was I shocked? I don't know if that's the right word, but I'll admit I honestly hadn't thought about the possibility of winning the race because it seemed so far-fetched to me.

It didn't really sink in until the next day, when my phone started ringing. One of the callers was Kenny Woodruff, the gruff and rough mechanic whom I had worked with on the Gambler cars 10 years earlier.

"Hey, bud, I heard you won a race last night…" Kenny said, and I was so surprised. First of all I was surprised he called, but also surprised he would have any idea I won at Jackson, Minn.

"Oh, yeah, we were out at the Devil's Bowl (or wherever it was) and I heard some of the racers talking on the CB radio about you winning that race. So how'd it feel?"

I can't begin to tell you how much that meant to me, Kenny taking the time to call. This was before cell phones, and he would have had to stop at a pay phone to make the call. And to think anyone would know what happened at a little race track in Minnesota, that was amazing to me.

* * * * *

Winning that race inspired me. It got me to thinking that maybe, just maybe, I could try to race again on a consistent basis. It made me realize I still wanted to race, after all. I knew I had no business trying to race with the Outlaws, because they were out of my class at that point. I had to ease into things.

Phil Durst, a dear friend of mine from Lincoln, Neb., was a racing geek from way back and had sponsored Max Rogers a little bit. Phil is a genuine good guy, and we began talking on the phone a little bit. One thing led to another and pretty soon he says, "I'm helping Bob Richardson and Ray Lipsey with a car, maybe you ought to come and drive it a couple of times!"

I grew up with Bob—we always called him "Buns"—and when I moved to Lincoln to work with Don Maxwell all those years ago Buns was living in Lincoln as well. He had an old race car at that time which he let me drive a time or two, and later on he was the first guy to take me to the Knoxville Nationals.

Well, I wasn't bashful. I was eager to go racing with Buns again. I don't remember our first race together in 1993, but we ended up running Rapid Speedway in Rock Rapids (Iowa), Jackson, Sauk Center in Minnesota, over at Rapid City, strictly local tracks.

Before the year was out I had won a couple more races, including Cheater's Day, the big race here in Sioux Falls at the Sioux Empire Fairgrounds. Say! Maybe I've still got some potential...

I definitely wasn't Doug Wolfgang again, but I wasn't a slug, either.

That fall we decided to build a new car for 1994, and went to Florida the following February. It carried Speedway Motors stickers from my good friend Bill Smith, although the car officially belonged to Ray Lipsey. We ran all nine nights of Florida Speedweek, and I sucked all nine nights. But afterward Bob Trostle pointed out, "Doug, you're the only guy to make the feature on all nine nights. You didn't miss the show one night."

In the midst of returning to racing, my life was continuing to change. I still had significant physical challenges, and had undergone a couple more surgeries. My feet and legs were still an absolute mess, but I was walking around all right and for the most part felt stronger every day.

Somewhere along the way in 1993 I began building and repairing race cars. I didn't go into the business with the thought of making a lot of money (good thing!) but more than anything just needed something to occupy my time and energy. I always liked messing with race cars, and was a decent welder, so I figured I could build a few race cars and maybe even support my family with the earnings at some point.

In terms of finances, we were okay. I wasn't thinking of racing simply because I needed to make money. Frankly, I knew where my skill level was at that point, and I knew I wasn't going to make any money at that level. Plus, I wanted to be Doug Wolfgang again. I didn't care about the money, but I wanted to be a star. I wanted that feeling you can only get when you win a race, a feeling that no amount of money in the world can buy.

Making a living as a race driver had been my life. Boy, I just wanted to get my life back. But as time passed I knew for sure that wasn't going to happen. No matter how much I wanted it, it wasn't possible. Any time I didn't want to believe that, all I had to do was get into the shower and look down at my legs and feet. In one millisecond I was reminded of what reality was.

Jeri and I had always been conservative people in terms of money, and we never lived an extravagant lifestyle. We'd spend what we needed, and bank the rest. My earnings from the mid-1980s until the time of my Lakeside accident had been very good, so we had some money in the bank. In the early 1990s the investment market was still very good, and that worked in our favor, too.

We didn't feel like the world was going to end because we ran out of money. That wasn't on our radar screen. Frankly, we were naïve; we figured the market would stay good forever, and didn't understand the realities that it takes a lot of money to live in these modern times. But in 1993 we weren't worried about it.

I'll tell you one thing, though: As the winter of 1993-94 came, I had finally accepted that my life was never going to be like it was. I had pictured myself as this fit, active race driver who could provide for his family with his winnings. But the picture had changed.

I now saw myself as a working man. A guy who welded and worked in the shop all day, and went home to his family.

Did I still see myself as a racer? Yeah, but the kind of racer who does it for the joy and experience, not because he's trying to make a living at it.

As that winter progressed a lot of things were going through my mind. Including a strange, far-fetched idea that had never in a million years entered my realm of imagination: I was contemplating legal action based on the circumstances surrounding my accident in Kansas City.

26

Agonizing Decision

If you've ever suffered a catastrophic injury where you're unconscious for several weeks, it's hard to grasp the feeling of mystery that surrounds the accident. It's like a big blank space in your life, and in the months that follow you slowly begin to piece things together, like trying to solve an intricate puzzle.

To this day I have no memory of the events of April 3, 1992. Maybe that's God's way of sparing me from replaying some truly awful moments, I don't know. I have a very faint memory of Jeri and I stopping at a McDonalds earlier that day as we drove down from Sioux Falls, but that's the only moment from the entire day I can recall. And of course I have no memory of the weeks that followed, when I was unconscious.

After I woke up and began the long healing process, I didn't think much about any of the specifics. I just knew I had been in a very bad accident and had been terribly burned. I knew absolutely nothing about what happened, why it happened, and so forth. It's hell when you're the central player in a drama, but you don't know the plot, the lines, the scenes, nothing. It was all built around you but you're clueless. It's a weird thing.

After I went home the second time in July I began to think back to the accident. I wonder what happened? How'd the fire start? How did I hit my head? Why'd I get burned so bad? Stuff like that.

Sometime in July we were invited to visit the Knoxville Nationals in mid-August. By then I was beginning to walk with a cane, so I was proud of myself. I thought I was "coming back," not to race but to become a normal person again, able to walk and have a normal life. I had already resigned myself that my racing deal was pretty much over. I never flinched on that issue, because I knew.

I didn't go to Knoxville to show off, or anything else. It's just that it had been a *loooonnng* summer for Jeri and me. We just wanted to get back to our normal life, which was going to races. We took our motorhome down and had a nice visit with a lot of people.

As I visited Knoxville, and Jeri and I visited a few other races in the weeks that followed, something interesting began to happen. A steady stream of people who were present that day at Lakeside approached us, and said with total earnestness and sincerity, something along the lines of, "What happened to you wasn't cool." Like something was very wrong. Over time, I began to realize it as well: What happened to me wasn't cool.

A lot—and I mean a lot—of people kept telling me that. People who you normally wouldn't think would say such things. For example, gruff and tough Lenard McCarl said to me, "I watched that whole thing, and I watched you die. I knew you were dead. That just wasn't cool at all."

The recurring theme from everyone there that day was that there was no fire crew. There was nobody on hand who could put out the fire, or get me out of the car. In fact, three other drivers—Mark Kinser, Steve Beitler, and Lee Brewer— ultimately got me out of the car. That's the thing everyone kept telling me: "Wolfie, there weren't any firemen there!"

At the time of my crash, nobody had been killed in major-league sprint-car racing for quite a while. I guess we all figured it couldn't happen any more. There isn't any doubt that watching somebody burn to death was a very traumatic episode for a lot of people. It *affected* people. No doubt about it.

For example, my car owner, Max Rogers, didn't even come by the hospital that night. Hey, I'm not knocking Max, not at all. He was so traumatized by the experience of watching his driver burn to death right before his eyes that he immediately loaded up that burned-up hulk of car and hit the road. He blistered that highway back to Iowa and was home in bed by midnight. Now, to make that trip in such a timeframe, you've got to absolutely haul ass.

Max drove like a maniac that night because he was so eaten up by what he saw. Goddam it, he stood there and helplessly watched me sit there in the fire and just burn up. Watched them take my charred carcass out of his car, and haul me away. Do you realize how difficult that had to be for Max? For anyone?

But the thought of a lawsuit had not yet entered my mind. However, I had come to the conclusion that something in our sport needed to change. I picked up the phone and contacted a few prominent promoters in hopes of getting some discussion going, thinking we could get together and get something organized so that what happened to me wouldn't happen to anyone else. We could make this a better deal.

But those conversations with the promoters lasted only a few moments. They were polite and cordial, but they also made it very clear that they weren't interested in having Doug Wolfgang tell them how to do things at their track. I can understand that; nothing against them, but promoters are in this for a different reason. They're in it to make money. It's very much a business, and the only way you make money is to not spend it. And they could figure out very quickly that whatever we might do to address the subject of fire safety was going to cost them money.

After those phone calls I started to become a little bit angry, and bitter. That's when I figured out they weren't hearing me, and I realized Doug Wolfgang didn't mean shit any more. It probably hurt my feelings as much as anything, because it was another reminder that I wasn't the great Doug Wolfgang any more. That's a big change in your life, really, to go from being somebody special to being nobody.

To offset some of that anger and bitterness, the fans helped me a great deal emotionally. I remember two or three 30-gallon cans full of cards and letters we received. Several people sent money. Four bucks, five bucks, 20 bucks, a hundred bucks. They'd explain in their notes that they wanted to help us, me and Jeri and the kids.

There was no way we could respond to all the letters. It was hopeless, overwhelming. When I went home in July, I read every card. It took weeks, but I read every one. Some I still have, from people whom I especially admire. Kenny Schrader sent four or five cards. A.J. Foyt called me on the phone a couple of times. Johnny Rutherford sent me a handwritten letter, with his superb penmanship. I got letters from Petty Enterprises. Hendrick Racing. People I never dreamed had heard of me. Joe Amato, the drag racer, sent me a get-well card. How could Joe Amato know me from Adam? But he sent a card.

Even a year after the crash, I still drew from the emotional lift those people gave me with their cards and notes. Although my recovery was coming along, I still had bad days, and it wasn't just the burns. I had a significant brain bruise, and the doctors told me the only prognosis was that the brain injury would take 18 months to heal. I kind of scoffed at that number, thinking, "Huh, what do they know? In three or four months I'll be all right."

Well, I wasn't all right. I'd jump rope and my head would ring. A year after my crash I hopped on a bicycle with the idea of using it as part of my fitness regimen, and I couldn't keep that bicycle between the curbs on a four-lane highway. My balance was junk. My head would ring and I'd get disoriented and lose my balance. It was amazing, and weird.

I went back and had all kinds of tests done on my eyes, my inner ears, my throat, an MRI of my head and brain, and they'd say, "Hey, Doug, there isn't anything wrong. Just hang on!"

You know, they were right. About a year and a half from my accident—November 1993—the dizziness and ringing in my head finally began to subside. As I raced a few more times, it bothered me less and less. That was a real breakthrough, because I didn't feel like I was going nuts any more.

In early 1994 I began to think very seriously about filing a lawsuit based on what happened at Lakeside. I can't begin to tell you how agonizing this thought process was. This went against everything I believed in: personal responsibility, the love of the sport, and so much more. This was a completely foreign idea to me and I didn't even want to think about it. I didn't know anything about lawyers and lawsuits and I didn't *want* to know anything.

But after many soul-searching nights of thinking it over, I came to the conclusion that filing a lawsuit was something I needed to do. There were two very powerful reasons, both very strong but somewhat unrelated.

First of all, I kept hearing reports from people who were present at Lakeside, and to a man or woman—and I mean unanimous—those people vehemently insisted that what happened to me was flat-out wrong. Frankly, at first they felt more strongly than I did; I guess the trauma of watching me sit in that car and burn was very powerful. These people were emotional and they were adamant. I kept hearing their words: *What happened to you wasn't cool.*

At the same time, Robby was getting to be about 18 months old. You know how it is with little boys who grow up in a racing family, when he was old enough to play with a toy car he immediately learned the words "race car." Probably before he could say anything else.

When he said "race car," something deep inside struck a chord with me. Something very powerful jolted me and said things aren't right. Just ain't right.

I looked at my son, and I wondered if someday he might want to race sprint cars. Maybe God had given him all the talent of Steve Kinser, Sammy Swindell, and Doug Wolfgang, all rolled together. What if he had? Then my son would probably want to race. If he raced, what if someday he burned up because that's just the way it is?

There's a saying that's common throughout our sport: "That's racing." People say it like they're resigned that you can't do anything about bad things that happen. Goddam it, you *can* do something. You can have a fire crew on hand. You can have water to put out a fire. That's all I was asking.

Anyone who has a child feels a sense of responsibility, an instinct, to protect that child. I looked at my son and wondered how I would feel if someday he burned up in a race car, because I just said, "That's racing," and didn't try to right something that was a terrible wrong. How would I feel?

If I don't stand up for Robby's rights, who will? Who will take steps today to protect him from what happened to me? Who will stand up and do that? Who will?

I'm his dad. What happened to me might have been wrong, but it would be more wrong if I didn't stand up for him.

Someday that bad thing might happen to Robby *because* I didn't stand up. I wouldn't be much of a father if I didn't stand up for the right things, even it's unpleasant and difficult.

Jeri and I talked earnestly about what we should do. Tom Nicholson had sent me a get-well card after my accident, and I remembered him from when we used to work out together at the YMCA. I didn't realize he was an attorney, and didn't really think much about it when I saw him again at the gym once I got back into a workout regimen.

As I began to think about things, Tom was probably the only lawyer I knew on a first-name basis. So one day at the gym in early 1994 I told him of my thoughts of looking into filing a lawsuit.

I asked him what my options were. Would he know anyone to help with this situation, to determine my options? He said yes, he could refer me to the right person.

We consulted with several attorneys based on Tom's referral, and my education began immediately. The first thing I learned was that Kansas has a very strict liability cap of $1.3 million. That means that no matter what the circumstances of the case, the award could not exceed $1.3 million.

The first three law firms I met with politely declined the case. It was too costly to win, they explained, among other things. Too difficult, too uncertain, and with the liability cap in place the potential reward was not large.

Man, this was an agonizing process. Agonizing! We didn't want to file a lawsuit. I loved racing; the sport had provided me with a living, and was filled with people we cared a great deal about. They were my friends. In a sense, filing a lawsuit was like suing my friends. It didn't feel good.

Finally we were referred to Victor Bergmann, and we met with him. He listened as I told him my situation, and he said he might be interested. He didn't know anything about racing, but he said, "It definitely sounds like you might have a case." He wanted to make some phone calls and study it a bit, and he would call me.

But as we were finishing our conversation he said something very strange.

"Son, you *don't* want to do this. You absolutely don't."

"What do you mean?"

"During your career, have you ever put your hand on a trophy girl's ass?"

"I don't think so."

"Have you ever put your hand on the waistband of her pants?"

"I don't know…what are you driving at?"

"Have you ever joked with a trophy girl about sleeping with her or tried to pick her up?"

"No…I mean, maybe when I was first starting out, maybe I flirted, but I never slept with any trophy girl…what are you trying to get at, anyways?"

"I'm telling you this…if you file this lawsuit, they are going to find somebody, *anybody*, who could sit on that stand and say that you're the most dirty, rotten son-of-a-bitch who's ever lived. They are going to drag you through the mud and make you look like you're the devil. It ain't nice, son. You ain't gonna like it. It's going to hurt you and it's going to make people hate you, maybe for the rest of your life."

I sat there and thought about it. What he was saying was very disturbing. I'm no angel, and I've got warts like everybody else, but I never felt like anyone hated me. Not anyone, ever. I don't think I ever gave anyone a reason to hate me. So what he was saying was awful.

But then I thought about my son. I pictured him sitting in a race car, burning to death. I pictured myself and his mother, crying and trying to get to him to help him. I pictured everyone standing around watching him burn, because there were no firemen, and there was no water. I pictured them pulling his charred body out of the car, and the entire sport shrugging their shoulders and saying, "Well, that's racing."

I looked at Victor.

"I'd like to go forward."

A few days later Victor called me back.

"Did you know you were Doug Wolfgang?"

"Sure I'm Doug Wolfgang. What do you mean?"

"But did you know you're Doug Wolfgang?"

"Yeah, I know. What are you talking about?"

"Well, I've been on the phone with about a dozen people, and son, you *really* don't want to do this."

"What do you mean?"

"You're famous, son. You're big. You're *very* big. Everybody knows who you are. When you file this lawsuit, they're going to hate your guts. Because they figure you're big, and rich, and you only care about yourself. It's not going to be pleasant."

"I don't care," I said. "I'm ready to do this."

"Then I'll take this case," he said. "I'm into cases like this. What happened to you needs to change. This lawsuit can change it. You're in a unique situation, and your voice can affect change. But it isn't going to be pretty."

The lawsuit was filed in late March 1994, just a couple of days within the two-year period following the accident. Although the information was public record, it took a while for it to be known I had filed a lawsuit. The courts don't send out a press release, it seems.

It wasn't long before people began hearing about it. None of my friends, or the people in my circle, told me I was wrong. Not that I'm loaded with friends, but they stood by me. The negative feedback was mostly from Dick Berggren of *Open Wheel Magazine,* and other people within the media.

You can brace yourself for the negative response, but until you experience it you don't really understand what it feels like. I'll admit I was surprised at first. For example, I was surprised that Dick took the position that he did. He was not only very much against the lawsuit, but against me personally. I didn't understand that; I thought Dick and I were buddies. We were on a first-name basis, and had a sandwich together a few times, things like that. I thought we were friends, and it hurt my feelings when he was so critical. But in some ways I understand, because Dick had a business to run—a couple of magazines that depended on racing—and it seemed that many in the media orchestrated a "circle the wagons" kind of reaction against me.

It didn't matter. Yes, it hurt my feelings, but in the end I was committed to doing something to better the sport, to prevent some other poor sap from sitting in a burning race car simply because there isn't anybody there to put the fire out.

So I just kept my head down and my mouth shut, and waited for things to play out. My attorneys advised me against any kind of media interview or comment, so all the things being said and written about me, I could not respond or defend myself in any way. It was frustrating because people were taking a position against me personally, and they truly did not hear or understand my side of it.

That period of time—from April 1994 to the trial, which came in August 1995—was the most lonely and painful period of my life. I was an outcast from the sport I loved. It was like I had become the ultimate bad guy.

But I had to see this thing through. No matter what was said, no matter what a worthless piece of shit the reporters made me out to be, I knew I was doing the right thing.

They say that sometimes there is nothing more painful or difficult than doing the right thing. By the end of 1994, I would have told you they were 100 percent right.

27

The Trial

As I mentioned before, the moment I filed the lawsuit against Lakeside Speedway, it began my learning experience. Well, on a warm August morning in 1995 in Kansas City, my education *really* began. That's when I saw, up close and personal, how the legal system works in the United States.

I'll never forget that morning. The one thing that stands out is the fact that the attorneys on both sides had obviously worked very hard preparing their cases. It's easy to bash lawyers and make fun, but the fact is these guys had spent an incredible amount of time building their cases. Several knew almost nothing about racing before they took this case, but by the time the trial rolled around they had really done their homework. I was impressed.

Those days in the courtroom were incredibly important for me in terms of learning what happened on April 3, 1992. When you're under oath, and they swear you in with your hand on a Bible, that's when the truth really comes out. Most of the time, anyways; throughout the trial I know of only one person whom I feel did not tell the truth. All the other people, on both sides, told the truth to the best of their ability.

The trial began, and each side took their turn presenting various witnesses and pieces of evidence to support their positions. I was amazed at the level of detail and the amount of information that had been put together to reconstruct what happened. I soaked it all in, because it helped me understand many things from that day.

They had assembled almost 300 photographs taken by six or seven different people that day, and recreated the entire process in chronological order, from the moment I hit the fence to the moment I was removed by helicopter. I was amazed at their ability to pinpoint the exact time and sequence of events.

I learned that the EMTs—Emergency Medical Technicians, who served on the ambulance crew—aren't there simply to save your life, but rather to get you stabilized and transported to a medical facility, where doctors *can* save your life. The EMTs are dispatched from a home base, with two-way radios linked to their computer system. This is used to keep precise records on what is happening in the field, 24 hours a day. Each radio transmission is recorded in terms of the time it was received. The personnel are trained to adhere to a very precise regimen so their actions can be tracked, because that information is important from a medical standpoint.

When my car hit the wall that day, one of the two EMTs knew from experience that this was not an average crash. The first thing he did was key his microphone for a moment, which both recorded the exact time of impact on their home base computer, and also turned on a mechanism that recorded every subsequent radio conversation. This was something like 4:30.35 p.m. They are trained to put on gloves and be ready for the first moment they have an opportunity to work on you, and that's what they did. Everything was precisely recorded.

The next thing that particular EMT did was write down on his glove the exact time he was first able to touch me. We learned that it was eight-and-a-half minutes from the time of the crash until he could begin providing care to me. That's the amount of time they had to stand by, because the fire prevented them from rendering care.

That's the behind-the-scenes stuff that amazed me. I had no clue this kind of process was in place for medical people.

There had been much legal wrangling that took place prior to our case going to trial.

I was adamant that it wasn't money I was after. I knew going in there would not be a financial windfall, because of the Kansas liability cap. That was fine by me.

I was also not looking for revenge. No amount of money, or no verdict in court, could change what happened. Nothing could bring my body back to the condition it was in prior to the crash. I had accepted my fate and that was that.

What I was after, ultimately, was to change the system. I wanted the sport—short track racing—to step up and address the matter of fire safety, and inadequate fire protection. There were no standards of any kind in place at that time, and I felt strongly there should be. The only way to force the sport to change, I felt, was to win a lawsuit. This, I believed, would get the sport and the insurance industry to put some standards in place.

The point of my lawsuit was very simple: I wanted to force the sport to change their bush-league approach to safety. It was as simple as that. There's usually only one way to get a business, or an entire industry, to address something like this: You hit them in the pocketbook. I figured if I won, the insurance industry would have no choice but to take steps to prevent losing future lawsuits.

We officially filed suit against Lakeside Speedway, because the promoters there were responsible for providing the fire protection. We also named the World of Outlaws in the suit, because as the sanctioning body it was also responsible for making sure the track's safety crew was adequate.

I was not aware of most of the legal details, but my lawyers consulted me on key issues. I was shocked early on when they explained that we couldn't just name Lakeside Speedway and the World of Outlaws, but several other parties as well.

For example, the three men who comprised the fire crew at Lakeside were technically not employees of the track. They were considered contract laborers. This was huge, because it meant that if the track were found negligent, their lawyers would immediately try to defer the judgment to the firemen. In other words, the track could say *they* weren't responsible for what happened, but it was the firemen—who were not officially employed by the track—who failed.

This would have been catastrophic for these three men. I absolutely did not want that. Besides, this was exactly what I wanted to change in our sport: It isn't right if a promoter or a track can simply lay off their responsibility onto another party.

If this would have happened, those guys could have lost their homes, everything. That was truly that last thing I wanted to see happen. I didn't want any money from them, or their kid's bedroom furniture. So we named the three men as parties in the lawsuit, and then I signed papers letting them out of the suit. I don't understand all the legal stuff but my lawyers assured me that this would prevent these guys from having to shoulder the blame if we won our case.

This led some of my detractors to claim that I was "filing suit against the very people who tried to save his life." What a bunch of bullshit. These people had no idea what they were talking about.

Another party named in the lawsuit was the manufacturer of the steering equipment on our car. One of the reasons they struggled to get me out of the fire was because the release ring on the steering wheel was made of plastic, and as soon as the car began burning that little ring melted, making it impossible to remove the wheel. Same deal: If we won the case, the track people could then say it wasn't their fault the steering gear was plastic, and therefore the judgment should be deferred to this manufacturer.

This is the kind of stuff I had no idea went on. How would I? How could I know that when you sue someone, they can counter-sue other parties? I sued the track and the Outlaws for "gross, wanton negligence," and their lawyers immediately took the position that the reason I couldn't get out of the car was because the steering wheel wouldn't come off, and therefore the burden of liability should fall on the manufacturer of that piece. Hey, that wasn't my idea; that was the defendant's legal strategy to shift the liability to somebody else.

This meant that if I were to win the case, the jury would then have to decide what percentage of liability each party bore. In other words, it was very possible that the manufacturer could be on the hook for the entire judgment. Was it the manufacturer, or the firefighters, Lakeside, the World of Outlaws, or any other parties? Who was ultimately going to be viewed as liable? I had no control over this.

So my lawyers asked me how I wanted to handle this. They explained what would happen, which way it might go, and so forth. Well, I didn't want the steering manufacturer to be involved. So we made a motion to let them out if they paid $80,000 up front. That sounds high; it *is* high, because they didn't have insurance to cover this. And it hurt them, I know that. But listen, if they had been voted by the jury as being 33-percent liable, it would have cost them $300,000, $400,000. So they got off as light as we could make it. It wasn't completely their fault, I know that. But it was one of those very painful situations where because of the law, they were going to be involved even if I didn't want them to be.

By the way, there were rumors floating around that we had specifically ordered that plastic hub in an effort to save weight. That isn't true; we ran the same piece everybody else was using. Hey, I'll bet I'm like everyone else: I never would have put two-and-two together and realized that a plastic hub on a steering release is a very bad idea. We don't think along those lines; it was something that you almost had to experience to realize the implications. Who would have thought to figure out what happens in the event of a fire?

I felt really bad for the manufacturer. They haven't spoken with me since. Sure I felt bad, from day one. I didn't control the system, and that's just how it is. The lawyers knew that if they paid a settlement, we released them from any further liability. Their settlement was applied to some of my out-of-court expenses, which I have to admit were considerable.

From the time I filed the lawsuit in March 1994 until our trial began some 17 months later, a lot of behind-the-scenes work was going on. This is called the "discovery" period, I learned. Attorneys on both sides interview dozens of people under oath, recording all of their information and building their cases. The lawyers also research things like legal precedent, and other elements that might strengthen their case.

One of the things my lawyers did was research what it would take to make the sport less bush-league. One solution was to create a traveling safety safari, like what the NHRA or IndyCar series each have. They go to all the races with the proper equipment, the proper personnel, the proper training, with the ability to extinguish a fire.

Prior to any case going to trial, the parties meet in pre-trial arbitration. During our session, we put that proposal on the table. If the World of Outlaws would commit to forming such a traveling safety safari, we were prepared to drop the lawsuit.

But they wanted no part of that, and weren't interested in those conditions at all. Maybe they thought they were sure to win, or maybe they didn't want to incur the expense, I don't know what their reasoning was. I think some of the issue was that Ted Johnson of the World of Outlaws didn't want to have Doug Wolfgang telling him how to deal with safety in his series, which I understand.

I wish the circumstances could have been different but there we were, sitting at the table trying to avoid going to trial. I was absolutely prepared to settle out of court on two conditions: one, they commit to funding the traveling safety team, and two, pick up my remaining medical bills. That's all I wanted. I would have accomplished my goal of changing the way the sport looks at safety.

A lot of people at the time had no idea of this behind-the-scenes stuff. They just saw this as another guy trying to scam the system, trying to hold somebody up for money. That's where I was very frustrated. I felt that much of the media clearly dropped the ball in covering the story. They had the power of the press, and they presented the position that I was wrong because I was suing auto racing for millions of dollars.

In fact, anybody who had done some basic investigative reporting would have known that you can't get "millions" in Kansas because of the liability cap. You can't get $7 million for dumping a cup of coffee in your lap; it can't be done. In other states, maybe, but not Kansas. This was never brought out in the newspaper or magazine stories, and it led people to form opinions when they didn't have all the facts.

When we did go to court, do you know how many reporters were there to cover the proceedings? None. Zero. People would write stories and columns saying what a scumbag I was, when they weren't willing to cover the story and get the facts. And that ain't fair.

If you're not going to cover the story, fine. I understand you don't want to go to the expense of sending a reporter to Kansas City. But if you're not going to cover the *entire* story—and I mean going to the effort to uncover facts and report them objectively—then don't cover it at all. Don't present only one side, and make me out to be a jerk who is trying to ruin auto racing. That wasn't accurate and it wasn't fair. I feel very strongly about that. The way it played out just wasn't right.

Along about the time this was all happening, O.J. Simpson was the talk of every news program after he was found not guilty in October of 1993. It seemed that everybody in the United States knew O.J. was guilty. Except me. And the reason they all knew he was guilty because they read it in the newspaper and heard about it on the news. They were totally convinced he did it. Which he may have, I don't know. But because they formed their opinion based on what they learned from the press, I was skeptical.

I witnessed firsthand what the press can do to you. I saw what they did to me in my court case. They took national magazines and made me a butthead. That's the power they have.

The trial spanned a couple of weeks, with dozens of people taking the stand. A complete sprint car was rolled into the courtroom as an exhibit to illustrate some of the specifics that were being discussed.

It was somewhat complicated, and very detailed. It was easy to get overwhelmed by all the information that was presented.

However, if I had to boil everything down to the simplest term, I would say we won the case on the very first day, when a very nice lady took the stand. She had been on the EMT crew at the track on the day of the accident.

This lady had been an EMT for many years at the time of the accident. But on the Monday following the crash, she walked into their office and quit her job. I had no idea this had happened, but the lawyers uncovered this along with many important facts.

Her testimony was very poignant. It almost made me cry. That poor woman was utterly traumatized by the experience of standing there watching me burn, and it was painful to hear her tell about it. I actually felt sorry for her, very much. That day literally changed her life. She never again worked as an EMT. She put it this way: "I took this job to help people, not to sit there and watch them die." She kept saying they were there to help me, but all they could do was stand there and scream, "Where are the firemen? Who is going to put out this fire?"

They were ready to do their job, but they had to stand by for eight-and-a-half minutes.

It wasn't just the matter of inadequate fire protection; it was the fact that it was all so elementary, so basic, and yet it happened. For example, to show you how inept the situation was, of the three guys on the fire crew that day, only one had received any training in firefighting. He wasn't a fireman, but had some training. The other two had none. They readily admitted this under oath. And when that fire got going, they didn't want anything to do with what they saw happening. It was way too catastrophic for them to deal with.

Was I mad at those firemen? Not particularly. They weren't really the problem. The *system* was—and is—the problem. How can a sport that prides itself on being professional hire these three men and say they're an adequate fire crew? As individuals, those men weren't bad guys. They didn't want me to burn to death. But the whole thing illustrates how amateurish and bush league racing is in some ways.

When somebody says a small little thing like, "Aw, that's racing," well, "that's racing" includes a lot. That covers a lot of amateur things, the bush league things of the whole system. And that's what I hoped to change.

There was a lot riding on this case. Many people in the media said that if I won the case, "racing would be destroyed as we know it." On the other hand, I stood to suffer a very significant financial blow if we lost.

At the bare minimum I would have been on the hook for $500,000 in legal fees. The case cost more than $100,000 up front, and that would have been lost. My total medical bills were something in the neighborhood of $800,000—it's hard to pinpoint because I still incur expenses from treatment and surgeries to this day—and my insurance covered $500,000. So we were also in line to pay maybe $300,000 in medical expenses that were beyond my insurance coverage.

Plus, my ability to make a living as a racer was finished, over. I could be marginally competitive at a much lower level, but any racer in the country will tell you it's impossible to make a living at that level. So not only was I in line for a significant financial hit if we lost, I did not have the capacity to earn money to cover it. See, in the past I could make money pretty easily as a professional racer. But now I was just a working man and a hobby racer, so how hard it is to earn $50,000, $100,000, $250,000? A whole lot harder for me than it used to be, I can tell you that.

Essentially, Jeri and I would have been broke for the rest of our lives. No doubt about it. So we were very anxious about what the outcome was going to be.

I've said a hundred times, my lawsuit was not about the money. But if you really back me into a corner, yes, some of it was about money. That not why I filed; that was never the first thing on my mind. But as the trial progressed and the expenses continued to pile up, the money was very much a worry for us. Plus my medical future was very uncertain at that moment. We knew there would be many reconstructive surgeries in the years to come but nobody could tell us how many or how much they would cost. So the money was important in a literal way, but it was never first and foremost in my mind.

Was I nervous about losing? No, because I never allowed myself to think about it. Other than I understood very clearly that we *might* lose. We really didn't know the outcome right down to the bitter end.

Plus, we were the plaintiff; the burden of proof was on us. We had to show beyond a shadow of a doubt to the entire jury that the defendants were guilty of gross, wanton negligence. If even one person on the jury isn't convinced, we've failed. That was a scary proposition, because you don't know what those people are thinking. You never know, not until they reach their verdict. And they make sure when they select the jury that we *don't* know what they're thinking. There were many people dismissed during the jury selection because they had remotely heard of me. It took all day long to pick a jury, maybe two days.

As the trial progressed, I never found it boring but it was hard for me to follow. Some things I didn't understand. But it was pretty damned interesting. Other stuff made me mad or hurt my feelings.

For example, Ted Johnson was on the stand and he said something to the effect of, "Well, Doug is 39 years old, did he expect to race forever?" That really hurt my feelings. I realize Ted was just trying to protect his position, but think about that: My ass got burned off, and he's basically saying, "Well, hey, at least you got to race for that long! But you wanted to race longer? Are you greedy or something?"

As the trial progressed the lawyers continued to pore over those 300 photographs, building a minute-by-minute case on what happened and why. More than 50 people were called to the stand to support this or that fact or position.

Those photographs were very important, because they were silent testimony of precisely what happened. When you go through a traumatic event your memory is often confused, and sometimes people testified that they remembered something-or-other but the photographs showed different.

In my eyes, it was all very obvious. All those photos show me sitting in that burning car, but often the firemen were in the background. It was my fellow racers, along with several brave onlookers, who eventually got me out of the car. In fact, I remember when one of the fire crew was on the stand our lawyer asked him to point out in any one of the photographs where he was actually lending assistance. He could not.

The whole thing was very depressing to me. For example, the track had a big water truck there, and after the fire started somebody thought to drive the water truck to my car and spray the fire out. But the water tank on the truck was empty. I sat there and wondered, "If only..." Maybe things could have been different.

The verdict came in on a Friday afternoon. We had been sitting around for two days while the jury deliberated, and suddenly they returned and everyone rushed into the courtroom to hear the verdict. The jury filed into the box and a foreman came forward.

The jurors had found that we had proven our case, and that the defendants were guilty of gross, wanton negligence. We had been awarded a judgment of $1.2 million, the maximum allowed by law.

The defense said they would immediately appeal. So we all stood up while the judge left the room and that was it. It was really quite anti-climactic. The first chapter was over.

Several of the jurors requested to talk to me following the announcement. They told me they didn't know anything about racing, but had come to be interested in the sport, and me, through this trial. They congratulated me on the verdict.

And then it was all over. Everyone began filing out of the room, and soon it was time to go. Jeri and I walked to our car in a nearby parking garage. We were standing near our car when a big Lincoln came rolling by. It was the judge.

He had apparently suffered from polio or some such ailment as a boy, and was able to walk only by utilizing two small aluminum crutch-type aids. I noticed this each day when he entered and exited the courtroom.

The judge stopped, and rolled down his window and I walked over.

We had seen the judge every day for three weeks, but he was not someone you could get to be friends with because of the situation. But I liked him, respected him. He was professional and fair and I believed he was trying to do the right thing by the law.

The judge looked at me, and for a moment neither of us spoke.

"Son, from the very beginning I could sense that you were doing this for the right reasons," he finally said. "You weren't here because of the money, and I admire that."

"Thank you."

"Congratulations on the verdict," he said.

I thanked him again.

He kind of chuckled, and pointed to a tall building across the river in Kansas City, Mo.

"You see that building there, that tall one? Do you know what that building is?"

I said I didn't.

"That's the courthouse over there, and if your accident would have happened in Missouri, that's where your trial would have been held."

"Really?"

"If your trial had been in that building, the verdict would have been about $7 million," he said. I noticed that he was studying my face as he spoke. "Not that it matters."

I just smiled.

"No, it doesn't matter," I said.

I thanked him, and we shook hands. He rolled up his window and in a moment his Lincoln was out of sight. Jeri and I got into our car and drove away, headed north on Hwy. 29 toward Sioux Falls. The long, draining trial was over. The rest of my life awaited.

28

Aftermath

Through the years that followed the lawsuit, a few people have asked if I felt a sense of relief that day as the verdict was read. Not really. I was glad the trial was over, but I didn't feel any particular sense of accomplishment. Of course there was an immediate appeal, so it wasn't over. It wasn't like winning a main event and they write you a check for $1.2 million; it was much more complicated.

The appeals process eventually took another year, maybe 18 months. I wasn't involved in any of those proceedings, and didn't travel to any courtrooms. They were just arguing technicalities, I guess.

The verdict was upheld on appeal, and eventually in early 1997 the judgment was paid. It had been almost five years since the accident at Kansas City.

After that I just tried to move on. There were occasional letters and things from people who were very critical of me, calling me names and so forth, but I tried to distance myself from all that, and avoided situations where it might happen.

The strong feelings and negative feedback didn't really surprise me, partly because my attorney warned me ahead of time that it was likely to happen. I don't know if I was fully prepared mentally, but at least I had a heads-up that it was coming. I would have been in total denial to not see it coming, in fact. He said, "These are the facts of life…this is the 11th commandment, son. You will go to the ground."

I was very sour on the media at that point. I wasn't interested in interviews or that kind of thing, and didn't talk to anyone for quite some time. I stopped reading all racing publications, and pitched almost all the issues I had accumulated at my house, including every copy of *National Speed Sport News* from about 1964 to 1995.

I went through a lot of very difficult days from 1992 to 1996 or so. When I first woke up after my crash, I suffered from a serious depression, and my emotions were up-and-down for a long time.

One day when I was feeling particularly bad about things, I loaded up almost all of my racing stuff in my truck. Trophies, helmets, memorabilia, piles of stuff. I drove out to the city dump, backed my truck up to a big pile, and swept that stuff right out of my truck. I got back into the cab and drove away, and did not look in the rear-view mirror.

I regret that very much. I wish I had that stuff back. But I was feeling so blue, so sad, so despondent, so angry, that was the way I vented my emotions. I was mad that I was so scarred, I was mad that I still had a lot of pain, I was mad that people wrote letters to me saying how much they hated my guts…I was just *mad*. Even though I tried to put up this big armor barrier around my emotions, and act like nothing bothered me, deep inside I was really hurting.

I couldn't understand why people hated me, when I was trying to do something to ultimately make the sport better, to help protect guys coming along behind me from the hell I went through. And then to have people say they hated me because of it…I could not connect the dots, I really couldn't.

Taking my stuff to the dump was my way of lashing out at the sport. If the sport hated me, well, then, I'll hate the sport right back. It didn't work, of course. I love racing, and I'll love racing until I die. As time passed I came to realize that as complicated as everything was, I knew I did the right thing by standing up for what I believed was right.

If you had asked me in late 1995 about things, I would have told you that my situation was never going to change. It was clear that some people were totally against me, and it would be that way forever. It was never going to get any better.

But I was wrong about that, because time changes things. I softened up in my views of the world, and as the years passed the hate mail quietly subsided. I guess people rethink things, or maybe they just lose interest and forget.

For example, during his playing career in the NBA, Charles Barkley was viewed as the biggest smart-ass out there, and a lot of people didn't like him. But then one day he retired from playing, and faded from the scene, and people forgot about him being a smart-ass. Then a while later when he started doing some television work, and had toned it down a little, all of a sudden he wasn't a bad guy at all. People *liked* him being a smart-ass, because he was funny and sometimes made a lot of sense. So it seems that anything is possible if you give it some time. Today by and large I don't have much negative feedback. Most people who know me don't say anything about the trial. It's like they forgot about it. It didn't have much of an impact on anything.

And that, boys and girls, is the unvarnished truth. In the long and short of everything, my lawsuit didn't really have an impact on anything.

Does that surprise me? Yes, absolutely. Because I was sure that a verdict in our favor would have forced the sport to examine how a track should be prepared to fight a fire.

But in fact nothing changed. You can still burn up in a race car today because a track does not have adequate firefighting personnel and equipment. Not every track, of course; let me be very clear on that. But there are still too many tracks where fire preparation—and a lot of other things related to safety—is an afterthought.

There were people who predicted that if I won the lawsuit, it would "end racing as we know it." They said it would destroy the sport. Those guys were wrong, too. My lawsuit didn't have the effect I thought it would, nor the effect they thought it would. In the end it was nothing more than a tiny hiccup.

It did have a small effect at first, and it seemed like a few people wanted to look at the issue and see what could be done. Or at least they were thinking about it. But then it seemed the topic faded in terms of interest.

In fact, I think things might be worse today than in 1992. I have a very strong suspicion of that. Think about it: It costs so much more money to do business these days, and it's hard for any small business to make it. Running a race track is one of the most challenging businesses out there, and it's not hard to imagine that at some tracks corners are being cut in order for the business to survive. There are still no laws, no rules, no guidelines that track operators are required to follow in terms of safety. There is still not a traveling safety team with any short-track series today.

That's when I feel a sense of futility. A sense that it's hopeless. Because the fact is, when it comes to safety and being prepared for the worse, you're on your own. The rest of the world isn't really looking out for your best interests. That's just how it is. When you've got it on your mind, it's your deal, but the rest of the world is thinking about a different agenda. Not your agenda, but a different agenda. I don't care how you look at it, it's true.

Want to know something? If I had it all to do over again, I would not file the lawsuit. It definitely was not all it was cracked up to be. People think I got a pile of money; when it was all said and done, my net was about $700,000. And I would have much rather raced for that $700,000. When you consider the anxiety, the emotions, the heartache of going through the lawsuit, and the fact that it didn't bring change to the sport like I wanted it to, it simply wasn't worth it.

But at least I know I did what I felt was right. That much I can hang my hat on.

The entire episode reinforced my belief that the world is sometimes kind of hard, kind of tough, and it's impossible for everyone to be nice and friendly to each other. Even though I want things to be on a friendly basis, the hard world doesn't work like that.

For example, Tom Nicholson, the attorney here in Sioux Falls who referred me to other trial lawyers, is still a friend of mine. From the beginning, Tom said I had to get an attorney licensed in Kansas, and he made the referrals. Once he made the referral, he was out of the case. On two occasions he traveled to Kansas City with me, and I drove and paid the gas and bought our meals. On a couple of occasions my Kansas City lawyers came to Sioux Falls for depositions and things, and they set up in Tom's office. Other than that, Tom was not involved.

When we eventually received the judgment proceeds, Tom was paid $60,000 for making the referral. That ain't a bad wage for two trips to Kansas City and letting somebody use your office for a couple of days, wouldn't you say?

A couple of years ago I needed some routine legal work done—some title work or something like that—and I asked Tom to take care of it. He did, and then he sent me a bill.

Now, I'm not telling this story to complain, and certainly not to badmouth Tom, not in any way. But the point is this: In this big, hard old world, business is business. We're friends, and my case helped Tom make a tidy amount of money, but that doesn't mean I'm entitled to free legal work for the rest of my life.

It's like when I first started racing, I wanted the world to be like this: Me and the car owner and our mechanics would be good friends, we'd all like each other and go have hamburgers together after the races. On Sunday afternoon I'd want 'em all to come to my house for lunch. That's what I thought the world should be like. But it didn't take me long to discover that ain't how it is. That's not real life. That's la-la land. Real America ain't la-la land.

So if you ask me if I've toughened up a little bit along the way, I'd say yeah, I have. I'm a little rugged on the edges, much more than I wanted to be. I like things to be easy, friendly, generous, kind, nice. But it can't be that way all the time. Business is business. Life ain't peaches and cream.

Maybe that's my defense mechanism kicking in, to help me survive. You figure people care about you, and think everybody is nice, and then you discover that lots of times people don't really care all that much. That hurts my feelings, so from now on I'll assume nobody cares, and that way I won't get my feelings hurt again.

But I'm not quite that hard yet. I still want to like everybody, and I want them to like me. I'd rather get pushed around now and then and have my feelings hurt than turn against the whole world. It's corny, but I like it better like that. I'd rather get abused now and then rather than get so hard I won't let anyone get close to me. I'd rather lighten up and run the risk of getting used now and then.

The good news is this, and I find it out more every day: Most people don't push you around or use you. Most people are genuinely cool. And I like that.

There were a lot of things written and said during and after the lawsuit, and it cost me some friendships. You didn't hear me say anything against anybody, but then again I wasn't doing any interviews at the time. When people started being very critical of me personally I probably would have blasted back a little bit, except that my lawyer said it wasn't good to do any interviews while the outcome was still uncertain.

Even after the trial was over, I didn't say much. I went about my business and kept my opinions to myself.

A couple of people were especially vocal about things, people who had been friends of mine. Cary Agajanian, for example, is a prominent lawyer who does a lot of work for race tracks and promoters. I had driven Cary's dad's car at Ascot several times, and considered him a friend. I was shocked and hurt when he was so vocal.

I also mentioned Dick Berggren earlier. Dick was another person whom I considered a friend and it hurt my feelings very much to have him write things that were so critical of me personally.

I bumped into Cary at Milwaukee during an IndyCar race a couple of years ago, and I got the impression he didn't want to have anything to do with me. That's fine, of course. I don't object. But if I saw Cary—or Dick, or anyone else—in the right setting I would have no problem offering a handshake and asking how things are going. I don't bear any grudges, I really don't. It's over and done with, behind us, water under the bridge.

Others might not feel that way, and I respect that. I would never force the issue. I'll just keep a low profile and let things go.

Ten years ago I couldn't have said that. I was still an angry person then, a bitter, disillusioned man. But time has a way of healing us, and that's been my experience. Today I can honestly say there are no hard feelings on my part toward anyone.

29

End of the Line

Part of the fallout from the Lakeside lawsuit was that my racing career was put on hold for almost two years. My attorneys told me it would be better if I kept a low profile, so I dropped out of sight. I concentrated on my chassis business, WolfWeld, back in Sioux Falls.

The layoff through 1994 and most of 1995 didn't hurt me much, actually. I was working hard in the gym, building my strength and stamina, and by the time the trial rolled around I was in fairly decent shape.

I had a setback along the way when my big toe got infected and they ended up having to amputate it. That was a tough recovery because it affected my balance, and I had to work a little bit to learn to walk properly again. That's part of the ordeal when you're badly hurt, because each reconstructive surgery means a recovery period. The surgery might only take an hour or two, but then you're in a cast for eight, 10, 12 weeks. That happened to me several times during 1994 and '95.

When the lawsuit was over Jeri and I got back to Sioux Falls, and I suppose I realized that for the first time in almost two years I had a life again. I didn't have to sequester myself in my shop any more. I had a complete race car sitting there, ready to go, and it seemed natural that I still felt an urge to go racing.

By this time I had probably built 15, 20 race cars, and was starting to pick up a little business here and there. One of my customers was Gary Zitterich, a guy from here in Sioux Falls. Right around the first of September Gary asked if I'd run his car at Rock Rapids, Iowa, for a two-day show. I had also talked with Buns Richardson and Ray Lipsey about getting back together with them.

I ran Gary's car at Rock Rapids in Iowa on a Friday night, and right away I noticed a couple of things the car needed. The brakes weren't quite right, so I fiddled with them a little bit, and sorted out a couple of other things. I piddled around and won that night, which I suppose surprised me as much as anybody.

A number of people got bent out of shape about me winning a race a week or so after my trial. They were angry, and took the position of, "He sued because he couldn't race any more, and he goes out right away and wins a race!"

I never, ever said I couldn't race any more. Nor did my lawyers ever say I couldn't race any more. Of course I could race…I won races in 1993, long before the trial. That wasn't the point at all.

My real motivation behind the lawsuit, as I've said before, was to force the sport to address the issue of fire safety more seriously. But in order to sue someone, first you have to show damages. My loss from the crash was that I could no longer make my living racing at the top level of the sport, which is obviously the World of Outlaws.

If I had won $100 million in my lawsuit, I still couldn't compete with the Outlaws. Nothing in the world could ever bring back my feet and legs and make me like I was before. Nothing.

But for people to get all riled up because I won a piddly weekly race at Rock Rapids, Iowa, and say I was as good as before, I don't really know how to respond to that. If that person can't see the obvious difference between winning at a local level and beating the best in the World of Outlaws on a consistent basis, I guess they just don't understand what sprint-car racing is all about.

It was so late in the 1995 season that I never really got going with Buns and Ray, so I wasn't sure what I wanted to do for 1996. In the meantime winter came and I got busy in the shop, building and repairing race cars. I was kind of enjoying this business thing. It kept my mind occupied and gave me a challenge. I liked it.

There was a local IMCA sprint car series that was going pretty good, basically an entry-level series. Feature races paid $400 to win, and the rules were very strict. They had an $800 claim rule on the engines, with the idea that guys would be hesitant to put a bunch of money in their engines just to watch them get claimed.

My friend Jack Trigg and I decided to build a car for the IMCA series, just to see what happened. More than anything it looked like fun. It wasn't serious in terms of blood-and-guts competition, but it was a bunch of guys who loved to race but didn't have tons of money.

Jack and I built this little IMCA limited sprint car, and started racing. I didn't have any notions that I'd get any better, not when I started. But as I started racing every week and really getting into it, it wasn't long before at *that* level of racing I was Doug Wolfgang again. We won 26 out of 41 races in 1996.

It made me feel weird to be in a beginner class, but I had convinced myself I wasn't good enough to be a pro again, and of course the mental aspect of racing is huge. If you don't think you can do it, you can't. So it didn't really bother me that I was racing at this entry level, because I didn't care what anybody else might have thought.

Naturally, when we started winning there was some controversy, even among some of my friends here in town. My engines got claimed several times, and the guys making the claims were expecting to get World of Outlaws-level 410 engines for $800. They quickly realized that my engines were as big a piece of shit as everybody else's. We spent the absolute bare minimum to put those things together. We had cast iron blocks, crankshafts, two-bolt-mains, stock rods, flat-top pistons; it was all very basic stuff.

I had some help with some of the pieces and parts, that's true. I still knew a lot of people, after all. But we built those things ourselves, and built them as cheaply as we possibly could, right down to the penny. Then we tuned them up to run good. See, that was worth a lot, because my experience helped me understand fuel systems, timing, magnetos, and things like that. Relatively speaking my engines hit hard, even though they were put together with basic parts. But they were running free, and nice. They wouldn't have lasted forever, of course, because sooner or later all of 'em blow up. And luckily we only blew one up, because the rest all got claimed first.

But we hung in there and won the championship. How about that! The great Doug Wolfgang wins the limited IMCA sprint-car championship in Sioux Falls! People probably made fun of me, but I didn't care. I was having fun and it felt good to be racing again.

By this time it had been more than four years since my accident, and I was clearly past the idea of ever being a pro again. I had accepted the reality of the situation, you might say.

I had discovered something very important, but it was a sad discovery. It was one of those things that should have been obvious, but it wasn't. It took me a long time to fully realize and understand what had happened.

I haven't told this to many people, and to be honest it's difficult to talk about. But for me to tell my full story I guess it's only right that I talk about it honestly here.

It all stems back to the first time I got into a race car, back in the days when I drove for Darryl Dawley in that first modified. I was young, and adventurous, and I wanted the idea of getting into a race car to get me so charged up that it made my palms sweaty with excitement. That's what I wanted. I was a thrill-seeker, you might say. I wanted a race car to be the best thrill ride in the whole world.

But I was actually disappointed. They looked so fast from the grandstand, and I thought it would scare me. I *wanted* it to scare the absolute dog piss out of me. But it didn't. Even in Darryl's car, I realized that the faster I went, the more things seemed like they were coming at me in slow motion.

At first I hated it, and of course I still overdrove the race car at times and crashed, because the cars can only do so much. I didn't have enough sense to realize I was going that fast.

But the whole racing experience just wasn't that big of a deal to me, because everything seemed easy, like slow motion. Not fast, but s-l-o-w-w-w-w-w. I was almost, at one point early in my career, ready to quit because the whole deal wasn't very exciting. You know, "This ain't all it's cracked up to be."

And then one day, many years later, it came to me: I had been given a gift. My brain was somehow wired so that no matter how fast things were happening in front of me on the race track, everything got processed in slow motion. I had an ability to see things very clearly, and to mentally know what was going to happen even before it happened. I know it sounds weird, but it's true.

For example, during one period we were using two-way radios when I raced with the World of Outlaws. Sometimes I would radio my crew, "Look down toward turn three, because there's gonna be one helluva crash there on the next lap." And sure enough somebody was doing the end-over-end thing. I could envision it one lap before it actually happened.

I began to understand that things came to me differently than maybe some of the other guys. It probably took me 20 years to fully get onto this, but as time passed I understood it more clearly, and tried to channel it properly and use it to help me race. I realized it truly was something special, and that's exactly how I looked at it: It was a gift from God.

But guess what? When I got hurt, the gift from God was gone. Where everything had come to me in slow motion, and was easy to process in my brain, now everything was coming at me in fast motion. And my brain was behind the processing point all the time. It was like I was in a foreign country and didn't understand the language. I was just lost.

After all those races I had run, and all the stuff I had experienced, now things were coming at me so fast I couldn't deal with it. Even with my level of experience I was completely over my head.

As I slowly progressed in the years after my crash, it did get just a little better. I got to where I wasn't completely lost, but it was never, ever like it had been before.

Other guys might have had this same gift, I don't know. I've never brought this up to anyone. Or maybe they're like me; they have the gift, but don't recognize what it is. It seems natural so they think everyone can see things in slow motion.

A gift from God is sometimes fleeting. There's no guarantee you'll have it forever. In time I realized that the gift was gone and was never coming back, and while that made me very sad, it helped a lot when I could finally accept it. I didn't feel sorry for myself, and could actually think in the right way of being grateful for all the years I had it instead of crying that it had been taken away.

After my season in the IMCA limited class I hadn't thought much about my future in the sport. I was 44 years old, definitely no spring chicken. I felt like I was getting a little better, and began to wonder if maybe I could be competitive in a 410-inch sprint car.

Dan Motter of Minnesota had been a longtime friend of mine, and Dan campaigned a car on the Outlaws tour with Stevie Smith as his driver. Dan and I would talk on the phone every now and again, and then one day I heard Dan and Stevie were parting ways. I might have called Dan, or maybe he called me, I don't remember. But the gist was I had sold my IMCA car, and wasn't sure what I was going to do. Dan was also unsure of his plans, so maybe we could go racing together.

The whole idea was pretty intriguing to me. I was ready for another challenge, I think. I didn't want to run the World of Outlaws circuit, because I wasn't interested in the travel and night in and night out, I couldn't compete with those guys. I just couldn't.

Somehow in my conversations with Dan we decided to get together, and our schedule would include running every Saturday night at Knoxville and every Sunday here at Huset's. My proposal was that we would field the car out of my shop, and Jack and a couple of other guys would mechanic it.

Dan wasn't sure about that. He had always kept his race car close by, and I think he had some reservations. I totally understood, and respected that. Not much more was said that winter, and I kind of figured Dan wasn't interested after all.

But he called and told me that's what he wanted to do. He said some very kind things about having always admired me from a distance, and that he was excited about having me drive his car. He also said he wanted me to drive with this in mind: If I felt like I was making progress, and wanted to try the World of Outlaws the following season (1998), he would try to find a sponsor. I said that's fine; if I feel I'm up to it, that's what we'll do.

We got going that spring, and actually won a race at Knoxville in the 410 class. I'll never forget winning that race, because when I got to the front straightaway after the race everyone was cheering. For a moment, it was like being the great Doug Wolfgang again. Just for a moment. It really was a special feeling, maybe because I never thought I'd experience it again.

I saw a friend of mine, A.J. Mottit (he runs the Dingus Lounge in Knoxville), and his girlfriend was crying. I thought they were so excited that I got them teared up, and that was cool. But then Jeri came to victory lane from where she had been sitting in the Hall of Fame suites with Allie and Robby, who were still very young kids.

Jeri had tears running down her cheeks, and I instantly knew something was wrong. *Very* wrong. She had just gotten word that her dad had passed away. I just cut the winner's interview off right away, and got right into our car and drove back home, through the night, so we could be with her mother. I'll always remember it as not just the last race I won at Knoxville, but one of the saddest days of my life.

I was happy that I had won, but I was also concerned about a reconstructive surgery on my left Achilles tendon that was scheduled right around that time. I had a cast up to my knee for a while, so just when I got to the point where I was encouraged a little bit I was on the sidelines, plus Jeri's dad died. It was a tough couple of weeks.

I had also hooked up with another friend of mine, Mark Burch, to drive his 360 sprint car when my schedule allowed. A 360 car has 50 cubic inches less than the 410-inch car, and they typically race for quite a bit less money. But I quickly found that I really enjoyed running Mark's car. I don't know if it was because maybe the competition wasn't as intense or whatever, but everything seemed to suit me. Plus, I had the busiest schedule since my 1992 crash, and all that track time was making me a little bit sharper.

I won some races in Mark's car, and continued doing okay in Dan's 410. I was never again a standout at Knoxville, although we made the trip to the Nationals in August and I made the championship event on Saturday night. I was better at Huset's, and won probably seven or eight features for Dan that summer.

I'm not sure why I couldn't get back on track at Knoxville. We started the year with a Hoosier Tire sponsorship, but Dan was a World of Outlaws guy and he wanted to go to Goodyear. We made the switch but discovered it didn't help us any.

It was actually at the Nationals when I came to the conclusion that I was finished driving 410 cars. I had decided that it was more fun in the 360s, and at this point since I'm not gonna be a pro, why not just have fun? I was better on top of a car in a 360 than in a 410, and it seemed that time had finally passed me by.

I guess I was starting to revert back to my old-old self, the guy who would beat himself up over every mistake. In the back of my mind I was telling myself that I was all right, but I just wasn't as much as I should be. It was the mental game again. It ain't the car, it ain't the tires, it's me. I'm the weakest link.

The fact is, everything in the sport had changed, and I hadn't changed with it. The engines were different, the tires were different, the cars were different. Not much, but enough that I was behind. If I would have just eased up and felt what the car was doing, and responded accordingly, I would have been better. But I was trying to race in 1997 with a 1992 setup, and forcing myself to learn how to drive differently. If I would have just shut up with the mental anguish and paid attention to what the car was trying to tell me, I probably would have been all right. Not a stud, but better than I was.

Pretty soon I was telling myself that I couldn't drive worth a damn any more. The more I kept telling myself that, the less I progressed. That was a big part of my problem.

I had made a commitment that I'd run Dan's car for the full season, so that was my plan. Finish up with him, then focus on 360s with Mark Burch from here on out. That's where I would finish out my career, I figured.

But then I got dumb. Instead of finishing out the season at Knoxville and Huset's and calling it quits with Dan, I decided we would travel a little bit through that autumn. I hadn't told anyone yet that this was my last few weeks in 410 racing, only Jeri.

We decided to try a couple of All Stars races. The first was at I-96 Speedway in Michigan, where I made a dumb mistake by touching an inside guardrail while racing for the lead with my friend Keith Kauffman. I should have won, but I messed up. The next night we ran at Findlay, Ohio, where we were just okay.

The next weekend I won two 360 races in Mark's car at Eagle, Neb., which reinforced my decision to concentrate on 360s the next season. But just a few more All Stars races…

Jeri and I vacationed for a few days in Las Vegas, and the plan was to fly home early on Friday and drive to Granite City, Ill. (near St. Louis), on Sept. 20 for a Saturday-night race. We would arrive home, hop in our motorhome when the kids got home from school, and make it a leisurely drive. Jack and the guys would have the car waiting at the track.

Everything went wrong. Our flight was delayed, and we didn't get back to Sioux Falls until 12:30 a.m. Saturday. We hurried right to the motorhome to begin the 10-hour drive to Granite City, stopping in Des Moines to catch some sleep. The whole deal was a bad omen from the beginning.

We blew our engine in hot laps, and had to thrash to get it changed. I got one qualifying lap at the end of the order, and it seemed like the whole night was going to hell. They had a red flag with five laps to go in the feature, and I was hanging on to seventh or eighth, not going anywhere.

While we waited for the restart I was thinking I might finish fifth, or maybe even fourth. We restarted and Gary Wright blew a tire in front of me, and I clipped his right rear. My car jumped into the air and kind of spun around, and another guy hit me hard and flipped me over backward.

I lost track of maybe two or three seconds of time, and don't remember anything after I touched Wright's car. The next thing I know is that my car had landed on its wheels, and I'm sitting there, completely awake. A piece of dirt was in my eye, and my brain told my hand to lift up my visor and flick this piece of dirt from my eye. But I couldn't do it, because I couldn't feel my arms or legs.

My hands were on the steering wheel, and my brain continued to tell my hands to move, but nothing was happening. I'm thinking, "Come on, let's rock here, let's get this piece of dirt out of my eye!" But nothing was happening.

That's when I got this sinking little idea that something ain't cool here. I'm thinking, "Aw, no. Not again…"

I realized I couldn't feel my belts, or my butt. About that time my feet began to tremor and burn. My first instinct was, "Holy shit, now this thing is gonna catch on fire! I don't *need* to be on fire!"

Right then a burning, shuddering feeling swept through my body, beginning in my feet, moving up my legs, through my midsection, and up my arms, out through the back of my hands. And then all of a sudden my feet weren't burning any more.

All of this happened in an instant, before the first safety worker approached the car. A matter of just a few seconds.

A guy ran up to the car and stuck his head in the cockpit.

"You all right?"

"Yeah, but don't jerk on this car."

"How come?"

"I think I broke my neck, and I don't want anybody to move this car."

"You sure?"

"I'm positive. Just don't let anybody move this car, please."

The safety team was right on top of things, and they did a great job of carefully removing me from the car. After the burning sensations subsided, I could feel my feet again. I was actually quite calm, considering I had narrowly missed a good chance to either kill myself or be paralyzed.

They got me to a local hospital, where X-rays determined that I had fractured a couple of vertebra in my neck and back. This was a very serious injury and was going to require extensive treatment.

Late that night a physician came to see me.

"Son, it's not my job to tell you what to do or what not to do," he said. "But we can tell from your X-rays that you've broken your neck before, in another spot.

"You probably should decide not to keep doing what you're doing."

I can clearly remember saying to him, "You don't have to tell me that, doc. I have already decided that I've had enough."

And I did. I had had enough. That was it for me. I didn't want to have to go through the rehabilitation that I did before, not again. I don't know exactly what I was feeling, because I was a sick dog. I got hit hard, and I wasn't operating too well. But I was thinking clearly enough to know that absolutely, positively, I was finished as a race-car driver.

Forget about it. No more 410s, no more 360s, no more racing, period. Don't matter if you're talking trying to be a pro or just putzing around for fun. I would not ever drive a race car again.

I was actually pretty messed up. I was hospitalized in St. Louis for about a week, then sent to Sioux Falls, where I spent another week in the hospital. I was on very strong pain pills, had severe headaches, and in general I was a complete mess. Within a day of the crash I was fitted with an orthopedic halo, which was a huge hindrance to deal with.

When they put the halo on they placed me in a ward with a bunch of guys who had suffered spinal injuries, all of whom had varying degrees of paralysis. Most were young guys, and they all wanted to die. That's all they talked about. They wanted me to help them die. They promised me money if I could make it happen. That was absolutely a very bad experience, seeing those young boys in that condition. God, it was heart-wrenching.

It took me a long time to feel good again. I don't know when I told Jeri that this one was it, but she knew. I hadn't come to my decision simply because of me, either. I could see what it was doing to my family. I could see a lot of pain in my children's eyes. Our oldest, Niki, was with us, and Allie was absolutely bawling. She was seven years old, and it was very traumatic for her.

I wasn't going to be a pro—I already knew this—and I was doing it for fun. It wasn't hard to figure out that it just wasn't worth it any more. The spending money I got from running like a hobbyist, it just wasn't worth it.

I remember lying there in the hospital the first night, beat all to hell, and closing my eyes to pray. "God, if you'll let me off just this one time, I promise I won't do this any more."

That was the end. He held up His end of the deal; I eventually recovered. And I've held up mine: Since that night at Granite City, I never raced again.

About a month later my mother died after fighting cancer. A few days after she had passed on, Jeri and I went to her apartment, along with a couple of her sisters, to go through her things. We sorted out a bunch of old photographs, and later that night took them back to our home.

That's when I did another dumb thing. Very dumb. I was still wearing the halo, but naturally I tried to act like a normal person even though I was far from it. I decided to carry this box of pictures downstairs to a storage room. I lost my balance on the stairs, and tried to quickly sit down so I wouldn't fall. But the box was too heavy and I tumbled backward.

The halo went through the wall behind the stairway, then was torn from my head. It broke my eyebrow sockets, and I had to go back to the emergency room again. They refitted the damned thing but I never again got comfortable with it. Of course, things could have been worse. *Much* worse.

That was a blue period. Losing my mom was difficult—my dad died in 1995 after a long, painful struggle with cancer—but then I had this accident, plus winter was setting in. It was a gloomy time.

In January 1999 Jeri and I were all set to celebrate our 25th anniversary. Hey! We made it for 25 years! That's really very cool. It was also cool that I was feeling better. I was scheduled to have the halo removed just a couple of days before our

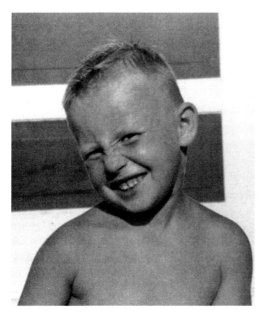

Summertime, and I'm about eight years old. I had an ornery look about me, didn't I?

A high school senior, facing the big ol' world without a clue!

In 1971 I finally got a break when Darryl Dawley let me
run his modified. This is our 1972 car, which I built.

Well, nobody could accuse me of not trying hard enough.
The key word here is, "Ooops!"

I wasn't a stud, but I did win a few races early on.

My boyhood pal Doug Clark helped out a lot on those old race cars. Ain't that a cool hat?

Don Maxwell was a very cool guy, and when he hired me to work in his Lincoln, Nebraska shop it was a big break for me. This photo is from around December, 1974.

Darryl Dawley was a great hero and mentor to me, and was also a great friend. This is Darryl in 1978.

On my way! Winning at East Alabama Motor Speedway with Bob Trostle in 1977. (Tony Martin)

Winning at Sedalia, Missouri in 1977. Left is Dub May, while a youthful Sammy Swindell is in the middle.

Cool glasses, eh? I wore glasses until I got gonked on the head in a crash in the late '70s and it corrected my vision.
(Gene Marderness)

Bob Trostle and I winning at the Florida Winternationals, 1977. That's Mary Tobias to my left. (Tony Martin)

I realized a lifelong dream at this moment. It's February, 1978, and my first outing in Bill Smith's Speedway Motors No. 4x.
(John Mahoney)

March, 1978, and the very first World of Outlaws race at the Devil's Bowl in Texas. I'm pictured with car owner Speedy Bill Smith, mechanic Tom Sanders, and good friend and racing writer Bill Hill.
(John Mahoney)

Winning the Knoxville Nationals in 1978. That's Paul
Pitzer on the left, runner-up Steve Kinser, myself, Jeri,
Eddie Leavitt, and announcer Jack Miller. (Kirby Laws)

Attacking
Eldora in 1978.
(Tony Martin)

Granite City, 1980, sharing victory lane with car owners Doug and Joanne Howells. (Tracy Talley)

Knoxville Nationals, 1981, and I'm preparing to warm up the car. I eventually finished third behind Steve Kinser and Sammy Swindell.
(John Mahoney)

Australia, 1979, and I won at the Sydney Showgrounds. That's Larry Burton on the far left, and see if you can also spot Steve Kinser and Jimmy Sills. Jeri is on my right, and our daughters Niki and Cori are in front holding the banner.

This is as close as I ever got to Indy. I'm trying on Sheldon Kinser's car in 1979.

I figured I'd win a lot more races in this car than I ultimately did. This is a World of Outlaws race at Grandview in 1983. (Jack Kromer)

Springfield, Illinois, 1982, and I'm running a USAC Silver Crown car for Bill King and Gary Stanton. That's my buddy Stanton in the red shirt. (John Mahoney)

Times were changing. This is how one of the top sprint car teams in the country went down the road in 1978... (John Mahoney)

...while five years later, this was the Gambler team's rolling operation. (Jack Kromer)

At speed in the Gambler car, 1983.

A very cool picture from I-70 Speedway in 1982. That's Shane
Carson in the cowboy hat, while Sammy Swindell is wearing a
spotless white uniform. (Shane Carson collection)

During my brief stint in the LaVern Nance house car, 1984.

Landing the Weikert Livestock ride was a huge break in my career.
This shot is from the Knoxville Nationals in 1984. (Max Dolder)

Bob Weikert and I share a conversation at Eldora Speedway's Kings Royal in 1985. (Jack Kromer)

Williams Grove, September 1985.

With Brad Doty at the Devil's Bowl, March 1985. (Max Dolder)

I can't say enough good things about these two guys. Davey Brown Jr. (L) and Sr. were great mechanics, and great friends. Our years together on the Weikert team were among the finest I ever experienced. (Jack Kromer)

Lealand McSpadden is truly one of the coolest guys I know. He's been a friend for more than 30 years and I enjoy talking to him at every opportunity. He was also one helluva race driver. (Tony Martin)

I was never a guy who wanted to just show up and drive. I wanted to be involved, and one of the reasons was that I enjoy working with my hands and staying busy. (Tony Martin)

Believe it or not, this is me! I'm at the Latimore Valley Fairgrounds in Pennsylvania, near the Eastern Museum of Motorsports. I'm wringing out a vintage racer, complete with open-face helmet and goggles, no roll cage, and racing in shirtsleeves. Wild! The guys who raced these cars back in the day were studs, for sure.

I'm pictured with two great Pennsylvania racers. Lynn Paxton is on the left, with the late, great Tommy Hinnershitz entertaining us.

Winning the Williams Grove National Open, 1984 or '85.
Victory lane sure is a happy place! By the way, the young
girl in the white jacket behind the car is Bobby Allen's
daughter Dana. (Marty Gordner)

If I had a time machine, I'd rewind to a moment just like this at Williams Grove in 1985. I'm talking strategy with Davey Brown Jr., and this photo reminds me of what a great friendship Davey and I enjoyed. We connected from the get-go, and this was probably the greatest period of my racing career. (Jack Kromer)

Manzanita Speedway, November 1988. It's the first event for the USA sprint car organization, and I ushered in the new deal by flipping out of the place. (Bill Taylor)

It's a whole new team: East Alabama Motor Speedway, March 11, 1989. It's my second outing in the brand new DP Motorsports car, pictured with Deuce Turrill, who put the team together. It was the single most successful season of my career, and was a very memorable and cool experience. (Max Dolder)

En route to winning at Flemington, New Jersey on May 31, 1989. (Max Dolder)

Checking out the surface at I-55 Raceway in Missouri in August with
Deuce and Robert Hubbard. Those guys were a major part of our
success as a team in 1989. (Max Dolder)

I was smiling *a lot* in
1989. (Jack Kromer)

Winning the Selinsgrove Nationals in 1989. Deuce sure
looks happy! (Jack Kromer)

When you race against Steve Kinser, you'd better bring your "A" game every night. This is Eagle Raceway in 1990, and I'm now in the Williams Bros. No. 8. (Jim Fleming)

In the Max Rogers-Bob Olsen car in 1991. (Jim Fleming)

Early 1994 in Florida, trying to come back after my 1992 accident.

This was my low-buck IMCA car in 1996.

The very last win of my career, at Eagle Raceway on Sept. 13, 1997, in Mark Burch's 360. It's cool that Robby and Allie were there to join me in victory lane. (Joe Orth)

With longtime friend Jack Trigg in my first WolfWeld Chassis shop.

Sept. 20, 1997, and my last ride in a sprint car. A few minutes after
this picture was taken I was badly injured, and that was the end.

(Mark Funderburk)

I'm grateful that throughout my career, the fans
have always been there.

In my Sioux Falls shop, putting together a
WolfWeld chassis.

Thirty years after he hired me to drive his sprint car (and
weld!), Bob Trostle is still my good friend. He stopped by
recently to visit my shop.

This, folks, is the center of my universe, the people who make
my life a wonderful place to be. From L-to-R:
Son-in-law Jarl Sjovold; daughter Cori Wolfgang Sjovold;
daughter Allie; grandson Alex Sjovold; myself; grandaughter Anni
Sjovold; wife Jeri; grandaughter Carly Wheeler; son Robby;
daughter Nicole Wolfgang Wheeler; grandson Carson Wheeler;
son-in-law Chris Wheeler. When all these people are together
in one place and I'm there, I'm lovin' it!

anniversary—January 6—so we decided to have a party at a local banquet hall.

It was a party with two reasons to celebrate. Obviously, our anniversary was the big deal, but we were also celebrating the conclusion of my racing career. See, I didn't have any second thoughts. I was 100 percent comfortable with my decision, and had no qualms about saying I really was done.

It was a wonderful night. I was feeling good because the halo was off, and my body was healing up quite nicely. I probably didn't look worth a shit, but I felt good. I had already gotten back into a fitness regimen, even when I still had the halo on. I was going to the gym every day, building my strength, and that really accelerated my recovery. I laugh when I think about being at the gym wearing that damned halo, sweating like a dog, working the Stairmaster. Guys would look at me and shake their head, saying, "Man, you *are* crazy!"

Many of our good friends came to the celebration. Bob and Dorotha Trostle, Bill and Joyce Smith, Phil and Mary Durst, and lots more. It was great to see all those people. They were more than former car owners or sponsors; they were friends. Plus a zillion of our friends from around Sioux Falls, and it was terrific to walk around the room and visit, and see all those smiling, familiar faces.

Second thoughts? I've never thought about getting back into a race car from that moment on. Not once. I've had several guys ask me to drive their car, even to this day. I don't know why they would, because they know I'm out of shape.

It was the first time in 24 years that I didn't look upon the upcoming summer and think about which car I was driving.

You know what? I guess, like anything else, at a certain point my thoughts changed and I got over the idea that I couldn't be Doug Wolfgang any more. You know, the big stud race driver. But enough time had gone on, I think, that I was beginning to like the new Doug Wolfgang.

At first I wouldn't give the new one a chance. I was angry, and bitter, and resentful, so I spent too much of my time thinking about what I *wasn't*, instead of looking forward to decide what I was going to do with the rest of my life.

What was different about the new guy? He was more calm, more likable. Through a big part of my life I could live on four hours of sleep, and the 20 hours I was awake I was consumed with being the best race driver I could be.

I was consumed with racing and I expected a great deal from myself, every day. That makes you hyper-competitive. You're on top of it all the time, because you think you have to be. But this new guy, he knew how to relax a little bit and let life come at him easier, gentler. If it snowed a foot and you can't run today, no big deal. Get over it. Don't sulk and rant and rave because you missed a workout. Matter of fact, relax and look around. You might find out you like other things, different things. Things you never noticed before, because you went through your life with blinders on.

My entire life had changed, one final time. I had been evolving steadily for a lot of years as I matured and my family grew up, but this time the change was profound. Stepping away from being a race driver literally changed me as a human being.

That night was like a new set of gates opened up for me, and a whole new world was on the other side. No kidding. Something swept over me, and it was like 24 years of tension just eased away.

I didn't have to prove anything any more, at least not to myself. I had a great wife, four great kids, a ton of friends, and all things considered my health was okay. I was a little crispy here and there, but I felt pretty good and life was all right.

It's kind of like that silly cliché: Today is the first day of the rest of your life.

The great Doug Wolfgang was gone. All but buried. The new guy had finally, officially taken his place. I wasn't the star any more. I was just a guy who went to work in the morning at his shop, building and fixing race cars. Instead of being the star, I was a husband. A father. A friend. A neighbor. No big deal, just another guy.

The day finally came when I was officially, totally, no longer a race driver, and never would be one again. Even though just about every racer denies this, the fact is the sun still came up in the morning in the East and later that day set over the Western horizon. Nothing of consequence had really changed. The world kept right on going without a hiccup.

You might not believe this, but...I liked it! It felt pretty damn good. All the anger and bitterness was gone...for good!

30

Life After Racing

My "retirement" party was about nine years ago, and life has hummed right along for me and my family. I'm actually pretty lucky in that when I decided it was time to quit, I had something to fall back on, which in my case was building and repairing race cars.

My business, WolfWeld, is as big as I care for it to be. I'm not into it to make a lot of money. If I wanted to make money at this business I'd expand and build 200 cars a year, running three shifts and five welders, four or five CNC milling machines, and so forth. That's how you make money, by mass production and getting your product out there. I could probably get out there and market it, but I don't really care to do that.

Instead, I'm happy building 15, 18 cars a year and taking in repair work. That's enough to keep me busy, along with my friend Jack Trigg, who comes to the shop most days to help out. Jack has been a lifelong friend who also enjoys this kind of work, and we enjoy each other's company.

When it comes right down to it, I like to be in the shop, and I like to work with my hands. I don't want to use the phone all day to keep 10 people working. That's how it's done. As far as business goes, I'm not really into business. Yes, I have to approach my work as a business, but I want to work at my pace. Now, I work hard; there are many days when I work 12, 13 hours a day. But there are other days that if I want to go home at noon and mow my lawn, I can do that. If Robby wants to go ride motorcycles, we go.

I'm probably not as good at customer relations as I ought to be. I enjoy people, and I'm definitely not rude to anyone, but sometimes I'm too blunt, too direct with my assessments of things. If a guy is asking me why his car isn't working, sometimes I might tell him it's because he isn't developed enough yet as a driver. Of course nobody wants to hear that. Everyone in racing today seems to think it's all about the race car.

I say that with authority because that's how I used to think. When I raced you couldn't convince me that I didn't need the very greatest and latest stuff. I was obsessed that the next guy might have some kind of mechanical advantage through some trick piece, so I had to have that trick piece. If I didn't have it, I was convinced I was beaten before I even got into the car.

I wasn't alone. Lots of racers still think that way today. If in their mind they think you've got to have a Maxim chassis to win, then they'd better get into a Maxim or they're going to struggle.

This sounds weird coming from a car builder, but it ain't the car. It's the driver. That's still the most critical component in sprint-car racing, and probably in most other forms of racing.

One thing that has not changed in racing in 30 years is that it's mostly mental. Most of the customers I have—and I expect it's the same with Chuck Merrill at Maxim or Brian Schnee at Schnee, Jack Elam at J&J, or Jerry Russell at Eagle—are interested in the physical equipment they get, and why it is or isn't good. And I believe the equipment out there today is nearly equal, so it's a matter of whether that driver wants to badly enough. It still matters if you really want it or not. I'm positive of that.

Somebody asked me the other day, "What is it about your chassis that attracts customers?"

I think it's because I build a nice car that's proven to be good. They look at my workmanship and see that it's fitted nicely, it's welded with concern, and I'm right here in town where they can get service. Not just nuts-and-bolts service, but advice and guidance. I'm here at the shop, and I'm accessible. They can call me or come by and discuss what the car's doing, what's working and isn't working, and we can talk about several ways to make it better. Usually we can get 'em going.

In dirt racing it's never cut-and-dried with regards to what works. However, I can almost always tell you what's *not* gonna work. There are certain things that will work for sure, so I usually begin a process of elimination to narrow it down to what will work for that particular racer.

In terms of the business, I'm a very tiny player. The big guys build hundreds of cars each year, and I build 18. Most of those companies promote their products by giving away stuff to the top guys in hopes that people will see how good they're going, and will then want to buy one for themselves.

It was the same when I was racing. When I was doing all right, a lot of people would approach me about using their products. They would give it to me free, and after a while you figure out this must be valuable for these manufacturers because they're awfully eager to have you run their part. So when I needed something I was not shy about asking for a free deal.

I see things from a little different perspective today. When a young boy comes to me—and I do get approached from time to time—and tells me I need to give him a chassis, my question is this: What has he produced so far? What has he put up in terms of numbers to justify someone giving him a deal? If he's a young boy, probably not very much. The fact is, I had to buy my stuff when I was starting out.

But what if someone very successful wanted a free chassis in order to promote WolfWeld? Let's say Terry McCarl, for example, came to me and wanted to get a free chassis. I'd have to tell Terry I just can't do it. I'm not into mass production. I just want to build 15 to 18 cars a year. I'm not overpriced, and I'm not cheap. But if I gave two or three cars away each year, I'd have to build a lot more cars to get the money back for those two or three. And a successful guy like Terry might sell me a hundred cars. But I don't want to build a hundred.

So when guys come to me looking for a free program, I send them to Jerry Russell or Brian Schnee or Jack Elam or Chuck Merrill. I'll be glad to sell 'em one, but I'm just too small to do the free deal.

The other day I got a phone call from a kid in Florida who somehow wound up with one of my WolfWeld chassis. Bought it used from a guy, so forth, you know the drill. This boy was a pretty good little local racer, and he was trying to figure out some things on my car that he didn't understand. He was more familiar with another type of car, and he was trying to learn what my car liked in terms of setup and adjustments.

I probably spent 45 minutes on the phone with the guy, talking about what the car was doing. He was very excited because right off the bat he figured out some things that will probably help him quite a bit. I told him to call me after he ran the car again this coming weekend, and tell me how the car worked, and we'll try to help it even further.

He had a lot of enthusiasm in his voice and you could tell how eager he was for the weekend to get here, because he was bustin' to go racing. It was really cool. I can hear myself through guys like him in those conversations, because that's how I used to feel.

Never mind that I don't make a dime from that boy. That's not the point. First of all, it's still my chassis, and I feel a responsibility to provide service and support, whether he's the original owner or not. Most of all, though, I enjoy the process. I really like talking specifics with somebody, and thinking of ways to help set the car up to someone's different style, or for a particular race track. It's cool.

I don't get all ate up on making money, anyway. I'm never going to be a wealthy person. That's fine, because Jeri and I don't have a lavish lifestyle. We're like any other family in that our primary expenses are our home and providing for our kids.

When I started my chassis business it was mostly to have something to do with myself each day. To have a purpose, you might say. It wasn't a matter of making a lot of money, it was about having a reason to get out of bed in the morning.

It turned out to be okay, and I've made a decent living. I had to, because the stock market changed a helluva lot from 1996 to 2006. You can't just sit on some money and coast any more, because it costs too much to live. We were at 90 cents for a gallon of gas not all that long ago, and now it's over three bucks.

We had a little bit of money in the bank, but a lot went to medical expenses and just plain living. So pretty soon I had to look at myself as a working man who needed to have a business of some kind to at least bring in some money.

But I'm very much okay with that. I like working in the shop, so I don't dread my work at all. I feel good about going to work each morning. That makes me a lucky, lucky guy. If you can be in business for yourself and like what you do, and manage to provide for your family, what more can you ask for?

My situation is somewhat unusual because my brother-in-law, Brian Schnee, is also in the chassis business right here in Sioux Falls. Things sometimes get awkward with family when it comes to business, but it doesn't seem to bother me or Brian. We get along great. We don't see each other a lot, but we talk on the phone fairly frequently.

Brian is a very hard worker. He and his wife, Jean, who is Jeri's younger sister by 10 years, are really good people. Jean was a nine-year-old flower girl in our wedding, and now she's a 40-something mother of two whose oldest son is out of high school and off on his own. Our family has grown, too, as our older daughters married and had children, so we now have our own Christmas and Thanksgiving celebrations, as do Jean and Brian. It's the natural thing as families and their children mature.

Brian's philosophy about the chassis business is very different than mine. Brian's business is much larger, and he builds a lot of parts. He's really gotten after it, and he's built a bunch of race cars, probably 750 by now. It's kind of amazing when you think about it. He has CNC machines, and he's a self-taught welder as well as a self-taught operator of the computerized CNC machines. Nobody helped him much, he did it on his own. I have the utmost respect for him. And he builds fantastic race cars, his workmanship is second to none.

When I got hurt, people asked me, "Why don't you just go to work for Brian?" The answer is simple: I was a self-employed race driver my entire life, and I don't feel comfortable as an employee. Even with Brian, who I first met as a snot-nosed high-school student who was dating my sister-in-law. It certainly wasn't because I'd be uncomfortable working with Brian, it's just the fact that I'm a loner, and I wanted to be on my own. I'm a lone wolf.

The only thing I really knew was race cars. So it seemed natural for me to go into the race-car business. And I certainly didn't create WolfWeld to run Brian out of business, and he knows that. And we've never had a problem. First of all, he's into business in a way bigger way than me. I doubt he loses a half-ounce of sleep over WolfWeld.

Racing continues to change and evolve, just like it always will. It's different than when I started, and in another 30 years it will be different still.

It's kind of interesting how sprint-car racing has developed two different levels with the 410- and 360-cubic-inch cars. I kind of caught this in the tail end of my career, when I got going real good in Mark Burch's 360. The level of competition is a little less in 360s, but don't kid yourself, it's still tough.

There is still a big difference between the cars. It kind of reminds me of the rodeo. Have you ever noticed that it pays $1,000 to win the bull-riding competition at the local rodeo, but it pays only a belt buckle for the saddle bronc competition? They'll be 30 riders signed up for the saddle bronc deal, but just six or seven for bull riding. Why is that? Because those goddam bulls will kill ya! They're mean, and they ain't for everybody.

Well, those 410-inch sprint cars are mean, too. They ain't for everybody. And that's my observation as a former professional driver. They definitely ain't for everybody.

The 360s are no piece of cake, and I didn't win all of 'em. But I felt more comfortable driving Mark's car than I did Dan Motter's 410. It wasn't that Dan's car wasn't good; I mean, we took care of that car ourselves and it was top shelf. It was just the fact that things happen quicker in 410 racing. They're more violent, more intense, more difficult.

Sometimes I'm asked what it takes for a young boy or girl to get started in racing today. That's an easy question.

First of all, get the best education you can get. Get a good job. Don't get married. Stay living at your mom and dad's house, and give them $5 per month—not per week, per month—for rent. Keep the rest of your money. Spend every waking moment of your life, and every penny, on your race car. Go win 200 main events, and you'll have a free ride the rest of your life. Now, you'll have to buy the first car yourself, and spend every penny of your money, but that's how you start.

If you want to drive in the Indianapolis 500, don't start out in a street stock. If you want to drive sprint cars, get in one. Get in a 305, a 360, a do-it-yourselfer. If you don't pay your dues, you're faking it and you won't come out in the end.

It's getting more difficult to find young people willing to do all that. There are too many other things out there today. When I grew up, there was nothing to do. I was almost 10 years old before we got our first television, and it was black-n-white and got one channel, if you were lucky. Kids grow up with so much more to do. When I grew up in Sioux Falls, Sunday night was race night at Huset's Speedway. That's what you did every Sunday, and you grew up that way. There was no pro basketball, pro baseball. They didn't have a league with 175 softball teams in town. There was nothing else to do here on Sunday night, so you went to the races. This was before I really even got the bug while living in Wisconsin; I'd be sitting in our driveway on Sunday afternoon, waiting for my dad to take me to Huset's. I was maybe six, seven years old.

That's one of the biggest changes I've seen. Actually, it isn't a change so much within racing, it's just that the world outside racing has changed, and our sport hasn't figured out what to do about it.

Sometimes when I reflect on my career I'm amazed at how long I raced, and how many different tracks I saw. At the time you're so focused on winning the next race you don't have an appreciation for the many places you see, or the many people you meet along the way. It's only later when you look back do you realize something.

Man. I traveled a lot of miles up and down the road, didn't I?

People ask me now and then what my least favorite tracks are. I can name three of 'em: Kokomo, Kokomo, and Kokomo. That little Indiana track puzzled me for my whole career. Nothing against the place, but it's just that I could never get that place mastered. It had me completely whipped.

I always liked the big, fast tracks better, much more than the bullrings. I worked hard on being smooth, and if nothing else the big tracks rewarded smooth. Down through the years I heard a lot of people say that the big tracks suited me and my style, and I'd have to agree with them.

The faster, the better. I think some guys were uncomfortable at the super-fast places like Syracuse, N.Y., or Springfield, Ill. But I loved those places. And Knoxville, which is a fast place.

I remember reading one time, and I don't think Steve would even remember this, where Steve Kinser said about a particular track, "Well, you just ain't gonna whip Doug on a big slick track, because they don't get any smoother than him."

I don't know why it was like that, because I never tried to be that way specifically. After a period of years it just came to me. I was interested in winning, but I didn't care much if I was spectacular. I recall a few times when after the races people would come down out of the stands to visit with me in the pits. I remember one old farmer in Ohio in particular.

"When did you pass him to win the race?" he asked.

"Oh, with about three laps to go."

"I know you won, but I didn't notice that you'd passed him. I didn't even see you win!"

To me that was a compliment. What he was saying is that I did it so quietly and smoothly, he missed it. That's when you're really racing right, when you can sneak by and win and nobody even knows you won, except you. Sure, you can come through and knock the shit out of the guy, knock him into the fence, sparks flying, and that's spectacular. But I felt like the other way was better. More complimentary.

After a while I shined on the big tracks, and I think it was because I was smooth. Smooth means being under control, and not being erratic. On those big tracks, where your speed is so great, if you make an erratic move it can cut your speed a bunch in one move. It doesn't take much to lose a lot of ground.

Actually, I learned something interesting after I was finished racing. One day I got a small piece of metal in my eye, and I went to the eye doctor to have him take a look. I was sitting in the waiting room, and there was a magazine about vision care sitting there. I picked it up and started leafing through it, and came upon an article that said the average human takes 1.7 tenths of a second to blink their eye. Not 1.7 seconds, but 1.7 *tenths* of a second. Round that off to two tenths.

At Knoxville, you're running 30 laps for the national championship. A lot of guys qualify at around 15 seconds. If two guys take off at the same time, dead even, running 15 seconds per lap, except that one guy loses two tenths each lap. That's the blink of an eye. That's how close it is. In five laps you've lost one full second. That's six seconds for the entire race, all because of two-tenths of a second per lap.

So you win by a half-lap, and you're the greatest sumbitch who ever lived. But it was really only the difference of a blink of an eye each lap, you were actually only that much better than the other guys. That's how close the competition is on the race track.

That's why smooth was so important. If you made an erratic move and lost a couple of 10ths here and there, next thing you know you're a full straightaway behind. I tried to concentrate on being ultra smooth with the wheel, because every twitch, every move, scrubbed off some of your speed. I focused on thinking ahead, so I could make a minimum of moves and turns, keeping my momentum up. It was beyond just driving around the track.

I wasn't the greatest natural talent out there, not by a long shot. But I had a lot of desire, and I tried to listen and learn and improve, and be smart in my approach. I guess all of that paid off, because as I look back I'm pretty happy with my career.

It all seems like a long time ago, and today I don't mind saying it: I was all right. I really was.

31

Reflections

In my WolfWeld shop in Sioux Falls you'll find the typical assortment of stuff you'd see in any chassis shop. Milling machines, a welder, a rack of tubing, drill presses, benches, the usual stuff.

I use the small area above my office for storage, and in front of all the stuff I've got four of my Knoxville Nationals trophies. These things are probably six-foot tall. I don't even notice them any more, because they're just sitting there quietly, blending in with all the other stuff.

One day a local kid came in to have his sprint car repaired. This boy was about 18 years old, and he had been racing sprint cars for just a couple of years. He walked into the shop and was just looking around when he noticed those trophies. He looked up at them, squinting, and he could read the small print: "Knoxville Nationals Champion."

The kid pointed at the trophies.

"Who won those?" he said.

I was a little red-faced and I cleared my throat.

"Well, uh…I did."

"You used to race!!?? Cool!"

I chuckle at that story, although some people don't believe it. They still think of the great Doug Wolfgang and they're amazed someone—especially a kid from Sioux Falls—hadn't heard of me. But they forget that time marches on, and it doesn't wait for anyone.

No matter how great you are, people forget you. The quicker you accept that, the better off you'll be. Don't have any illusions that just because you accomplished some nice things some years ago while driving a race car makes you special forever. It doesn't. Now I'm just another guy with a chassis shop.

I can say all this without malice or bitterness, because I'm actually a happy person with a nice life. I don't need for people to ask me for an autograph to be happy. I'm just as happy being a regular person, going to lunch every day with Jeri, just being normal.

A few months ago, we had a family get-together at the Wolfgang household. Our grown daughters and their families came over, we had a nice meal, and Jeri and I enjoyed doting on our grandchildren. It was the type of gathering that we have many times each year, as often as we can.

We were talking about a bunch of different things, kidding each other and having fun. Somehow the subject came up about how Steve Kinser and Sammy Swindell are still going pretty good in sprint-car racing, or something like that.

Our daughter Cori teased me, "Gee, dad, I wish you hadn't gotten burned…just think how much more money you'd have by now!"

She was kidding me, of course, but I have to admit that the thought has crossed my mind more than once. I've said this all along, and I mean it sincerely: Racing was never about the money with me. Still, now that I'm just another working man, you think more about money because you worry that someday you might run out, and be destitute. What if Jeri and I were broke, and our kids had to support us? That's probably every parent's greatest fear, and we're no different.

Sometimes when I let my guard down and allow myself to slip into a bit of self-pity, I wish things had worked out differently for me and my career. I was almost a superstar; I was pretty good when I got burned, and if I could have stuck with it for another three, four years I think I would have elevated my career standing a notch or two. Plus, we would have had another few years of earnings at my peak level, which would have definitely made a difference. In fact, if I could have squeezed another 10 years out of my career, I think Jeri and I would be set financially for the rest of our lives.

But you know what? If it would have worked out like that, I might be a rich, unhappy, divorced guy. No kidding. Because I was so self-absorbed in winning races, I wasn't a very nice person, and I think Jeri would have had enough of it by then. It's true that I began to soften up and adjust my priorities a little bit before I got burned, but I was still a focused, self-centered person. I was still tormented by the demons of intense competition, still torturing myself mentally after every loss, making life difficult for those around me.

Maybe the fire at Lakeside was God's way of getting my attention. I've thought of that. And I look up and smile a little bit and say, "Well, God, couldn't you have chosen a more, uh, subtle way to get my attention? Maybe just a lightning bolt or something? Did you have to season me to well-done?"

But you have to realize, we aren't talking about the average person here. I was so intensely consumed with racing, and my own goals and agenda, I didn't listen to God or anybody else. I can distinctly remember times in my life when someone—and I'm talking about someone I liked and respected—was trying to tell me something, give me advice. While they were talking, I was thinking, "Listen, sonny, I stopped listening to my dad when I was 16 years old, and I'm damn sure not going to listen to you."

That was my attitude. I might do it wrong, I might screw it all up, I might make a total mess out of things, but I was gonna do it my way. That shows you what a dumb jerk I was.

The fact is I'm a very happy person today, maybe more than at any point in my life. I've got a great wife; Jeri is way beyond simply being my wife, she is literally my best friend. We have lunch several times each week, or go out for a sandwich in the evening, just so we'll have some nice time to visit and talk. No big deal; but I love those minutes we spend together. And I totally love her. I still think she's hot.

We've got four great kids, and four wonderful grandchildren. I like spending time in my shop, working at my own pace, and I've got a number of friends whom I enjoy.

Money? I ain't worried about it. Not when I think about it in the right perspective. Yes, you need money to live, but life ain't about money. Or at least it shouldn't be. We're comfortable enough that we can pay our bills and get the things we need, and that's enough as far as I'm concerned.

So you're probably wondering: Would I go through the fire again, if it means getting to this point of my life? That's too hard of a question. The ordeal was too painful, too difficult, to think about it in that context. Instead, I kind of look at things as they are, and figure things worked out like they were supposed to. I've had far more good things in my life than bad, so I've got no kick. Really, I don't. I'm a happy cat.

I don't have very many specific regrets about my racing career. I do regret that it took me almost 20 years to gain the right perspective of racing, so that I could have enjoyed it more. I regret that my attitude wasn't better and I didn't have the peace-of-mind that I began to figure out right there at the end.

I really wasn't all that good in a stock car, and it wasn't all that interesting to me at that point in my life. So I don't regret that it didn't happen for me in NASCAR. I haven't looked over my shoulder and wished things could have been different.

The only time I thought much about stock cars was right after I got burned. When I was laying there feeling sorry for myself, I would think, "You know, dummy, you should have gone down there because then you wouldn't have gotten burned and would have maybe another five years of racing in you." But that's shoulda-woulda-coulda. It don't matter.

There are still things that I don't feel are right in our sport. Do you realize that the racers on the track have about $5,000 in accidental death coverage, and no liability, yet if you're in the grandstand and you get hurt there is a million dollars of insurance on you? What's wrong with that picture? I know there are probably insurance people who can explain why this is, but to me something isn't right. I realize I'm just one person, and maybe I'm looking at it from the wrong perspective, but I truly feel that isn't right. I feel like the racers aren't being looked after, I really do. But I don't get on the soapbox much these days. I have accepted that my responsibility of trying to change the world has come and gone.

I still struggle with health issues related to the fire. For the most part things are fine: I can work all day on my feet, and even though I have pain I can deal with it. I've learned to accommodate the effects of my injuries and it doesn't prevent me from doing most of the things I want.

But just this past summer I required more surgery. Something was wrong and I was constantly sick, but the doctors couldn't figure out the cause. It was only after a lot of trial-and-error and research that we discovered a serious infection on my left kneecap that was caused by some leftover debris from the fire. They put me on the table and lanced the infection and opened up the area and cleaned it out again. But even little things like this are a big deal, because the skin on my legs is so thin and scarred—from a combination of the burns and the grafting— that it's painfully slow to heal. I was very frustrated this past November when I fell and skinned it open again, because I bled like a pig and I knew it would again take months to get it healed back up. Things like that are disheartening because the process is so slow.

Still, I don't dwell much on that. I think back to how much worse it could have been. Hey, I had many opportunities to kill or maim myself, but I was lucky. Falling down the stairs and knocking my orthopedic halo off, for example.

Matter of fact, any time I feel sorry for myself I think back to that week in the spinal injury ward in St. Louis, and listening to those poor young men who only wanted to die. That reminds me that in the big picture I've been one very lucky man.

Writing this book turned out to be a good experience for me. About a year after I was burned someone approached me about writing a book, but I dismissed the idea. I don't know what my reasoning was at the time, but now that I've done this book and can look back across a lot of years, I see why that time wouldn't have been right to tell my story.

After I got burned I didn't take much stock in myself. I was depressed and sad and actually quite cynical. I'm not cutting myself down, I'm just being honest. At the time I saw myself as just a sprint-car racer, and I wasn't even the best one at that! I wasn't Steve Kinser. So how can you think much of yourself in that perspective? I didn't think I was all that worthy of being talked about.

As time passed I began to realize how lucky I was. I had a fine career, and actually won a few races, and some of 'em were pretty big races. I got to see some cool places, and meet a lot of really nice and interesting people. I mellowed out, and my attitude and perspective on life changed.

2007 turned out to be a much better time for me to contemplate my life and my career, and I've enjoyed the process much more than I thought I would. It's enabled me to be honest with myself and say, "You know, you weren't a bad little race driver!"

If there is a moral to my story, it's this: If you want something badly enough, you can achieve it. I wasn't born into a racing family, spoon-fed from the womb to drive a sprint car. I discovered racing by accident and started from absolutely nothing. I didn't have much natural talent but I forced myself to learn how to do this. I was naïve and dumb, but what I had going for me was total desire. I wanted to be a professional race driver.

I hope somebody who is reading this book can take that moral from my story. If there is something you want—a career, an adventure, an experience, an education, a business, whatever—don't be afraid to go for it. You can do it. Young or old, rich or poor, it don't matter. Just set your mind to it and don't be afraid. If you fail in the beginning, try again. You might be surprised at how much you can accomplish toward your goals if you work hard enough.

America is great, isn't it? Still to this day it's great.

The process of writing this book was actually therapeutic for me, which I never saw coming. I never took much time to be proud of myself, because I figured that was the kiss of death. In fact I'd beat myself up mentally, even when I didn't deserve it. And then after I got burned and decided to file the lawsuit, my career spun into something many people criticized. I discovered that it doesn't feel good to have people think you're a butthead. I went from not thinking much about my career to thinking I might have been a bum after all, so I never got to sit back and enjoy looking back at my career.

In the end this book helped me through some of that. It was nice to remember the good times, and the good people. And—now I can grin a little bit and say this—on a few nights along the way, we kicked their ass! On the race track, that is. That's pretty fun to think about some of the races we won, because those were really good nights.

This book made me proud again of who I am. I've got my warts, sure, but I'm no more of a butthead than anybody else. I realize that now. The only real criticism that I ever received was because of the lawsuit, and that whole deal was completely misunderstood and blown clear out of proportion. It left a sour taste in my mouth, for sure. But not nearly so much now.

Why did I write this book? Honestly, I thought maybe a few people wondered where I went off to. See, my career ended pretty abruptly, and basically I disappeared from sight. That was 15 years ago, and I was on top of the game that day. At that time I'm not sure sprint-car racing wasn't actually a bigger deal than it is today in terms of popularity. I'm not sure but it just might have been. So in some ways it was the heyday of the sport, and I was with a couple other guys on the top of the ladder. At 4:30 in the afternoon I was one of the best, but one hour later that same day it was all over.

So I got to thinking about it and figured maybe some of the people might have wondered whatever happened to me. You know, "Say, Clem, whatever happened to ol' so-and-so?" "That boy from South Dakota? Hell, I don't know…"

At the very least this book settles the question of whatever happened to ol' so-and-so, the boy from South Dakota. And maybe a few people enjoyed some of my stories.

A book is kind of permanent, and it's kind of cool to think that 30 years from now somebody might pick up this book, after I'm probably long gone. If you do, know this: Boy, I had a great life, all those years ago.

Each segment of my life was a learning process. When I was a hired driver I went through phases of what life taught me. Life is a continuous learning situation, and there were times when I thought being a race driver was all I was or ever would be. In the end I discovered I'm much more than that: I'm a husband, a dad, and a grandpa. I wasn't sure I enjoyed that job very much at one point. I enjoyed being a racer more, to be honest. But in the end I was lucky enough to come back to earth and have people help me understand that the best gift I ever had was to be a family man.

For all the fans who supported and cheered for me, I want you to know how much I treasure you. I always felt I was just the same as you; just another guy, other than I could drive a race car. Beyond that we weren't any different, and I hope I always treated you like my equal, because that's how I felt. I had good days and bad days, had a wife and kids, and most of the time when you saw me at the race track I had my family with me.

That's probably just like you. You probably enjoy going to the races with your family or your friends. So we're alike in many ways, you and me.

As you get older you're often better able to reflect on your life, and can put things in a better prespective.

Racing is a violent, tough sport, and I saw that many times throughout my career. If you're going to make it as a racer you have to develop just a bit of hardness, hopefully just enough to help you get through the painful things without changing you too much as a person.

But I never kidded myself: I knew this business was dangerous and that it could take me out on any given night. That's just the way it was. I saw several guys killed at this deal, some of them right before my eyes. Some were very dear friends of mine.

Many years ago I was talking to a reporter and he asked me what happens at the end of your career.

"In sprint-car racing," I answered, "if you're lucky, at the end you get to go home."

In the end, I was lucky. I got to go home.

One more thing…

A Racing Legend

By Alex Sjovold

He's my grandpa and he's famous around here in the world of racing. My grandpa won a lot of races in his racing career. My grandpa's name is Doug Wolfgang.

Doug Wolfgang started liking sprint car racing when he was a boy because his dad always took him to sprint car races. Doug Wolfgang started sprint car racing in 1975 in Knoxville, Iowa. Quickly he became a star.

Doug won five Knoxville Nationals. "That's like winning the Super Bowl," says Doug. In Knoxville history Doug became the driver with the most wins! In one race Doug got a bad burn in a fire.

Sprint car racers race on oval dirt tracks all over the U.S.A. To some people, Doug Wolfgang is a racing legend, but to me he's just my grandpa.

Prepared for Mrs. Hill's second-grade class - 2007
Challenge Center School
Sioux Falls, S.D.

Index

232, 236, 240, 241, 249, 252, 262, 264, 273,
278, 295–303, 311, 312, 313, 315, 316
Wright, Gary - 318

Yarborough, Cale - 247
Youngstown, Ohio - 169

Zitterich, Gary - 310

Dave Argabright has covered auto racing since 1981 for publications including *National Speed Sport News*, *Sprint Car and Midget Magazine*, *Speedway Illustrated*, *OPEN WHEEL Magazine*, *Car and Driver*, *Road & Track*, *On Track*, and *AMI Auto World*. His background in broadcasting includes work as a pit reporter for Speed Channel, the Indy 500 Radio Network, and TNN television.

His professional honors include the "Frank Blunk Award for Journalism" from the Eastern Motorsports Press Assn., the "Dymag Award of Journalism Excellence," the "Outstanding Contribution to the Sport" award from the National Sprint Car Poll, and the Hoosier Auto Racing Fans "Media Member of the Year" awards. He is a six-time recipient of the "Media Member of the Year" award from the National Sprint Car Poll.

Dave and his wife Sherry have four children, and reside in Fishers, Ind.

Also by Dave Argabright

Still Wide Open
with Brad Doty

American Scene
a collection

Hewitt's Law
with Jack Hewitt

EARL!
with Earl Baltes

Let 'Em All Go!
with Chris Economaki

Reorder information:
American Scene Press
P.O. Box 11578
Indianapolis, IN 46201-0578
(317) 631-0437
www.americanscenepress.com
www.daveargabright.com